REVIVAL FIRE

REVIVAL FIRE

REVIVAL
FIRE

WESLEY L. DUEWEL

ZONDERVAN

Revival Fire
Copyright © 1995 by Wesley Duewel

Requests for information should be addressed to:
Zondervan, 3900 Sparks Dr. SE, Grand Rapids, Michigan 49546

ISBN 978-0-310-35744-5 (softover)

ISBN 978-0-310-35745-2 (ebook)

Library of Congress Cataloging-in-Publication Data
    Duewel, Wesley L.
      Revival fire / by Wesley L. Duewel.
        p. cm.
      Includes bibliographical references and index.
      ISBN 978-0-310-49661-8
      1. Revivals—History. I. Title.
    BV3770.D84 1995
    277.3—dc20   94-43260

All Scripture quotations, unless otherwise indicated, are taken from The Holy Bible, New International Version®, NIV®. Copyright © 1973, 1978, 1984, 2011 by Biblica, Inc.® Used by permission of Zondervan. All rights reserved worldwide. www.Zondervan. com. The "NIV" and "New International Version" are trademarks registered in the United States Patent and Trademark Office by Biblica, Inc.®

Any Internet addresses (websites, blogs, etc.) and telephone numbers printed in this book are offered as a resource. They are not intended in any way to be or imply an endorsement by Zondervan, nor does Zondervan vouch for the content of these sites and numbers for the life of this book.

First printing October 2018 / Printed in the United States of America

DEDICATION

This book is gratefully dedicated to all prayer warriors and hidden intercessors who have invested holy hunger, fervent intercession, and Spirit-led obedience that God might send revival. Their faithfulness is not forgotten by God. It has been their eternal investment. If they did not live to see the full answer to their own prayers in their own lifetime or locality, they will see the result and their reward in the records of eternity.

All holy longings and prayer for revival are kept by God and united in His reservoir of revival blessings with other seemingly unanswered intercession. They are added to the mighty intercession of the Son of God on heaven's throne. Their prayers for the extension of God's kingdom are answered in some subsequent revival outpourings and finally in the great climactic millennial revival outpouring.

CONTENTS

FOREWORD

"If there isn't a revival in this country of some sort . . . we're moving toward a state that would be very much like pagan Rome." This spiritual assessment of conditions in our land today is the insightful conclusion of John Whitehead, president and founder of the Rutherford Institute. His words are frightening if we take them seriously. Rome was pagan. We only have to read the first chapter of Paul's epistle to the Romans to see the picture. The fact is there is a moral law that teaches that if men and women are left to the consequences of their own freely chosen course of action, they will go from bad to worse—unless this tendency is reversed by divine grace. So we read those words of doom, "God . . . gave them up," "God gave them up," "God gave them over" (Rom. 1:24, 26, 28 KJV).

This is where revival comes in, as Dr. Wesley L. Duewel's book, *Revival Fire*, abundantly illustrates again and again. When the tide of evil threatens to overwhelm the church, "The Spirit of the LORD [lifts] up a standard against [the enemy]" (Isa. 59:19 KJV), and spiritual recovery and revival ensue.

I have read, researched, and recorded the movements of God in revival throughout more than fifty years of ministry, and I have prayed and preached to see revival in our time. I have been privileged to discuss this vital subject with men like Evan Roberts of the Welsh revival (1904–1905), Duncan Campbell of the Hebrides revival (1949–53, 1957), and in more recent years Dr. Edwin Orr, whose works on revival are classics. I list these names in order to say that knowing these men and their literature has been enriching and enlightening; but nothing has stirred my heart to pray and preach for a mighty invasion of the Holy Spirit in our time like *Revival Fire*. My friend Wesley Duewel has compiled, in brief chapters, a mass of material on revival that informs the mind and ignites the heart. No pastor, lay leader, or church member should fail to read this book. I heartily commend it.

Throughout Scripture "fire" is a symbol of God's presence (Gen. 15:17; Ex. 3:2; 13:21–22, et al.), God's power (Ex. 19:18; 24:17; 1 Kings 18:24, 38), and God's purity (Isa. 6:1–6). It is not without significance that the words *purify* and *purge* come from the Greek word for fire. What a call this is to Christian people to purify themselves by the fire of the Word of God (Jer. 5:14) and the fire of the Spirit of God (Acts 2:3) to be the instruments of a mighty conflagration that burns the barriers to revival and brings the blessing of revival! It was Dr. W. Graham Scroggie who once said that "there never has been a spiritual revival which did not begin with an acute sense of sin. We are never prepared for a spiritual advance until we see the necessity of getting rid of that which has been hindering it, and that, in the sight of God, is sin." God's promise is clear: "If My people who are called by My name will humble themselves, and pray and seek My face, and turn from their wicked ways, then I will hear from heaven, and will forgive their sin and heal their land" (2 Chron. 7:14 NKJV).

Revival fire—that's it! God stir us to pray, "Oh, that You would rend the heavens! That You would come down! That the mountains might shake at Your presence—as fire burns brushwood, as fire causes water to boil—to make Your name known to Your adversaries, that the nations may tremble at Your presence!" (Isa. 64:1–2 NKJV).

Stephen F. Olford
Stephen Olford Center for Biblical Preaching
Memphis, Tennessee

INTRODUCTION

Welcome to these pages that describe some of the unusual outpourings of God's Spirit in holy spiritual revival over the past centuries. May God use them to cause you to hunger for His salvation power in our day. May they lead you to a deepened prayer life and closer walk with God.

Revival days are not normal days in the life of the church. They are supernormal, supernatural. They are the great days of the church when God manifests His presence in overwhelming reality. They leave you with a profound realization of God's greatness and transcendence and of your own unworthiness and dependence on Him.

God's presence and power are so mightily and extensively at work during revival that God accomplishes more in hours or days than usually results from years of faithful nonrevival ministry. Revival usually involves some preaching and evangelism. But revival is far more than evangelism. Man can evangelize; only God can give revival.

During revival people are moved toward Christ, people who can be moved in no other way. Many prayers that have gone unanswered for years are gloriously answered. Often the very atmosphere seems awesomely filled with God's power. Christians recognize it as the holy presence of God. Sinners feel a fearsome awareness of God's presence and their own sinfulness.

God may reveal His presence in unexpected ways. Accompanying His deep work in the soul may be other surprising occurrences. There may be such a sense of God's presence and power that some people tremble. Some may be moved to weeping before God; some at times sink to the ground in physical helplessness. Others may feel almost irresistibly drawn to attend revival services or to convene at a place and time where no service has been announced.

Man-made enthusiasm and emotionalism is superficial and cheap. In real revival emotion is not produced or manipulated by man. It is a response to the unsought, unexpected, but powerful working of God's Spirit upon the inner depths of people's souls.

Some have become so aware of God's presence that they could not move for some minutes. Some have been unexpectedly and instantly healed, to the amazement of unsaved people nearby. Such demonstrations of God's power may lead to repentance and the salvation of unsaved friends or relatives.

Some have been so filled with the joy of the Lord that they have sung hymns or choruses over and over with joy almost too deep for words. Some have praised God with loud voices because they felt themselves almost bursting with holy joy and gratefulness.

Many people fear revival because of these unusual manifestations. There is nothing to be feared. If occasionally someone is too unrestrained or overexpressive of his sorrow over sin or his joy at Christ's forgiveness and God's overwhelming presence, this can be understood and accepted. People are accustomed to unrestrained exuberance at sports events or upon seeing loved ones after a long absence.

Says Dr. A. T. Schofield, "One thing to be borne in mind is that since the days of Pentecost there is no record of the sudden and direct work of the Spirit of God upon the souls of men that has not been accompanied by events more or less abnormal. It is, indeed, on consideration, only natural that it should be so. We cannot expect an abnormal inrush of Divine light and power, so profoundly affecting the emotions and changing the lives of men, without remarkable results. As well expect a hurricane, an earthquake, or a flood, to leave nothing abnormal in its course, as to expect a true

Revival that is not accompanied by events quite out of our ordinary experience."[1]

Revival converts tend to be lasting converts. Again and again it has been noted that the people who have been profoundly convicted of their sin in a time of revival remain faithful over the years after their conversion. They have a permanent reverential awe of God and an abiding love for Christ. They have a deeper understanding and appreciation of the grace of God.

In the words of Job, "My ears had heard of you but now my eyes have seen you. Therefore I despise myself and repent in dust and ashes" (Job 42:5–6).

Come Suddenly
(Malachi 3:1)

Come suddenly again, O Lord; Your temple waits for You today.
Come in accordance to Your Word; come suddenly e'en while we pray.
O blessed, blessed Holy Ghost, bring the revival we need most.

Most graciously our hearts prepare for Your great work in this our day.
Help each of us to do our share; remove each hind'rance from Your way.
O Holy Ghost, our hearts inspire; descend in all Your holy fire.

We need You more than we can tell; we need You more than we can say.
Our worldliness and sin dispel; come, cleanse and fill us all, we pray.
O Holy Ghost, come on us now as we in need before You bow.

We pray, Lord, light the flame once more of Holy Ghost revival fire.
Come now as in the days of yore; for You we wait with great desire.
Come suddenly upon Your own and make Your holy presence known.

Come suddenly and do much more than we can do in months and years.
We plead Your mercy o'er and o'er; we praise You that revival nears!
Come, Holy Ghost, descend today! Come suddenly on us, we pray.

—Wesley L. Duewel

(Written in Moriah Chapel, Loughor, Gorseinon, South Wales, on
September 24, 1964. I was kneeling in prayer with John and Henry
Penry, converts in the first week of the 1904 revival under Evan
Roberts. After hearing their testimonies of how God came then,
Henry prayed, "Come suddenly again, O Lord." I began the poem
while he was still praying and while we were on our knees, and fin-
ished it after concluding with prayer myself. This is the same Moriah
Chapel where the revival broke out. The Welsh sing this poem to
the tune "Stella" in many hymnals.)

CHAPTER ONE

The God Who Blesses

It is God's nature to bless. He created us to be blessed by Him. The outpouring of God's Spirit upon a person, group, or area is one of God's greatest ways to bless. This book is all about such blessing. God poured out His Spirit in special abundance in Old Testament days from time to time and again in New Testament times. Throughout the history of His church, God has continued to do so in all parts of the world.

What shall we call these special times of blessing? Some like the term *spiritual awakening*. Others prefer to use the word *revival*. Sometimes it has been termed *spiritual renewal* or *the outpouring of the Spirit*. Perhaps the briefest and most time-honored term is simply *revival*. So this book is about God's grace, giving revival to His people.

VARIETIES OF REVIVAL

Sometimes God has given personal revival to a hungry-hearted, deeply devoted Christian. What a blessed experience of spiritual refreshment and new manifestations of God's grace and power this brings! It is always an experience to be remembered and cherished. Are you really hungry for personal or widespread revival? God is eager to come to you in grace and power.

Sometimes God gives revival to a local church or group of people. At times a whole community is blessed and changed by revival. On a few occasions an entire region or even a whole nation has become spiritually awakened and morally transformed by a widespread outpouring of God's Spirit in revival.

At times revival has lasted only a day or two. Yet God has been so powerfully present for that brief time that more spiritual transformation has resulted than from months and years of ordinary Christian life and witness. At other times revival has lasted for months.

GOD COORDINATES REVIVAL

In times of regional or nationwide revival, God's Spirit has worked in one church after another and in one community after another. These times of revival visitation by the Holy Spirit sometimes have begun almost simultaneously in various churches in a city or community, or sometimes in various cities of a given nation, and on occasion have even begun almost simultaneously in different parts of the world. I will describe such. Only God can plan that kind of coordinated divine working.

It is almost as if God's spiritual fire from heaven has touched down like a powerful tornado of blessing and leaped from place to place. All these divine manifestations have been marked by an unusually widespread awareness of God's presence, God's mercy, and God's transforming power in the lives of people.

God is infinitely original in His working. In no two places are the accounts of revival the same in their details. God's mighty work of salvation has transformed the most hopeless situations and the most spiritually damaged people. The more widespread any revival movement becomes, the more transforming are the moral effects in the areas where God's holy fire has burned.

REVIVALS OVER THE CENTURIES

God visited Israel with times of revival during the Old Testament period. He visited the early church with revival, and then over the centuries He has come again and again in revival to bless His people. In the early years of this century (1905–10), revival fires burned. God sent powerful awakening to Wales and many places in England, Scotland, Ireland, the United States, India, Korea, Manchuria, China, Japan, Australia, Madagascar, Norway, and in parts of South America and the Caribbean islands. In the middle of this century, God sent revival to some of the American Christian colleges and sent revival outpouring on some of the Hebrides islands.

Will revival sweep across our nation again? Do we need revival today? Revivals are the sovereign working of God, but they are always related to the obedience of God's people. Are you and I willing to prepare the way of the Lord by prayer, fasting, and obedience?

SPIRITUAL HUNGER

The purpose of this book is to thrill you with true accounts of how God has worked in powerful blessing over the centuries and around the world. May God increase our spiritual hunger to see Him bless our churches again with great spiritual renewal. May He bless our nation again with mighty spiritual awakenings.

God is the God of revival. Until Jesus comes again, "times of refreshing may come from the Lord" (Acts 3:19). Will you read these true accounts of revival and ask God to increase your spiritual hunger for God to visit us in grace again? Will you make intercession for world revival and world harvest a part of your daily fellowship with Jesus? He is even now interceding for us (Rom. 8:34; Heb. 7:25). Will you join Him in petitioning for a new, mighty spiritual awakening? Lord, send Your fire again!

CHAPTER TWO

When Fire Really Fell

"If God does not answer my prayer today with visible fire, then He is not real and you can forget Him." That, in effect, is how Elijah challenged the Israelite nation. Would you dare make such a challenge? Elijah stood up in a national assembly and called, "The god who answers by fire—he is God" (1 Kings 18:24).

Why would that grand Old Testament prophet Elijah stake all his future ministry and the faith and confidence of the people on God's answering his prayer by sending instant fire from heaven? It was the most crucial moment in his ministry. It was a moment that would decide the destiny of the nation. When had any prophet done such a thing before?

NEVER TOO LATE FOR GOD

Wicked Queen Jezebel and her compromising husband, King Ahab, had almost destroyed the worship of Jehovah throughout Israel. Ahab had been preceded by a succession of evil kings. But "Ahab . . . did more evil in the eyes of the LORD than any of those before him . . . and did more to provoke the LORD, the God of Israel, to anger than did all the kings of Israel before him" (1 Kings 16:30–33).

Elijah actually thought that he was the only faithful follower of Jehovah left in the nation (1 Kings 19:10). Was the

nation too far gone to be brought back to God? Of course
not. It is never too late for God to work. No situation is ever
so hopeless that it is useless to pray. No church can become
so compromising or backslidden that God cannot send fresh,
new blessing. No people has ever become so sinful that God
gave them up and no longer yearned to save them.

It was not too late for God, and it was not too late for
Elijah. Do you remember what Elijah was facing? He had
been in hiding for three years. Do you remember why? King
Ahab was obviously very successful in leading the nation
into the worship of Baal. Baal worship often involved
obscene sexual immorality as a religious act. Wicked Queen
Jezebel had commanded the execution of every prophet of
the Lord.

Imagine Ahab's surprise when a stranger dressed in the
crudest of apparel appeared before him and said, "As the
LORD, the God of Israel, lives, whom I serve, there will be
neither dew nor rain in the next few years except at my
word" (1 Kings 17:1). Elijah's statement proved true. The
nation suffered an awesome drought for three years. King
Ahab tried to find Elijah and even sent scouts to the surrounding nations, but he could not find him.

God was miraculously hiding Elijah and feeding him—
with the help of ravens. Never had such a thing been heard
of before. This was really living by faith. Then in an adjoining nation Elijah stayed with a widow and her son. Each
mealtime God miraculously multiplied the food. This was
not living by faith one day at a time. This was living by faith
one meal at a time.

After three years God told Elijah to go back to Ahab
and that He would now send rain. He guided Elijah to carry
out the most daring confrontation between God and Satan
ever recorded in Scripture. Baal was Satan's demon helper
masking as a god of rain, fertility, and nature.

Ahab was so desperately in need of rain for his devastated land, and it was so obvious that his only hope of rain was through Elijah, that amazingly he agreed to Elijah's commands. He summoned the nation together at Mount Carmel, some forty miles from Samaria, and commanded the prophet-priests of Baal and the Asherahs (fertility goddesses) to be present for a national confrontation with Elijah and Jehovah, Elijah's God.

Then Elijah took command, surrounded by Baal worshipers at a Baal center. He issued the challenge: "You build an altar to Baal and ask Baal to send rain today. But build no fire under it. You believe Baal controls lightning; let him light your fire. Then I'll put a sacrifice to Jehovah on Jehovah's altar and put no fire under it. The God who answers by fire—he is the real God."

Of course you know the result. Despite the priests' frenzied prayers and even self-abuse, Baal did not respond. The falseness of their god was blatantly evident to all.

Elijah then called the people to come close and watch his every move. He built an altar to Jehovah. He dug a trench around it probably at least a yard wide. Four times he had quantities of water poured on the sacrifice until everything was drenched and the trench was filled with water.

Then Elijah prayed a brief prayer, "O Jehovah, God of Abraham, Isaac, and Israel, let it be known today that you are God." He did not even get to say his "amen" before the holy supernatural fire of God descended from the sky. It burned up the sacrifice, wood, stones, and dirt, and evaporated the water in the trench.

Instantly the thousands watching fell on their faces in humble acknowledgment and worship of God. Over and over they shouted, "Jehovah—he is God! Jehovah—he is God!" Never in history was there so instant a revival. The people seized the false prophets who had been deceiving them and, in accordance with God's command in Exodus

22:20, Deuteronomy 13:5, and 18:20, put them to death. God had dealt Baal worship a tremendous blow.

FIRE IN THE DESERT

The first transforming revelation God gave of Himself to Moses was at the burning bush (Ex. 3:2). Moses did not immediately recognize what he saw: an ordinary desert bush was burning without being consumed. The flames he saw were like no other flames he had ever seen. They burned without destroying. God's fire in those He fully controls, who are totally and absolutely surrendered to Him, can burn on and on. It will transform, but it will not consume.

God's judgment fire can consume the sinner. But God's holy fire consumes the sin in repenting, surrendering believers. It cleanses them. It does not destroy them or their personalities. They become holy with a holiness that is Christlike. God's holy fire purifies believers and makes them more beautifully human, more like God originally created them to be. Any "bush" will be radiant when it burns with the fire of God.

FIRE ON SINAI

God's great visible manifestation to Israel as a nation was at Mount Sinai. Some five million people stood with Moses at the foot of Sinai, an almost two-thousand-foot high towering mass of rock. For two days, at Jehovah's command, the Israelites had prepared themselves for this moment. Now the whole of Mount Sinai shook and trembled violently from the presence of God (Ex. 19:16–20; Deut. 4:11–12; Heb. 12:18–21).

Volley after volley of crashing thunder reverberated through the sky. Lightning struck repeatedly. A piercing trumpet blast became louder and louder. Perhaps it was the same trumpet which Christ said will herald His second coming (Matt. 24:31; 1 Cor. 15:52).

The whole summit of Mount Sinai was covered with smoke, black clouds, and deep darkness. Then Jehovah descended in fire (Ex. 19:18). The top of Sinai blazed with fire, blazed up into the sky out of the bellowing darkness in the sight of all the people. That blazing fire burned for at least forty and perhaps even eighty days (Deut. 9:15).

THE FIRE OF GOD'S PRESENCE

God's holy fire is the glory of the church. God led Israel out of Egypt with a visible cloud of His presence by day, which became a cloud of fire by night (Ex. 40:36–38). At times God's fiery glory so filled the Old Testament tabernacle that not even Moses could enter it (Ex. 40:34–35).

That fiery glory-cloud was a forty-year miracle visible to all Israel. God's holy presence can be experienced repeatedly in His church today, not visible in actual flames, but visible in holy radiant living by God's people. The very demeanor of the apostles testified to those looking on that they had been with Jesus (Acts 4:13). In some similar sense God's holiness should be visible again and again in our personal lives and in our church assemblies. If it is not, we certainly need revival.

When Moses communed face to face with God in all His fiery glory, both on Mount Sinai and in the tent of meeting which he later pitched outside the camp, God's glory seemed absorbed into his very face. It was a visible testimony that Moses was in communion with God. Others saw it, but Moses was unaware of it (Ex. 34:29). Something wonderfully similar has occasionally been seen on the faces of believers, especially during revival times.

FIRE IN THE TEMPLE

When Solomon dedicated the temple, God again manifested Himself by sending fire from heaven to light the altar. All the Israelites saw the fire coming down and the Shekinah glory hovering above the temple, and they fell on their faces before God in worship (2 Chron. 7:1–3).

When Ezekiel had a vision of God and His throne, he was shown holy fire, radiance and brilliant light (Ezek. 1:26–28). In Daniel's vision of God, "His throne was flaming with fire, and its wheels were all ablaze. A river of fire was flowing, coming out from before him" (Dan. 7:9–10).

FIRE AT PENTECOST

John the Baptist prophesied that Jesus would baptize His people with the Holy Spirit and fire (Matt. 3:11). On the Day of Pentecost God restored to the church the Shekinah glory, which Ezekiel had seen before God withdrew it from the temple centuries before (Ezek. 10:4, 18; 11:22–23). This time God's fiery glory separated into individual flames of visible fire which then rested on those who were filled with the Spirit (Acts 2:3). This was the promised baptism of the Holy Spirit and fire that Jesus had foretold (Acts 1:5).

The fire of the Spirit can still cleanse, empower, fill, warm, enlighten, and reflect God's radiance. Often those truly living in the fullness of the Holy Spirit are easily recognized as men or women of God. There have been many times in different parts of the world that people have recognized a partially or even fully visible radiance on the face of someone who was specially endued by the Holy Spirit or during a time of revival.

FIRE IN INDIA

Very, very rarely the holy fire which flames but does not consume has been seen visibly during a time of revival. For example, during the 1905 revival in the Mukti center in India, the evangelist Ramabai had been teaching the hundreds of girls at the center about the Holy Spirit. As they were meeting together in prayer, girls began to be filled with the Spirit. Early one morning while all the girls were on their knees weeping and praying, suddenly a visible fire flamed around one of the girls. They all saw it, and one girl ran across the room for a bucket of water. She was about to throw it on the girl when she realized it was not literal fire.

The girl told them all that she had been filled with the Spirit, and she exhorted them to repent: "O Lord, I am full of joy, but forgive and cleanse my sisters as you have me. . . . O Lord, we must have revival, we must have it. Begin it today." As God revived them, many of the girls testified they felt a sensation of holy burning within them. They called it a baptism of fire. They were greatly transformed, and their faces were lit up with joy. Two little girls had such a spirit of prayer poured on them that they prayed for hours with a visible "heavenly light shining on their faces."[1]

We should not seek visible, spectacular, unusual experiences, or highly emotional ecstasies and visions. However, we must remember that in times of revival God has done most unusual things. We seek only more of God's presence, a greater awareness of His holiness and goodness, a deeper experience of His holiness, grace, and love.

You may ask why God on rare occasions pours out His Spirit in miraculous visible ways. I am not sure of the answer. Perhaps it is to remind us that He is still the God of fire. Perhaps it is to remind us that He is holy and sovereign in His working.

No, we are not to seek such physical or visible manifestations. But we are to long for and seek for mighty workings of the Spirit in transformation of lives, churches, and communities. Our God is still today a God of transforming reviving power. He is the God of revival fire. Lord, we need Your fire again!

CHAPTER THREE

Revival: Blessing or Judgment?

O ur God is the God of revival. Revival is an essential part of His plan of redemption. From the time God created Adam and Eve and they fell into sin, Satan has tried to alienate humanity from God. He has tried to get us to disobey God and sever our relationship with Him.

REVIVAL IS GOD VISITING IN LOVE

God is a redeeming, blessing, reviving God. Why? Because God is love. "This is love: not that we loved God, but that he loved us" (1 John 4:10). "We love because he first loved us" (1 John 4:19).

In the Old Testament period, Israel repeatedly forgot God, turned away from Him, and backslid into idolatry. But God did not give up on Israel. His heart was revealed by His words through Isaiah: "All day long I have held out my hands to an obstinate people" (Isa. 65:2). But Israel disregarded God's outstretched arms of love. God responded to stubborn, backsliding Israel, "How can I give you up. . . . For I am God, and not man" (Hos. 11:8–9).

From one viewpoint, revival is the manifestation of God to His people, convicting by His awesome presence and by His infinite holiness. From another viewpoint, revival is God holding out His arms of love to us and refusing to give up on us.

Again and again during the Old Testament period God held out His arms to Israel through prophets, righteous kings, or leaders whom He raised up to call Israel back to Himself. The greatest revival visitation in history was Jesus. "God so loved the world that he gave his one and only Son" (John 3:16).

God followed up Jesus' ministry with the mighty revival of Pentecost, in which Christ founded His New Testament church. The church was born in revival fire. It is the nature of the church to experience revival through the Holy Spirit.

The history of the church from Pentecost till today shows the repeated need for revival. Read the letters of Christ to the seven churches in Revelation 2 and 3. No church, no matter how holy or godly, has not at times needed refreshing and reviving. Even Ephesus needed to seek again her first love (Rev. 2:4).

God understands. God loves. God has provided an answer. Call it renewal, call it revival, call it refreshing, or call it whatever you will: God planned the ministry of the Holy Spirit to meet this great need of ours. We all repeatedly need God's reviving touch. But there are special times when the church needs revival in an unusually urgent way. I believe we need revival desperately today.

REVIVAL OR JUDGMENT?

In the long line of kings that followed Saul and David, after the division of the nation into Israel and Judah, most of the kings were not known as righteous kings. All of the kings of the northern and larger nation of Israel are said to have done "evil in the eyes of the LORD." Such words are found at least forty-six times in Scripture. The first king of Israel was Jeroboam. He set up idols in the north and the south, and the people bowed before golden bull calves. Although they kept a semblance of worship of Jehovah, the calves were an attempt to combine Baal worship with the worship of Jehovah.

God sent prophets to Israel and to its kings: Ahijah, Jehu, Elijah, Micaiah, Elisha, Hosea, Amos, Jonah, and Oded, plus an unnamed prophet. But neither the kings nor most of the nation truly repented. There was not one real revival in Israel.

When God calls for repentance and people refuse to repent, how can God awaken them to their danger? He has no alternative but to send judgment. Israel was eventually taken into captivity a century and a half before little Judah was. The nation as a whole never returned after captivity. When people who have had God's light reject revival, judgment is inescapable.

Judah, the tiny nation in the south, centered in Jerusalem, also had prophets, more than Israel had. Shemaiah, the son of Oded, Jehu, Jahaziel, Eliezer, Elijah, Zechariah, the son of Jehoiada, Joel, Isaiah, Micah, Nahum, Habakkuk, Huldah, Zephaniah, Jeremiah, Uriah—these were prophets before Judah was taken into Babylonian captivity. Ezekiel, Obadiah, Jeremiah, and Daniel were prophets during that captivity. Haggai, Zechariah, and Malachi were prophets after the remnant of Judah returned from their Babylonian exile.

Many of the kings of Judah were more responsive to spiritual things and more faithful to Jehovah. Five of Judah's kings were especially righteous. They cooperated with and responded to the prophets' call to repentance. Some degree of national revival or reformation was experienced during each of these five reigns. We will briefly examine three of these times of special revival in later chapters.

JUDGMENT CAN LEAD TO REVIVAL

Please let me repeat: God is a God of revival, a God of love. God desires to visit His people with revival rather than with judgment. God longs to bless, longs to forgive, and is slow to punish (Ex. 34:6; Neh. 9:17; Ps. 103:8–12). But when His people drift away from Him or turn away and refuse to repent, God may need to send punishment, wake His people up, and bring them back to repentance so He may be merciful to them.

Backsliding into idolatry was the constant danger and frequent sin of Israel and Judah until God finally sent them into awesome judgment during the captivity. Jerusalem and the temple of Solomon were destroyed. Most of the remaining Jews were taken into captivity to Babylonia, where they were forced to remain at least seventy years. Then through Nehemiah and Ezra, God sent a time of revival, and many went back to Jerusalem again. God was able to fulfill His plan as prophesied in Scripture, and in the fullness of time Jesus Christ became incarnate and provided salvation in His atonement on the cross.

When judgment is humbly accepted and people repent, God is always ready to forgive and to restore. The Jews learned their lesson through the judgment of captivity. Never since that time to this day have any considerable number of Jews ever gone back into idolatry. The judgment of God became a blessing to them as a nation.

In the next two chapters we will look at three times during Judah's history when God was able to send revival because He had a leader to whom the people responded. When they humbled themselves and returned to God, He manifested His grace and mercy. He is ready to do the same today.

CHAPTER FOUR

Renewal Under Father and Son

For a period of sixty-five years during the reign of King Asa and his son, King Jehoshaphat, there was a movement of revival and reformation. Sometimes God's presence and power were visible to all, and sometimes they were not. But this revival-reformation undoubtedly saved Judah from extinction and called the nation back to God.

HOW QUICKLY WE FORGET

The glory of King David's reign was succeeded by the materialistic prosperity and secular splendor of Solomon's reign. Solomon built a beautiful and majestic temple according to the pattern God gave to David. It was functionally similar to the tabernacle Moses had set up. At the beginning of his kingship Solomon served Jehovah. Twice God revealed Himself to Solomon in a special vision. But Solomon became materialistic and secular, and his many wives enticed him into compromise with idolatry. The book of Ecclesiastes, written by Solomon in his old age, is a sad commentary on his backslidden condition and outlook on life.

Solomon's son Rehoboam proved to be a foolish, stubborn, and sinful king who abandoned the law of the Lord and allowed idolatry and pagan fertility practices to spread across the land. After Rehoboam's sad and sinful reign, came the short-lived, evil reign of his son Abijah. Scripture says, "He committed all the sins of his father before him" (1 Kings 15:3).

What hope was there for Judah to be able to survive as a nation or for God's plan that the Messiah come through the lineage of David? What hope was there that the promises to David would eventually be fulfilled? Thank God that, in the long line of kings until Judah went into Babylonian captivity, there were times when kings served the Lord and followed more or less the example of David their forefather. Through them God sent times of national renewal, reformation, and even revival.

THE INCOMPLETE REVIVAL UNDER ASA

Thank God an evil father need not have an evil son. We do not know how the godly influence came into the life of Asa, son of Abijah, nor how old he was when he became king. He reigned for forty-one years. We do not know in what year of his reign he began to turn the nation to God, but apparently from the very time he took the throne he began to prepare to bring his nation back to Jehovah and to follow once more the example of his great-great-grandfather David.

The holy influence of a godly person can extend over several generations even if his or her prayers are rejected by one or two generations. Those prayers live on and may yet be answered in succeeding generations. Prayer is a tremendous treasure with which to endow descendants for generation after generation. David was a man of prayer. For David's sake, God blessed Israel again and again over the centuries.

Asa's first ten years were a time of peace, and he seized this opportunity to devote much of his energy to turning the nation back to God (1 Kings 15:9–24; 2 Chron. 14–15). He removed all altars and high places dedicated to foreign gods and destroyed the stone pillars and Asherah poles surrounding the altars. He removed the illegal altars to Jehovah so the nation would worship at the temple in Jerusalem as God had commanded.

Then Judah was invaded by Zerah the Cushite, an Egyptian military commander with an immense army. Asa, with a much smaller army, prayed and trusted God, and Jehovah gave him amazing victory. Asa and his army captured tremendous wealth from the defeated and destroyed foes. They came back to Jerusalem driving herds of sheep, goats, and camels.

When the victorious army reached Jerusalem, God raised up a previously unknown prophet to encourage Asa and all the people. The Holy Spirit came upon Azariah, and he called out, "Listen to me, Asa and all Judah and Benjamin. The LORD is with you when you are with him. If you seek him, he will be found by you, but if you forsake him, he will forsake you. . . . be strong and do not give up, for your work will be rewarded" (2 Chron. 15:2, 7).

How true this proves even to this day. God rewards and sends revival to those who seek Him. Encouraged by the great victory God had given and by the prophecy of Azariah, Asa renewed his reform and revival efforts. He destroyed all idols throughout Judah and Benjamin and the cities he had just captured. He repaired Jehovah's altar in front of the porch of the temple. Large numbers of people had emigrated from the northern kingdom of Israel and settled in Judah because "they saw that the LORD his God was with him" (2 Chron. 15:9). So in the fifteenth year of his reign, Asa gathered together all the people from the whole nation and held a service of sacrifice to Jehovah. Asa called on all to recommit their lives to the Lord by renewing the covenant with God that had been made in the time of Moses and the covenant established in the reign of David.

Asa and the people offered a multitude of sacrifices to God. "They entered into a covenant to seek the LORD, the

God of their fathers, with all their heart and soul" (2 Chron. 15:12). They took an oath to the Lord, calling aloud to Him, shouting with joy and blowing trumpets and horns.

It was a mighty revival. "All Judah rejoiced about the oath because they had sworn it wholeheartedly. They sought God eagerly, and he was found by them. So the LORD gave them rest on every side" (2 Chron. 15:15).

Asa removed his grandmother Maacah from her position as queen-mother because she had erected an Asherah pole to the fertility goddess. Asa cut down the pole, broke it up, and burned it outside the city. He would not permit his own grandmother to retain a position of honor because she had set an evil example and practiced idolatry. Then Asa brought into the temple all the silver, gold, and treasures which he and his family had.

Real revival can occur when we are willing to take a stand for God regardless of whether our loved ones and friends agree or even understand. Asa knew the land had to be cleansed at any cost. The Bible gives this summary: "Asa's heart was fully committed to the LORD all his life" (2 Chron. 15:17).

Unfortunately, there is a shadow at the end of Asa's reign. Baasha, king of Israel, after years of friction began to prepare to invade Judah. Asa turned from his total dependence on God to dependence on the military alliance with the king of Aram. He took the silver and gold from his own palace and from the temple to induce Aram to attack Baasha.

The prophet Hanani came to Asa and rebuked him. Hanani told Asa that if he had only relied on God he would have had an even greater victory and blessing. Instead of humbling himself before God, Asa imprisoned Hanani and, out of anger with God, mistreated some of his people. So God permitted Asa a severe foot disease. Instead of humbling himself and asking God to heal, Asa stubbornly went to the doctors and refused to pray. What might have been the deepest revival of Asa's reign ended in failure.

THE CONTINUED REVIVAL
UNDER JEHOSHAPHAT

For the last three years of Asa's reign, as his health deteriorated, his son Jehoshaphat was coregent. Thank God, Jehoshaphat had the same fiery zeal that Asa had during his early years. Perhaps revival fire burned even more brightly in Jehoshaphat's heart. His fervent devotion to the Lord echoed that of his forefather David.

Jehoshaphat sought the God of his father, and spiritual seekers are always finders. He had no use for Baal or the practices of backslidden Israel. "His heart was devoted to the ways of the LORD" (2 Chron. 17:6). He planned, worked, and prayed for national revival. God confirmed his rule. The people gladly followed him and brought gifts, and Jehoshaphat quickly became wealthy and honored. His leadership was fully accepted.

Jehoshaphat carried on many of the policies of his father. He removed the altars and Asherah poles from Judah. Asa had removed them, but during his forty-one years' reign, some may have been rebuilt. But Jehoshaphat did much more. In the third year of his reign he began a teaching ministry throughout the whole nation. He appointed five officials, nine Levites, and two priests. These men took the Scriptures and toured from town to town, teaching the people from the one end of the land to the other the commands of the Lord and the sacred history of their nation. Jehoshaphat knew the nation needed to be grounded in the Word of the Lord. Lasting revival can only come as people are blessed in soul and soundly grounded in God's truth.

There was an amazing result. Without winning one new battle to demonstrate his military prowess, all the nations around Judah began to respect Judah and

Jehoshaphat's leadership. Scripture says, "The fear of the LORD fell on all the kingdoms of the lands surrounding Judah, so that they did not make war with Jehoshaphat" (2 Chron. 17:10). The Philistines brought silver and gifts. The Arabs brought 7,700 rams and 7,700 goats.

Jehoshaphat's power grew. He built store cities and forts, kept supplies in the towns, and stationed military leaders in Jerusalem. He organized a tremendous army. But he made one great mistake. Jehoshaphat was tired of the years of friction and fighting with Israel on his northern border. After some years, he began a policy of cooperation with Israel. He married his son to a daughter of Ahab and Jezebel. That brought an evil influence in his son's life.

Then Ahab asked Jehoshaphat to accompany him in a mini-war against Syria. Jehoshaphat replied that he would help on the condition that they consulted a prophet of the Lord. This prophet warned that the war would be lost. But somehow Jehoshaphat permitted Ahab to persuade him to help. Ahab was killed, and Jehoshaphat almost lost his life.

When Jehoshaphat got back from the war, the prophet Jehu rebuked him. He warned him of Jehovah's anger, but acknowledged, "There is, however, some good in you, for you rid the land of the Asherah poles and set your heart on seeking God" (2 Chron. 19:3).

That was Jehoshaphat's priority: seeking God. He accepted the rebuke. Some time had elapsed since his teaching-revival team of sixteen had reached every town in the nation. Apparently King Jehoshaphat had also gone with them or had gone separately from them and himself reached the people. For the Bible says that Jehoshaphat "went out again among the people from Beersheba to the hill country of Ephraim and turned them back to the Lord, the God of their fathers" (2 Chron. 19:4).

We are not told of this king-evangelist's methods. Undoubtedly Jehoshaphat exhorted, taught, pled with, and prayed for the people. Never did a prophet carry out so thorough a crusade to bring people back to God.

In addition, Jehoshaphat tried to reform civil administration. He appointed Levites, priests, and selected heads of families to administer "the law of the LORD" and settle disputes. He commanded them, "Serve faithfully and whole-heartedly in the fear of the LORD. . . . Warn them not to sin against the LORD; otherwise his wrath will come on you and your brothers. Do this, and you will not sin" (2 Chron. 19:9–10).

Jehoshaphat also began to reform the judicial system. He appointed judges in each of the fortified cities. He ordered, "Consider carefully what you do, because you are not judging for man but for the LORD, who is with you whenever you give a verdict. Now let the fear of the LORD be upon you. Judge carefully, for with the LORD our God there is no injustice or partiality or bribery" (2 Chron. 19:6–7).

Jehoshaphat was doing everything he could to bring about spiritual and moral revival and just government and civil administration. The revival Asa had begun was now transforming the whole nation as it reached ever deeper and broader in the lives of the people.

As always, Satan is not happy when God sends revival, so he tried to interrupt the spiritual renewal by creating war. A vast army of Moabites, Ammonites, and Meunites attacked from the southeast. Immediately Jehoshaphat put his primary trust in the Lord. He proclaimed a day for fasting and prayer and convened a national assembly in Jerusalem to seek God's help. "They came from every town in Judah to seek him" (2 Chron. 20:4) and gathered in front of the temple.

Jehoshaphat led in a powerful prayer of intercession. At that very moment the Holy Spirit came upon one of the ordinary Levites who was standing in the assembly before the Lord. This man called out in prophecy, "This is what the

LORD says to you: 'Do not be afraid or discouraged because of this vast army. For the battle is not yours, but God's. Tomorrow march down against them. . . . You will not have to fight this battle. Take up your positions; stand firm and see the deliverance the Lord will give you'" (2 Chron. 20:15–17).

Jehoshaphat instantly bowed down with his face to the ground, and all the people followed his example, humbling themselves and worshiping the Lord.

Early in the morning they all began their march to the desert. Never in history had an army marched to battle led by a choir singing and praising God for the beauty of His holiness. As they praised the Lord, God "set ambushes" against the enemy army. How? Suddenly the armies of Moab and Amon began to attack and killed the army from Seir. Then the remaining two armies turned on each other and fought until all were killed.

When Jehoshaphat and his men reached the spot, there was no one left to fight. For three days Jehoshaphat's people took jewelry off the dead bodies and collected the loot and treasures that the armies had carried with them.

They spent the fourth day in a national assembly in a nearby valley. They named it Beracah—the Valley of Blessing. Satan intended for it to be their valley of death; God made it their valley of blessing. Joyfully they marched back to Jerusalem and to the temple of the Lord, carrying the great wealth they had gathered. They were led by harps and lutes and trumpets, praising the Lord.

Again the fear of the Lord came upon all the surrounding nations. The story was told and retold. God fights for Israel! God fights for and delivers His people! God gave them peace on all sides. God gives many great revivals to those who prepare the way for the Lord. But no two are the same. Lord, send revival fire again!

CHAPTER FIVE

Hezekiah: Never Too Late

Hezekiah came to the throne at one of the darkest moments in Judah's history. His father Ahaz was such a failure as a king, so wicked, and did so much that was destroying the nation that he was not even buried in the royal tombs. It was a relief to the nation to have him out of the picture.

Ahaz "did not do what was right in the eyes of the LORD." He followed the lifestyle and practices of the wicked kings of Israel. He participated in the idolatry of the nations around him.

Ahaz offered pagan sacrifices and burned incense at the high places of Baal which God had condemned. He worshiped "under every spreading tree" (2 Kings 16:4). This referred to the pagan, immoral, sexual rites held at shrines beneath large trees. The trees were looked on as symbols of fertility. Ahaz even sacrificed more than one of his sons, burning them to death on a flaming Canaanite altar (2 Chron. 28:3).

Eventually the kings of Aram and Israel defeated Ahaz. The king of Israel killed 120,000 of Ahaz's soldiers in one day. He also killed the son of Ahaz, his palace manager, and his second in command. Israel took all the plunder they could find, and they took 200,000 wives and children captive

37

back to Samaria. There the prophet Oded convinced them to release the prisoners and take them back to Jerusalem.

After their return, Edom attacked Judah and took away prisoners. The Philistines raided border towns in the west and south. Ahaz sought help from the king of Assyria but received only more trouble in return. Ahaz stripped the temple of its gold and furnishings to bribe Assyria to go away.

Throughout Judah's troubled period, Ahaz became more and more unfaithful to Jehovah. He removed the bronze altar and replaced it with an altar modeled after the pagan altar in Damascus. He took away the Sabbath canopy from the temple and removed the royal entryway (2 Kings 16:10–18).

Ahaz finally even shut the doors of the temple and set up pagan altars "at every street corner in Jerusalem." He built high places to worship pagan gods "in every town in Judah" (2 Chron. 28:24–25). Even the doors of the porch of the temple were closed, the lamps were put out, and all burnt offerings and sacrifices in the temple were forbidden (2 Chron. 29:7).

The nation of Judah was reduced to disgrace, attacked on all sides. Thank God, one son of Ahaz survived and became king. But what a hopeless situation to face a young king of twenty-five. But, wait, see what God can do for and through a young king on fire for God.

A PROPHET'S INFLUENCE

The very year Hezekiah was born God called Isaiah by a wonderful vision and made him His prophet. Isaiah lived in Jerusalem and was related to the royal family. He was keenly observant of all that was happening in the palace and in the nation. Isaiah was God's prophet in God's place at God's time.

Scripture does not record what the godly influences were that prepared Hezekiah for his great role. With a father so apostate and totally given to idolatry and the rejection of all Israel's godly heritage, how did Hezekiah reach such total commitment to the Lord?

Could it not be that God used Isaiah in a hidden but strategic role? Isaiah had unusual access to the palace. He was the eloquent prophet of the nation. Surely Isaiah became the counselor-pastor to the young prince Hezekiah. They may well have talked and prayed together often about how Hezekiah could turn the nation back to God once he became king. Most revivals have their roots in long periods of behind-the-scenes intercessory prayer.

Isaiah and Hezekiah probably prayed together again and again as Ahaz became more and more apostate and as God sent judgment after judgment on Judah because of the sins of Ahaz and the people. The nation was reeling from one attack after another by the surrounding nations. Would it be too late for Hezekiah to act? Would the nation be destroyed before he became king? Hezekiah had his much-prayed-over plans ready.

Hezekiah could hardly wait to begin working for a national revival. His father Ahaz may not even have been buried yet when Hezekiah started his reformation. The Bible says on the first day of the first month of his reign Hezekiah ordered the temple doors unlocked and the repairs begun. He called the priests and Levites together and charged them to return the temple to its holy state. Hezekiah told them, "The anger of the LORD has fallen on Judah and Jerusalem; he has made them an object of dread and horror and scorn, as you can see with your own eyes. . . . Now I intend to make a covenant with the LORD, the God of Israel, so that his fierce anger will turn away from us" (2 Chron. 29:8, 10).

The priests consecrated themselves and started to obey Hezekiah's command, "following the word of the LORD" (2 Chron. 29:15). How did Hezekiah get the word of the Lord? Probably through Isaiah.

For eight days they did nothing but purge the temple, carrying out everything unclean. This probably included not only the rubbish and dirt that had accumulated during the years the temple was shut, but also the idols Ahaz had made and put inside the temple (2 Chron. 28:2). All were destroyed and burned at the Kidron stream as Asa had done 150 years before (2 Chron. 15:16). For eight more days they cleansed and consecrated the temple itself and all its sacred vessels. Then they reported to Hezekiah.

This was the day Hezekiah had been waiting for. Early in the morning the very next day the young king led the procession to the temple. He had twenty-eight sacrificial animals ready to be killed for a sin offering for the nation. The king ordered that the sacrificial blood be shed for "all the nation." Then he immediately ordered the full temple worship to begin. The priests and Levites played instruments and sang, as David had commanded years before (2 Chron. 29:25–26). The whole congregation remained bowed in worship until the sacrifice was completed.

"Praise the LORD with the words of David and Asaph," Hezekiah commanded. What joy thrilled the hearts of all present. Their sins were forgiven and the people rejoiced. The king told them, "You have now dedicated yourselves to the LORD. Come and bring sacrifices and thank offerings to the temple" (2 Chron. 29:30–31).

So many sacrifices were brought that there were not enough priests to complete the sacrifices, so the Levites helped them. "Hezekiah and all the people rejoiced at what God had brought about for his people, because it was done so quickly" (2 Chron. 29:36).

AN INVITATION TO REVIVAL

Hezekiah was so thrilled he sent out letters to all of Judah and to all the Jews who survived in Ephraim and Manasseh, inviting them to come to Jerusalem and celebrate the Passover: "People of Israel, return to the LORD, the God of Abraham, Isaac and Israel, that he may return to you who are left. . . . For the LORD your God is gracious and compassionate. He will not turn his face from you if you return to him" (2 Chron. 30:6, 9).

Hezekiah's intent was to reunite the kingdoms. What thrills of excitement came to all the godly throughout the land. It was once more like the days of David and Solomon. True, many were so backslidden that they scorned and ridiculed the couriers who brought the message of invitation. But many humbled themselves and came to seek the Lord in repentance. Revival always begins among the people closest to God.

The people became so excited that they joined in the revival-reformation. They went around Jerusalem clearing out street by street all the incense altars that Ahaz had built. Then what a Passover they held! For more than a century they had not shared in such a time of Passover and revival. Hezekiah prayed for the people, the priests played, and the Levites sang as all the people rejoiced.

Hezekiah encouraged and thanked the Levites, telling them to keep up the good work. The people fellowshiped and praised God for seven days. Then they asked for more. They did not want to go home. So for a total of fourteen days they fellowshiped, praised, and sang. They sacrificed 2,000 bulls and 17,000 sheep and goats.

The people were so fired up, so revived, so blessed that they all wanted to help clean up the nation from idolatry. "The Israelites who were there went out to the towns of Judah, smashed the sacred stones and cut down the Asherah poles. They destroyed the high places and the altars throughout Judah and Benjamin and in Ephraim and in Manasseh. After they had destroyed all of them, the Israelites returned to their own towns and to their own property" (2 Chron. 31:1).

Then Hezekiah reorganized the priests and Levites for their ministry as they had served in David's time. He gave generously to the temple from his personal possessions and then called on the people to bring in their firstfruits and tithes. The response was so wholehearted and overwhelming that all the needs were met and heaps of grain were left over. Special storerooms were built to contain the tithes and offerings. When people are living in revival, God's cause is fully supported.

According to Ezra, the probable author of Chronicles, Hezekiah did "what was good and right and faithful before the LORD his God. In everything that he undertook in the service of God's temple and in obedience to the law and the commands, he sought his God and worked wholeheartedly. And so he prospered" (2 Chron. 31:20–21).

VICTORY IN THE NIGHT

Asa and Jehoshaphat had had their times of trouble, and Hezekiah was certainly not exempt. After all the revival and national reformation God brought about through Hezekiah, Sennacherib, the Assyrian king, came to attack little Judah. Hezekiah immediately began to strengthen the fortifications of Jerusalem, appointed officers over the people, and convened a national assembly. "Do not be afraid or discouraged because of the king of Assyria and the vast army with him," Hezekiah told them, "for there is a greater power with us than with him. With him is only the arm of flesh, but with us is the LORD our God to help us and to fight our battles" (2 Chron. 32:7–8).

Sennacherib sent his officers to shout threats and insults to the people, the king, and to God. Hezekiah and

Isaiah united in prayer. Sennacherib sent a further letter insulting Hezekiah and the Lord Jehovah. Hezekiah went to the temple and again poured out his heart to God.

That very night God sent His avenging angel. In the morning all Hezekiah and his people found were the bodies of 185,000 Assyrian soldiers. Sennacherib went back home in disgrace, and when he went into the temple of his own god to pray, two of his sons assassinated him.

Hezehiah's revival was characteristic of Old Testament revivals. Yet God can revive us again today! Lord, send revival fire again.

CHAPTER SIX

A Monk's Revival

When revival came to Florence, Italy, in 1496–98, God's human instrument was the Italian Roman Catholic monk Savonarola. When Savonarola's revival began, Martin Luther was just a small boy. Savonarola was shocked by the vice and immorality of the world about him in Italy and by the corruption he knew existed in the Roman Catholic Church. As a youth he would walk beside the River Po, singing to God and weeping for the sins, the injustices, and the poverty of the people about him. He wept and grieved over the lewdness, luxury, and cruelty of many leaders of the church. He would lie for hours prostrate on the altar steps in the church, weeping and praying about the sins of the age and the sins of the church.

What can one unknown monk do in an age of immorality both in society and in the only church existing at the time? Although he was a devout Catholic, Savonarola's prayers and spirit-filled life helped prepare the way for the Protestant Reformation. Martin Luther called him a Protestant martyr. His life is another glorious testimony that one prayer warrior by the grace of God can be used to turn the tide and prepare the way for a mighty revival.

AN OLD TESTAMENT PROPHET IN A NEW TESTAMENT WORLD

At the age of twenty-two, Savonarola wrote a paper, "Contempt of the World," in which he likened the sins of the current age to those of Sodom and Gomorrah. He slipped away without first telling his family and entered a monastery to begin a life of fasting and prayer. He was desperate to see God send revival.

For years Savonarola studied Scripture, waited for God, and prayed. Suddenly one day God gave him a vision: the heavens opened and a voice commanded him to announce the future calamities of the church to the people. Filled with a new powerful anointing of the Holy Spirit, Savonarola began to preach to the people.

When the Spirit of God came upon him, the voice of Savonarola thundered as he denounced the sins of the people. Revival power gripped the whole area. Savonarola's audience—men and women, poets and philosophers, craftsmen and laborers—all sobbed and wept. People walked the streets so gripped by conviction from the Holy Spirit that they were half-dazed and speechless.

On several occasions while seated in the pulpit, all in the church could see Savonarola's face seemingly illuminated with a heavenly glow, and he would sit in the pulpit lost in prayer or in a trance for up to five hours at a time.[1] The smaller churches could not hold the crowds that came to hear him, so for eight years Savonarola preached in the large cathedral in Florence, Italy. People came in the middle of the night, waiting for the cathedral doors to open so they could hear his message. Savonarola prophesied he would be with them only eight years.

CITY-WIDE REFORMATION

The Spirit of the Lord was upon Savonarola. He prophesied that the city ruler, the pope, and the king of

Naples would all die within a year, and so they did. For months he predicted that God would punish Florence with an invasion from across the Alps. King Charles VIII of France and his army crossed the Alps and prepared to attack. Savonarola went out alone to meet them. He faced the French army single-handed and twice persuaded Charles to turn back and not attack Florence.

The wicked city government was overthrown, and Savonarola taught the people to set up a democratic form of government. The revival brought tremendous moral change. The people stopped reading vile and worldly books. Merchants made restitution to the people for the excessive profits they had been making. Hoodlums and street urchins stopped singing sinful songs and began to sing hymns in the streets. Carnivals were forbidden and forsaken. Huge bonfires were made of worldly books and obscene pictures, masks, and wigs. Children marched from house to house in procession singing hymns and calling everyone to repent and empty their house of every "vanity."

A great octagonal pyramid of worldly objects was erected in the public square in Florence. It towered in seven stages sixty feet high and 240 feet in circumference. While bells tolled, the people sang hymns and the fire burned, reminiscent of Paul's revival bonfire in Ephesus centuries before (Acts 19:18–20).

MARTYRDOM

The corrupt pope, the cardinals, and the priests were outraged. In time, the political and religious enemies incited a rough mob against Savonarola. They battered down the doors of the sanctuary of the convent where he was staying and captured him.

Savonarola was severely tortured as his enemies tried to get him to confess to heresy. His hands were bound behind him. He was hoisted to a great height and then dropped almost to the ground when the rope snapped him up again, pulling his shoulders out of joint and tearing his muscles. Burning coals were put to his feet to try to get him to recant. He refused. This was repeated several times. Returning to his cell, Savonarola would kneel and ask God to forgive the people.

Finally Savonarola and two companion monks were brought out to be executed before a mob of thousands of onlookers. An awesome silence settled down over the crowd. Savonarola's last words were, "Should I not die willingly for Him who suffered so much for me?" He then communed so deeply with God that he seemed unaware of what was happening around him. He and his two friends were hanged in the public square, and then their bodies were burned.

ONE MAN CAN CHANGE THE WORLD

One lone man, totally surrendered to God, burning with passion for revival in the church and nation and the salvation of the people, had for several years turned the tide against evil in church, government, and the lives of the people. If God could use one Savonarola to bring such a mighty revival at such an impossible time, what could He not do in answer to a movement of truly prevailing prayer by the thousands of believers and Christian leaders who love Christ today? But will we prepare the way of the Lord through prayer like Savonarola did? Will we feed on God's Word and memorize much of the Bible by heart as he did? Will we spend the nights and hours in prayer and fasting as he did?

Savonarola feared neither men nor demons. He exposed sin wherever he found it. He was a pioneer of the Protestant Reformation, though he was a loyal Roman Catholic even when the pope excommunicated him. Savonarola replied from his pulpit that we must obey God rather than man. He said the pope was a fallible person like every other sinner and could make mistakes and sin just as any other person. Savonarola pointed out that the current church leader, Pope Alexander, had illegally purchased his office with money and was not even a believer.

Martin Luther, as he grew up, was greatly influenced by the life, ministry, and death of Savonarola. Certainly Savonarola is one of the greatest heroes in the history of the church and in the history of revival. He will stand before God's judgment throne one day to witness against all who in these days have compromised their conscience and kept silent in order to secure favor and position in church, business, and government. He will denounce the cowards who failed to condemn sin in high places, who watered down their convictions in order to secure promotion, position, or power even in Christian denominations and organizations.

CHAPTER SEVEN

The Great Awakening Dawns

In the 1500s another monk, Martin Luther, was guided by the Holy Spirit to lead a revival in Germany. His renewal movement spread into Switzerland under Ulrich Zwingli and John Calvin, and to Scotland through John Knox. From those areas it spread throughout France, Scandinavia, and the British Isles. Luther's renewal was more truly a reformation than a revival. Its leaders, though godly men of the sixteenth century, were thought of as reformers rather than as revivalists.

God did send real revival, however, repeatedly in the localities affected by these Protestant leaders. Through the newly revived hearts of individuals, the church, government, and society experienced much-needed change. The results were not thought of so much as various revivals but as part of a movement of widespread reformation.

THREE YOUNG MEN ON FIRE

Two centuries after God used Luther, Calvin, and others to bring reformation to Europe, the spiritual life in the churches largely died out. Sin engulfed the nations again. Civil unrest, rioting, smuggling, and violence were threatening England. The French Revolution almost destroyed

France. Now it was the 1730s, and the Spirit of God burned in holy fire in the hearts of three young Englishmen: John Wesley, age thirty-five; Charles Wesley, age thirty-one; and George Whitefield, only eighteen years of age.

The Wesleyan Revival, or "Great Awakening," moved in power across the British Isles and the American colonies. It launched a period in church history in which for nearly two centuries there were recurrent revival movements.

The revival began in England and spread across Wales, Scotland, and Ireland. It later spread to America through Whitefield and Methodist itinerant circuit riders like Francis Asbury. Wherever the Wesleys, Whitefield, or their successors went, salvation fires and revival fires began to burn. Nearly every denomination experienced renewal and growth, but for over fifty years it was the Methodist movement that most profoundly demonstrated God's revival fire.

ENGLAND BEFORE THE REVIVAL

The eighteenth century was a time of great moral and spiritual darkness, political restlessness, and social need in many parts of the world. In England, deism had had a devastating effect, and the authority of the Bible was shaken. Spiritual indifference and skepticism abounded, and liberty degenerated into license. Religion was emptied of its spirituality and power. Viewed with contempt, it became at most a code of ethics. The masses were largely untouched by the church. There were godly, faithful ministers here and there, but many clergy were mere figureheads who did not teach and actually opposed the doctrine of salvation by faith. Many were known for their drinking habits. At times some of them even led riots against the revivalists.

In higher circles of society, people laughed at the mention of religion. Most prominent statesmen were unbelievers and known for grossly immoral lives, drunkenness, and foul language. Marriage was sneered at. Lord Chesterfield's famous letters to educate his son instructed him how to seduce.

Many clergymen supported by the state did not live near the churches to which they were assigned. They enjoyed the revenue, but some never saw their parishes. One bishop boasted he had only seen his diocese once. He habitually resided at the lakeside. Church services declined, church buildings fell into disrepair, worship was neglected. Not more than four or five members of the House of Commons attended church. Lord Bolingbrooke reproved a group of clergymen for their lifestyle and called it "the greatest miracle in the world" that Christianity was surviving when it was committed to the hands of "such un-Christian men as you."[1]

The common people in prerevival England were, for the most part, ignorant and amazingly brutal. There were schools only for the elite. Few towns had any kind of police force; mobs ransacked and pillaged in London and Birmingham, burning houses, flinging open prisons, and terrorizing people.

The criminal classes became bold in intimidating the populace. Every third house in London sold liquor, and gin shops invited the public to "get drunk for a penny, or dead drunk for two pence and straw to lie on till the drunken stupor was gone."[2]

Londoners rarely traveled after dark, even to the nearest suburbs, except with an armed group. Smugglers operated along the coastal areas, and armed bands brought the smuggled goods to London. Even the sports were brutal: cock fighting, bull fights, bear baiting, and savage bulldog fights.

Despite an ineffectual police force, criminal justice during this time was quite ruthless. There were at least 160 actions declared to be "liable to death without benefit of clergy"—that is, instant death. Cutting down a cherry tree, snatching something out of the hand of a man and running away with it, stealing forty shillings or more from a home, stealing to the value of five shillings from a shop—all of these brought the death penalty until 1800. During one court session there is a record of forty to fifty people being hanged at one time.

Prisons were crowded, dark, and filthy, with the air offensive from the open sewers running through the prison cells. There was no bedding and insufficient water, and the only food supplied was twopenny worth of bread per person per day. Many prisoners died in the dark and filthy prison cells. It was in these prisons that Wesley and other members of his group began ministering early in the revival period.

THE HOLY CLUB

In the early 1730s the Wesley brothers gathered several student friends into John's room at Lincoln College, Oxford University, to earnestly seek to be holy. Membership ran ten to fifteen, and never more than twenty-five. After John Wesley left Oxford in 1735, the group disintegrated.[3] This group was initially called, in derision, the "Holy Club" and sometimes "Bible-Moths."

These young men sought to live by stringent rules designed to help them achieve holiness. They had a method of daily self-examination, partook of communion each week, fasted each Wednesday and Friday in imitation of the early church, and regularly visited the prisoners and the sick. They tried so diligently to please God and be holy by their methods that many began calling them "Methodists."

John and Charles Wesley went to America to minister to the Indians and colonists, but they had little success. Their high standards for holy living and direct preaching against the more popular sins closed hearts against them. They returned to England after a year and a half. But God saw these sincere and hungry hearts. George Whitefield, Charles Wesley, and, on May 24, 1738, John Wesley himself all received the assurance of sins forgiven and began to teach and preach instant salvation by faith.

Spiritually, in spite of reformation two centuries before, the possibility of immediate salvation or of assurance of salvation was unheard of in the churches. When the Wesleys and Whitefield began to preach this doctrine, they were scorned and nearly excluded from the church, although they were ordained ministers of the Church of England. But this was now their burning message and testimony, and they proclaimed it far and wide.

A REVIVAL IS LAUNCHED

On New Year's Day, 1739, John and Charles Wesley, George Whitefield, and four other members of the Holy Club, plus about sixty other like-minded people, held a love-feast in London at Fetter's Lane. "About three in the morning, as we were continuing instant in prayer, the power of God came mightily upon us, insomuch that many cried out for exceeding joy, and many fell to the ground (overcome by the power of God). As soon as we recovered a little from that awe and amazement at the presence of His majesty, we broke out with one voice, 'We praise Thee, O God; we acknowledge thee to be the Lord.'"[4] This event has been called the Methodist Pentecost.

Five nights later eight of these "Methodists" prayed and discussed till the early morning hours and left with "the conviction that God was about to do great things." Another night that week a group of them met and spent the whole night in prayer.

The next weekend, January 14, 1739, Whitefield was ordained. He spent the day before his ordination in prayer and fasting, praying on into the evening. Sunday morning he arose early to pray. "When I went up to the altar, I could think of nothing but Samuel's standing as a little child before the Lord. . . . When the bishop laid his hand upon my head my heart was melted down, and I offered my whole spirit, soul, and body to the service of God's sanctuary! I read the Gospel, at the bishop's command, with power."[5]

From that day on Whitefield preached with great unction and power. He was only twenty-two years old, but wherever he spoke crowds flocked to hear him. His rooms were filled with praying Oxford students. He wrote, "I sleep very little. Had I a thousand hands I would employ them all. I want a thousand tongues to praise Him. He still works by me more and more."

In the opening days of the great revival it was Whitefield, more than John Wesley, who dared to innovate and lead. When Whitefield preached at Bermondsey Church in February 1739, the crowd was so great that even the churchyard was filled. God led Whitefield to go outdoors to preach. In his clerical gown, Whitefield preached his first open-air sermon to a congregation of two hundred and launched a new day in gospel history.

Crowds swelled day by day until some twenty thousand gathered. Some of the wealthy sat in coaches and others on horseback. Some sat in the trees, and everywhere people crowded the ground to hear Whitefield preach. At times all were moved to tears as the Spirit of God gripped them.

Within six weeks John Wesley took his place at Whitefield's side. As a high churchman of the Church of England, Wesley had many prejudices to overcome. On the second day of preaching, Wesley's message was, "The Spirit of the Lord is upon me, because He hath anointed me to preach the gospel to the poor." He saw the masses as harassed and helpless, sheep without a shepherd, and he, like Christ, was moved with compassion.

Charles Wesley was the most emotional and appealing of the three. Tears would flow down his cheeks as he spoke, and his audiences were deeply moved. Whitefield was the preeminent orator of the movement and became perhaps England's greatest preacher-orator. John Wesley was not as powerful an orator as Whitefield, but he was more organized, had a more dominating personality, and outlived Whitefield by twenty-one years. They had doctrinal differences but remained close friends until Whitefield's death.

In the next few chapters, we will look more closely at the ministries of these three young men and the revival fire that burned through them to rekindle two nations.

CHAPTER EIGHT

George Whitefield: Ablaze for God

During the year and a half before he sailed for America, George Whitefield preached to crowds almost everywhere he went. He was only twenty-two, but his name became a household word across England. He was a man of prayer, a man of compassion, and a man of true humility. From his first message after his ordination until the end of his life, he maintained one goal: winning souls. Between sermons he spent much of his time counseling and praying with people convicted of their sins. People called him "The Awakener" and "The Fire-Bringer." The God who answered by fire in Elijah's day was still at work through George Whitefield.

In Bristol and in London, the multitudes were moved. At one place, the communion elements had to be consecrated four times because so many people kept coming forward. On some occasions, Whitefield preached up to four times on Sundays, beginning at 6:00 A.M., because so many people wanted to hear him. Churches were so crowded that constables had to be placed at the doors to maintain order. Thousands were turned away for lack of room.

On December 28, Whitefield sailed for America. Immediately God began to use him on board the ship as he preached and taught the Bible. The two smaller ships accompanying them drew close on either side so that all could hear. When they stopped at Gibraltar, Whitefield preached to soldiers and local people. The audience quickly shot up from three hundred to a thousand.

Reaching Georgia, Whitefield began the Lord's work. But three months later he returned to England to raise money for an orphanage he wanted to build in America. He reached England November 30, 1738, after a dangerous nine-week voyage.

REVIVAL COMES TO ENGLAND

While Whitefield was in America, John and Charles Wesley had kept the sacred fire burning at home. The reunion of the Holy Three upon Whitefield's return could be called the official launching of God's mighty movement of revival in Britain.

Jealousy among the ministers closed the doors of all the churches against Whitefield in Bristol. So he went to a notorious area of the city called Kingswood and preached in the open air. Kingswood was a rough four-thousand-acre district at the edge of Bristol where coal miners lived. The miners did not mix with the other laboring classes. People shuddered at their dirty hovels, calling the miners "sheer heathen" who lived like "utter savages." Some had suggested to Whitefield, "Why go to America to preach to the Indians? Go to Kingswood, to the Colliers."

Whitefield preached his first message to two hundred shocked people who had never seen a clergyman in a clerical gown speaking outside a church building. He felt so assured of God's presence and blessing that he went back, and this time five thousand gathered to listen. Crowds soon increased to twenty thousand. At times nearly the entire congregation wept with conviction. As one writer describes it, "White gutters made by tears plentifully fell down their black cheeks as they came out of the coal-pits."[1]

For six weeks Whitefield preached at Kingswood, and thousands were gripped by the Holy Spirit. He preached in the yards of the glass factories to Bristol's most sinful and desperate people. He went to Moorfields—one of the most vile and notorious pleasure parks and resorts in London— and then to Kennington Common, an outdoor resort also used by the government for public hangings. Thirty thousand gathered to hear him for the first message. The singing of the people could be heard across the countryside, and Whitefield's voice was so clear that people a mile away could understand him. All classes of people, from the nobility to the poor, gathered to hear him. Often the nobility sat in their coaches, while the common people thronged on the ground.

DOORS CLOSE BUT GREATER DOORS OPEN

Then Whitefield went to the Hackney Marsh race course and preached to the ten thousand people who were there for the races. The people largely ignored the racing and listened instead to the Gospel as Whitefield proclaimed it. A few days later he went to Marylebone Fields and thirty thousand people gathered. Later at Moorfields sixty thousand attended. By this time the more Whitefield preached, the more opposition he faced from the church.

Threats were made at these gatherings by ill-tempered ruffians that Whitefield would not come out alive. At times when he preached in the open, he had to push alone through the rabble to find a place from which to speak. Once the table on which Whitefield was to stand was smashed before he reached it. Yet he preached without molestation to crowds of thousands. In one place he preached to fifteen thousand in the morning and double that number at night, and yet the thousand stood so quietly, one would have thought there were only fifty people present.

Prominent clergymen were so incensed that they attacked Whitefield and published pamphlets against him. He boldly carried on. Meanwhile, Wesley preached to similar crowds at Bristol, and his messages received even more opposition. Yet the Holy Spirit ministered through Wesley's quiet messages even more than through the dynamic sermons of Whitefield, and numbers of people fell to the ground as if thunderstruck.

BACK TO AMERICA

After a preaching tour of England's cities, Whitefield embarked again for America. He spent the eleven-week voyage in impassioned prayer, self-examination, and Bible study. Reaching America, he began a warm and lifelong friendship with Benjamin Franklin, who published Whitefield's sermons and journals. Everywhere he went, Whitefield took up offerings for his orphanage project, just as he had done in England.

As Whitefield moved across America he had many contacts with the Presbyterians, and his theological position became more strongly Calvinistic. He traveled in triumph from town to town: New Brunswick, Elizabethtown, Maidenhead, Neshaminy, Abingdon, and back to Philadelphia. Considering the comparative sparsity of the U.S. population, Whitefield's crowds were phenomenal. At Neshaminy, three thousand people gathered, one thousand of them sitting on horseback while he preached. At Germantown there were six thousand. Two hundred horsemen accompanied him when he journeyed from there to Philadelphia. When Whitefield went to Chester, three thousand people came out to meet him. Two thousand people listened in the street at Newcastle, and later that day two thousand met at Christian Bridge. The next day ten thousand returned to Christian

Bridge, hundreds of them on horseback. Whitefield preached two sermons, with a small interval between them.

The governor of Maryland attended one of Whitefield's meetings, and a few days later Whitefield dined with the governor of Virginia. For five months he moved from place to place, across Virginia and Carolina and into Georgia. Reaching Savannah, Whitefield devoted himself primarily to his orphanage project. He was already supporting 150 orphans, but he continually struggled with bringing in enough funds to meet their needs. The small towns he preached in could not donate enough to keep the orphan project going. So Whitefield rode back to Boston, where twenty thousand listened and funds were again contributed for his orphanage.

A HOME AT BETHESDA

At Whitefield's orphanage in Bethesda, the day began for the children at 5:00 A.M. with fifteen minutes of private prayer. At six o'clock they assembled in the chapel for a hymn and the morning Bible lesson from Whitefield or the manager. They breakfasted at seven, after a morning hymn and free prayer. The hours from eight to ten were spent working. The girls learned domestic tasks such as spinning and weaving, picking cotton, sewing, knitting, cleaning, carrying water, and cutting wood. The boys were taught the trades: shoemaking, tailoring, carpentry, and other skills.

School lasted from 10:00 A.M. until 4:00 P.M., with a two-hour break at noon for lunch. From 4:00 to 6:00 P.M. the children returned to work. Supper and hymns were at 6:00 P.M. At 8:00 P.M., Whitefield taught the catechism, and at nine there was light refreshment and fifteen minutes of private prayer before retiring. Does this seem oppressive for the orphans? Compared to the cruel forced labor that other homeless children endured in those times, this was an almost blissful atmosphere of quiet, music, and method.

THE YOUNG SOUL WINNER

Whitefield had accomplished much during this brief time; he was still only twenty-five. By September he was back in Boston, preaching to four thousand, and the next Sunday to fifteen thousand at the Boston Common. The population of Boston itself was only ten thousand to twelve thousand. At one meeting, a Boston clergyman greeted him, "I am sorry to see you here." Whitefield replied, "So is the devil." On he went to Cambridge, where he was greeted by a crowd of seven thousand.

At times Whitefield's lodgings were so crowded with inquirers that he could scarcely find time to eat his meals. When he left Boston, his associate Gilbert Tennent carried on the ministry for four more months. Two Boston ministers each testified that more people came to them for prayer and spiritual help in one week than had come to them in the whole previous twenty-four years. Revival continued for a year and a half. Church services overflowed. Thirty religious societies were started, and nearly every night ministers held meetings in private homes.

Whitefield reached Northampton, where Jonathan Edwards was pastor. The awakening under Edwards had begun in 1737, and practically every person in town, younger or older, had been moved by that revival. The whole town was filled with the presence of God.

When Whitefield entered Edwards' territory, he poured fresh spiritual fuel on the fire. Edwards and Tennent had emphasized the terror of God, the judgment, and the darker side of the Calvinist mind. But Whitefield preached the consolations of God, the privileges of His children, and the outpouring of the Spirit on believers. Instead of continual distress over sin, people experienced a spiritual renewal as Whitefield preached a healing, tender, positive gospel.

Wherever Whitefield went, in city after city between Northampton and New York City, God "kindled the flame

of revival in each place." Upon reaching New York, Whitefield felt so needy and unworthy that he cast himself on the
ground humbly before the Lord. He was so weak that he
could hardly reach the church where he was to speak.

Whitefield had no more than begun his sermon when
the Spirit of God came upon the congregation. From all over
the building came the sound of loud weeping. Many fell into
the arms of others. Whitefield poured out his heart until he
could speak no longer. At Staten Island, "fire fell from
heaven on the crowds." Whitefield continued to Philadelphia and then returned to Savannah, Georgia. In spite of
offerings collected along the way for his orphanages, Whitefield still owed a considerable debt. So in January 1741, he
returned to England.

Whitefield's impact on the churches of America was
phenomenal. The Congregational churches of New England
were revived. The Presbyterian and Baptist churches of the
middle states received new power and aggressiveness. The
mixed colonies in the South received new zeal and energy.
Whitefield's published sermons led to the founding of the
Presbyterian Church in Virginia and beyond. The Baptists
of Virginia, the South, and the Southwest built on the foun-
dations of his ministry. Whitefield did not organize the
results of his preaching, but his ministry prepared the way
for Wesley's zealous itinerant preachers who came a few
years later.

CHAPTER NINE

Whitefield's Continued Ministry

During Whitefield's time in America, revival fires had continued to burn brightly in England. God used the Wesley brothers in London, Howell Harris in Wales, and Benjamin Ingham in Yorkshire. When Whitefield returned to England, the doctrinal differences between him and John Wesley became evident. At first, many to whom Whitefield formerly ministered refused to listen to him, choosing instead to follow Wesley. Whitefield and the Wesleys, however, remained close friends.

Whitefield went to Scotland for the first time, and wherever he went revival flames began to burn. He preached in city after city across Scotland. He interrupted this revival ministry to journey to Wales, where he married a widow of thirty-six. He himself was only twenty-six.

At the end of 1741, he returned to Bristol and then started across England, speaking to thousands with God's power upon him. From this time on, Whitefield's routine when he was in the British Isles was to preach at his Moorfields center in London in the winter and to tour other parts of England in the summer.

Whitefield describes his Easter Monday at Moorfields. At 6:00 A.M. there were already about ten thousand revelers in the spacious area. Whitefield, with a large congregation of praying people before him, began to preach. A hush from God came over the worldly crowd. Many were moved to tears. At noon Whitefield went out again. He estimates from twenty to thirty thousand people had gathered in the area. Opponents threw stones, dirt, rotten eggs, and dead cats at him. But as he preached on, most of the people became like "lambs." Whitefield announced a third service for 6:00 in the evening.

By then, thousands more than before gathered in the area. As Whitefield began to preach, people deserted the entertainers and clowns in other parts of the area. An enemy tried to strike Whitefield with a long, heavy whip. Other opponents beat drums to drown out his message. Despite numerous disturbances, Whitefield preached on for three hours. Three hundred fifty people were converted that day, and more than a thousand people handed notes to him asking for prayer.

The next day Whitefield held a similar daring program in Marylebone field, and the following day he was back at Moorfields.

MIGHTY REVIVAL IN CAMBUSLANG

Two years before Whitefield's return to Scotland, a godly but ordinary minister in Cambuslang, a suburb of Glasgow, had read to his congregation reports of Whitefield's ministry and the revival in America. Later this minister preached a series of sermons on the new birth. Suddenly, the fire of God fell upon the people.

The minister preached daily and, between the services, prayed with people convicted of their sins. In less than three months three hundred people were converted. Revival fires spread to four nearby parishes and eventually to Kilsyth, twelve miles from Glasgow.

When Whitefield arrived in Edinburgh in June 1742, seats to hold two thousand people had been erected in a park. He preached twice a day to great crowds and regularly visited three hospitals. On July 8 Whitefield arrived at Cambuslang, where he preached to large crowds in the afternoon and late into the evening.

Whitefield describes the event: "Such a commotion was surely never heard of, especially about eleven o'clock at night. It far outdid anything I ever saw in America. For about an hour and a half there was such weeping, so many falling into deep distress, and manifesting it in various ways, that description is impossible. The people seemed to be smitten in scores. They were carried off and brought into the house like wounded soldiers taken from a field of battle. Their agonies and cries were deeply affecting." When Whitefield stopped, the parish minister preached another sermon until after one o'clock in the morning. Even then the people did not want to leave. Throughout the whole night prayer and praise could be heard in the fields.[1]

THE COMMUNION OF SAINTS

Two days later, thirty thousand people assembled to hear Whitefield preach his Sunday sermon. Seventeen hundred people took the sacrament, which was administered in two tents. When the people returned that evening to their villages in the surrounding areas, they told the story of revival wherever they went. On August 15, a second communion service was held in three tents pitched for the occasion. Such a service had never been seen in Scotland, with twelve ministers officiating, three thousand taking communion, and those present numbering between thirty and fifty thousand. Many had come from England and Ireland. The

Cambuslang revival shook the whole of Scotland and sent its fire over all the country.

On October 3 at Kilsyth, twelve ministers officiated at a communion gathering that lasted from 8:30 A.M. till 8:30 P.M. Twenty-two separate services of communion were held. Whitefield reported, "I saw 10,000 people affected in a moment, some with joy, some with crying ... some fainting in the arms of friends."[2]

TO WALES AND BEYOND

Whitefield's friend Howell Harris had recently founded the Calvinistic Methodist movement in Wales. On January 5, 1743, Whitefield presided at the group's first conference. As moderator of this new denomination, he traveled the length and breadth of Wales, preaching to three thousand at Neath, four thousand in Swansea, and to several thousand in other towns. In just three weeks he traveled four hundred miles, preaching forty times in thirteen towns in seven counties. Whitefield and his followers faced angry mobs, and some of his followers were assaulted and wounded.

Whitefield returned to America on his fifth voyage, arriving October 26, 1744. He preached in and around Boston for three months, his average audience about two thousand. He traveled through Connecticut and Rhode Island preaching to thousands, usually twice a day. During this time God sent revival to the Delaware Indians through the prayer and ministry of David Brainerd.

Whitefield reached his Bethesda orphanage at Savannah in January 1746. At times he toured Maryland and Virginia, where a revival began through reading a volume of his sermons. His wife apparently stayed in Bethesda while he went back to New England. Whitefield's health was very poor, so he went to the island of Bermuda for rest. He found its climate too hot, however, so he took a ship to England, hoping to rejoin his wife at Bethesda in a few months.

MASS EVANGELISM

Thousands welcomed Whitefield when he reached London. In 1749 he surrendered the moderatorship of the Welsh Calvinistic Methodist Church. He preached to crowds during a short visit to Scotland. Returning to Plymouth, in the south of England, he was greeted ten miles from the city by a great cavalcade, and he preached to thousands each night for a week.

In the winter of 1749–50, Whitefield preached to huge congregations at six o'clock each morning before the business day began. He and Wesley exchanged pulpits at times. Whitefield was not physically strong and was, in fact, very sick. At times he preached with such passion that he vomited blood afterwards, but he would not spare himself.

As spring arrived, Whitefield started across the nation. In two months he preached ninety times to a total of about 240,000 people. In Ireland he preached to the largest crowds ever. He returned to England, and thousands heard him in Moorfields, Bristol, and Wales. The year of 1753 he spent "cross-plowing the land," drawing larger and larger crowds—up to twenty thousand each in Leeds and Glasgow. Whitefield opened his first tabernacle in Bristol but returned suddenly to London upon hearing of his friend John Wesley's serious illness. Wesley recovered and lived another forty years.

WOUNDED AND WEAK IN BODY

Whitefield spent another year in America, then returned to England for an eight-year period. During a speaking trip to Ireland, the Roman Catholics stoned him within "an inch or two of death." He suffered massive blows to his head, skull, and face, leaving him "almost breathless and all over a gore of blood." He bore the scar of the wounds on his temple the rest of his life.[3]

Whitefield's body was weakening, and by 1758 he could preach only once a day and only three times on Sunday. His health was so poor he had to travel by carriage rather than on horseback. Between 1763 and 1768, however, he made two more trips to America. In August 1768, upon the death of his wife, he returned to London to preach her funeral sermon. Shortly afterward, while preaching and writing in Wales, he burst a blood vessel and again almost died. The "Holy Trio"—John and Charles Wesley and Whitefield—began to meet together frequently in Whitefield's home. John Wesley mourned to see Whitefield's health in such a poor state. The three men sang together, prayed together, and shared "a feast of love," reveling in Christ's preciousness. In one letter to his flock at Tottenham Court Road in London, Whitefield wrote, "Had I strength equal to my will, I would fly from pole to pole. Though wearied and almost worn out, I am not weary of my blessed Master's service. O love Him! Love Him!"[4]

FAREWELL SERMONS

In 1769 Whitefield preached for the last time in place after place. He said in London, "It is now high time for me to preach my own funeral sermon. I am going for the thirteenth time to cross the Atlantic. . . . I might have been rich; but now, though this chapel is built, and though I have a comfortable room to live in, I assure you I built the room at my own expense. It cost nobody but myself anything, and I shall leave it with an easy mind. . . . I have a better land in view."[5]

He wrote to John Wesley, "What hath God wrought for us, in us, and by us. . . . O, the height, the depth, the length, and the breadth of thy love, O God! Surely it passeth knowledge!"[6]

Whitefield arrived back at Bethesda on December 14, 1769. On April 24, 1770, he left Bethesda for the last time. Reaching Philadelphia, he met Wesley's first two missionaries who had been sent to America and did all he could to help them. He preached for three weeks in Philadelphia and then traveled on to New York. During July he preached every day, traveling a five-hundred-mile circuit to large congregations moved by the Holy Spirit.

Whitefield wrote, "O what a new scene of usefulness is opening up in various parts of the New World! All fresh work where I have been! The Divine influence is as at the first." His preaching was "never more powerful or popular."[7]

Whitefield's last two months were "a grand itinerary of New England towns—a triumphal progress of impassioned evangelism."[8] On September 29 he preached his last sermon in the open air. Standing on a large cask, he spoke to a vast multitude for two hours. He then traveled on to Newburyport, Massachusetts. While he ate his supper, a crowd gathered outside hoping to hear him preach. "I am tired and must go to bed," he said. He took a lighted candle and started upstairs to his room. But as he saw the crowd standing, he turned and started to preach, continuing until the candle burned down to the socket and went out.

At 2:00 in the morning Whitefield awoke to a violent attack of asthma. Unable to sleep, he began to pray for his orphanage and for his congregation in London. By 5:00 he was panting for breath and went to the window. At 6:00 A.M. he awoke in heaven. It was September 30, 1770, and he was fifty-six. Whitefield had blazed until he burned out for God.

At the memorial service in Newburyport, six thousand gathered. Hymns could not be heard because of the crying and sobbing. Church bells tolled, and the ships in the harbor fired their guns in salute. In Georgia, the governor and council led a procession to the memorial service. As the news spread across two continents, many memorial services were held and large audiences attended in city after city. In London the multitudes crowded the tabernacle to hear John Wesley's eloquent tribute to his lifelong friend, George Whitefield.

Whitefield was one of God's elite men of fire. Like Wesley and Finney, wherever he went there flowed a mighty current of God's Spirit. Revival and harvest were integral parts of Whitefield's faithful, zealous ministry. May God give us more men of fire like George Whitefield.

CHAPTER TEN

Wesley the Revivalist

The Great Revival Awakening of the years 1739–91 is frequently called the Wesleyan revival. For though God greatly used George Whitefield, both Wesley brothers, and dozens of lay preachers to light revival fires, John Wesley preached in more places, to more people, and for many more years than the others. He also did more to conserve the fruit of the revival. John Wesley was clearly the God-chosen leader of this major spiritual awakening.

WESLEY'S CHILDHOOD

John Wesley, fifteenth child of Rev. Samuel and Susannah Wesley, was born June 17, 1703. Of the nineteen Wesley children, only six lived to maturity. Both parents were raised as religious nonconformists, but both were also independent. When Samuel and Susannah were about thirteen, they both decided to reject their nonconformist backgrounds and identify with the Church of England. John was the fourth generation in his family to attend Oxford University.

Susannah was the twenty-fourth child of Dr. and Mrs. Samuel Annesley. Dr. Annesley was the "Saint Paul of the non-conformists,"[1] and his ancestors included earls and viscounts. Susannah was a lady both by birth and by breeding.

John Wesley's roots sprang from both the nobility and the clergy.

Susannah relied on her strong Puritan background in raising her children. She enforced a detailed timetable, which included morning and evening devotions and regular times for meditation and self-examination before God. She kept a spiritual journal and strictly observed the Sabbath. Her children were expected to be obedient, quiet, helpful, and respectful, and she taught them all to read. She set aside a special time one night each week with each of the children to talk about the Bible, Christ, and their own spiritual attitudes. John said that until the age of ten he never consciously disobeyed his father in anything.

When John was six years old, enemies set their house on fire. The fire spread so rapidly that after the family escaped outside the house, they realized little John was still sleeping inside. Just then he appeared at an upstairs window. There was no time to run for a ladder. One neighbor stood on the shoulders of another and reached John just as the roof fell in. The Wesleys always considered him "a burning stick snatched from the fire" (Zech. 3:2).

When he was eleven, John was sent to a boarding school, Charterhouse, where he continued until he went to Oxford at the age of seventeen. At Charterhouse the senior boys "fagged" the younger boys, not only treating them as servants, but also taking away from them all the meat and many of the vegetables served. As a result, during much of John's early teens, he had a small daily portion of bread as his only food. He learned to suffer wrong with patience.

Wesley attributed his wonderful health throughout his long life to a simple diet and exercise. As a boy, he obeyed his father's instructions to run around the school grounds three times each morning. Throughout life he enjoyed walking.

THE HOLY CLUB

At seventeen, John was elected to Christ Church College at Oxford and entered in June 1720. He was diligent in his studies and skilled in logic, and he maintained a free and cheerful disposition. He was faithful in public and private prayer, and in his studies he became acquainted with and much influenced by *The Imitation of Christ* by Thomas á Kempis and *Holy Living and Dying* by Jeremy Taylor.

John received his bachelor's degree in 1724, was ordained in 1725, and became a Fellow of Lincoln College. The next year he was made a lecturer in Greek and moderator of classes. In 1727, he received his master's degree. During these years John read two books by William Law: *Christian Perfection* and *A Serious Call to a Devout and Holy Life*. He soon became a personal friend of Law and was tremendously influenced by him.

The holy and disciplined childhood John had enjoyed from his mother blessed and influenced him all his life. In spite of her large family and busy life as a mother, Susannah taught all the children until they reached primary school. She set the example by regularly taking an hour in the early morning, an hour in the evening, and often an hour at noon to be alone with God. For thirteen years after his ordination, John Wesley longed for the holy life. He sought to obtain salvation by his disciplined devotion, constant worship of God, abstention from sin, and acts of Christian service.

It was at Oxford, in November 1729, that John's brother Charles and two other students began to meet together for three or four evenings each week to discuss their subjects and their Christian life. As soon as John Wesley returned, he became the accepted leader of the group. They began their meetings with prayer, studied the Greek New Testament and classics, reviewed that day, and planned the next day. Then they prayed again, had supper together, and listened to John read. On Sunday they read devotional and theological writings. They fasted on Wednesdays and Fridays and celebrated communion once a week. A system of self-examination, arranged topically, was followed each day: for example, on Sundays they meditated on "the Love of God in Simplicity," on Mondays "the Love of Man," and so on.[2]

The men sought God's will in everything and prayed with fervor. Each day they strove to develop some virtue, such as humility, faith, hope, or love. Almost every hour they would offer a brief prayer for this particular virtue. They repeated printed prayers of the Church of England at nine, twelve, and three o'clock.

Many members of the Holy Club began to visit in jails, teaching the prisoners to read and to pray. They visited the sick an hour or two each week. It is easy to understand why the club's numbers did not grow rapidly. The most important one to join them, after several years, was George Whitefield. The group fluctuated in numbers, but there were never more than twenty-five. At the end of each year the members gave away all they had left when their own needs were met. They assisted poor families, read to them, and taught their children.

John Wesley urged the other members never to waste a moment. He himself was able to fall asleep the moment he lay down. Wesley said he did not total fifteen minutes a month in lying on his bed awake. In his old age when he would come in from an exhausting ride, he could lie down for ten or fifteen minutes and arise again fresh.

MISSIONARY SERVICE

On October 14, 1735, John and Charles Wesley sailed for America as missionaries to the colonists and Indians. For two years they ministered rather unsuccessfully in Georgia. Although George Whitefield reported that Wesley had made a great impact and that he was loved by the people, still Wesley found his ministry basically disappointing. He had hoped to see reproduced the same high standards of Christian living he had come to be familiar with in his Holy Club. He was constantly disillusioned, and his preaching against popular sin was never well received. On February 1, 1738, he arrived back in England. Charles had preceded him.

On the American trip Wesley had become acquainted with the Moravians and was challenged by their assurance of salvation and their fearlessness in the face of death. Wesley still did not have assurance of his own salvation. "I went to America to convert the Indians, but, oh! who shall convert me?" he mourned. "What have I learned myself in the meantime? Why (what I the least of all suspected), that I, who went to America to convert others, was myself never converted to God."[3]

WESLEY'S NEW BIRTH

After years of faithfully pursuing God and an assurance of salvation, Wesley finally became convinced by the testimony of his Moravian friend, Peter Bohler, and by his own study of the Greek New Testament. He believed fully that salvation is instantaneous and by faith, and he convinced his brother Charles also. Charles was the first to receive the joyful assurance of sins forgiven. Four days later, on May 24, 1738, John Wesley himself received the witness of the Spirit. It occurred while he was in a small society meeting, listening to Luther's preface to the book of Romans. Toward 10:00 P.M. John called, "I believe." His friends all joined together in a hymn of joy and then they parted with prayer.[4]

The next six months were spent in joyous ministry in whatever churches would open their doors to him, in religious societies, in prisons, and in homes. Whitefield returned from America on December 11, and Wesley hastened to meet him and join in fellowship. The little society at Fetter

Lane had grown to thirty-two members. Then came the great outpouring of the Spirit on New Year's Day, 1739, described more fully in chapter 7.

Over sixty people were present at the moment when the Wesleys, George Whitefield, and others received God's power in the Spirit. Waves of unspeakable joy passed over them, and they prostrated themselves on the ground in awe and adoration. God gave these men a deep conviction that He was about to do something great and wonderful in England. They were sure they had entered a glorious year of God's grace and power. God did not disappoint them.

THE WESLEY-WHITEFIELD REVIVAL

The dawning of the new year marked the probable beginning of the great revival. Certainly the Wesleys and others were instantly filled with the Spirit, and a new power and fruitfulness was immediately apparent. Within a month and a half Whitefield was preaching to the thousands, and within three months Wesley was doing the same.

George Whitefield was already popular as a speaker and had returned from widespread evangelism in the States. The churches in Britain were now prejudiced against him and the doctrines he and Wesley were preaching. On Whitefield's return to Bristol, not one church was opened to him, but God's call and message still burned within him.

Meanwhile, Wesley was fully involved in London, preaching to religious societies. The power and anointing of the Spirit rested on him in a new way. Here is one week's ministry: On Sunday, February 25, he preached to two crowded churches, to three hundred at a religious society meeting, then at a house service, then at a service of the Fetter Lane Society, and finally at another house service—six services that day. On Tuesday he preached three times, on Wednesday once, on Thursday to about three hundred at the Savoy Theater, and on Friday he preached three times.

Whitefield kept urging Wesley to come to Bristol and help. In April, Wesley stood at Whitefield's side in Kingswood, still questioning the appropriateness of speaking outside a church building. That night Wesley preached on the Sermon on the Mount. Suddenly he realized that Jesus had also preached out-of-doors. Whitefield returned to London, so the next day Wesley preached to three thousand in the open air in Kingswood. He remained in Bristol for two months, busier than ever before. His 7:00 A.M. Sunday services often had five to six thousand in attendance.

Here, to Wesley's surprise, he began to experience the Holy Spirit powerfully convicting people of their sins while he preached. Well-dressed, mature people suddenly cried out as if in the agonies of death. Both men and women, outside and inside the church buildings, would tremble and sink to the ground. When Wesley stopped and prayed for them, they soon found peace and rejoiced in Christ.

One Quaker, greatly displeased at the groans and cries of the people who were convicted of their sins, was suddenly smitten to the ground in deep agony over his own sin. After Wesley prayed, the Quaker called out, "Now I know thou art a prophet of the Lord."[5] Similar scenes occurred in London and Newcastle. Wesley did not encourage these emotional reactions and recognized that there could be imitations. He himself always spoke in a calm, unemotional voice. But he also recognized that God's power was at work, convicting and transforming person after person.

METHODIST REVIVAL SPREADS

Returning to London, Whitefield asked Wesley to preach in Black Heath. Wesley preached twice: at 7:00 A.M. in Upper Moorfields to a crowd of twelve to fourteen thousand, and at 5:00 P.M. at Kennington Common to fifteen thousand. Soon Charles Wesley also began to preach in the open air.

At first the two centers of Wesley's ministry were in London and Bristol. Then the work spread to Newcastle in the north, where Wesley found so much drunkenness, cursing and swearing, even by little children, that he felt compelled to stand in the open to preach. Crowds soon stood in rapt attention. When Wesley would stop at an inn or in a home, repeatedly people were converted within an hour or two. Small revivals seemed to spring up wherever he stopped.

Wesley reached his birthplace, Epworth, but the drunken minister refused to let him even read the Scripture lesson during the service. So Wesley spoke outside the church in the evening, standing on his father's tombstone in the churchyard. He found such spiritual need that he stayed for seven days, visiting in the surrounding villages during the day and preaching in the churchyard at night. A powerful revival resulted.

By Saturday evening the people were under such conviction for their sins that "many in the churchyard congregation dropped down as dead."[6] Wesley tried to preach, but the cries and praises of those repenting and receiving assurance of forgiveness almost drowned out his voice. On his last Sunday, masses of people from the surrounding area gathered to hear him. Again standing on his father's tomb, he preached for three hours.

About this time, Wesley also began to conduct one-day revivals. Here is a characteristic description in Wesley's words. "At seven I walked down to Sandhill, the poorest and most contemptible part of the town of Newcastle, and, standing at the end of the street with John Taylor, began to sing the Hundredth Psalm. Three or four people came out to see what was the matter; who soon increased to four or five hundred. I suppose there might be twelve or fifteen hundred before I had done preaching; to whom I applied these solemn words: 'He was wounded for our transgressions.'

Observing these people, when I had done, to stand gaping and staring upon me with the most profound astonishment, I told them: 'If you desire to know who I am, my name is John Wesley. At five in the evening, with God's help, I design to preach here again.'

"At five, the hill on which I designed to preach was covered from top to bottom. I never saw so large a number gathered together, either in Moorfields or in Kennington Common. I knew it was not possible for the half to hear, though my voice was then strong and clear; and so I stood so as to have them all in view, as they were ranged on the side of the hill. The Word of God which I set before them was: 'I will heal their backslidings; I will love them freely.'

"After preaching, the poor people were ready to tread me under foot, out of pure love and kindness. It was some time before I could get out of the press. I then went back another way I came; but several people got to our inn before me; by whom I was vehemently importuned to stay with them, at least a few days; or at least one day more. But I could not consent, having given my word to be at Birstal, with God's help, on Tuesday night."[7]

METHODISM BECOMES A REVIVAL MOVEMENT

Wherever Wesley went his "revival societies" sprang up. These were groups of converts who united together to worship the Lord. Wesley encouraged these converts to remain loyal members of the Church of England. He had no desire or intent to form a denomination outside of it. Wesley and his followers gathered together to seek more of God's holiness, to pray together, to receive scriptural instruction, and to watch over and care for one another. Believers rejoiced in the assurance of salvation.

As the numbers in the societies grew, some members became lax and others went to dangerous excess. Wesley was deeply burdened about discipline in the societies. He developed class meetings, led by lay leaders, that met an hour or two each week.

The class leader's responsibilities were to encourage all to comply with scriptural exhortation and to warn any who became careless or drifted into error. At times Wesley gathered the class leaders together for exhortation and guidance, and these groups became known as conferences.

After three years Wesley formed a staff of lay preachers. He nurtured them like a father, yet he also insisted on strict discipline. He directed them: "Never be unemployed, never be triflingly employed. . . . Be serious: let your motto be, Holiness to the Lord. Avoid all lightness as you would avoid hell-fire, and trifling as you would cursing and swearing. Touch no woman; be as loving as you will, but the custom of the country is nothing to us. Take money of no one; if they give you food when you are hungry, and clothes when you want them, it is enough; but no silver or gold: let there be no pretense for any one to say we grow rich by the gospel."

From the Moravians he met in Georgia, Wesley developed the concept of the love-feast, which involved partaking of bread and water and then fellowshiping together and sharing testimonies. Some of the people insisted on contributing to the cost of buildings where they met, so stewards were appointed to supervise the finances. Wesley sacrificed all for the work of God and reaped the love and reverence of the people.

Wesley wanted to keep peace with the leaders of the Anglican Church. He said he would do everything in his power to keep the movement within the borders of the Anglican Church, but these things he would not do: (1) he would not give up the doctrine of an inward and present salvation by faith alone, (2) he would not stop preaching in private homes and in the open air, and (3) he would not dissolve societies or prohibit lay preaching.

At first Wesley felt no one but an ordained minister should administer baptism or the Lord's Supper. He believed the ordination must be by a bishop. But in time he began to realize that the doctrine of apostolic succession was something that could not be proved, and that he himself was as scriptural a bishop as anyone could possibly be. So when the bishop of London refused to ordain Wesley's helpers, Wesley ordained them himself by laying on hands and granting them the power to administer the sacraments.

All Wesley wanted was to see new life pouring into the church. He loved the Anglican church to the day of his death. The Wesleyan revival was a revival of preaching. There were many sermons delivered in the churches of his day, but true preaching of the Gospel hardly existed. Through the revivals of the Great Awakening, preachers with hearts ablaze for God brought the living message. Methodism's leaders were Spirit-baptized, holy men of God who proclaimed the scriptural truth. Lecky, the great historian, declared that the evangelical revival "gradually changed the whole spirit of the English Church." Through Methodism, Christianity regained its rightful place in national life, gave great impetus to work among children, and instilled a new missionary vision.[8]

CHAPTER ELEVEN

The Revivals
of Methodism

Beginning in 1739 individuals and groups sought to disturb Wesley's meetings. At times hostile crowds closed in around him and made such a noise that Wesley could be heard by only a few. Often people who came to contradict, disturb, and blaspheme left in tears instead as Wesley preached on God's righteousness, the coming judgment, and the forgiveness of sins. Even King George insisted that the Methodist preachers be respected and protected.

Sometimes mobs tried to destroy the houses where Wesley spoke. Large stones were thrown through windows and roofs, endangering the lives of the people listening to Wesley's messages. Once a drunken clergyman tried to ride his horse into the crowd and stop them from listening to Wesley.

On one occasion Wesley was mobbed by first one and then another crowd of rioters who shoved him, pulled him by his hair, threatened his life, and shouted and struggled for five hours. But God convicted several of the rioters, and they suddenly came to Wesley's defense. One of them was almost killed. Stalwart men struck at the back of Wesley's head with large clubs, but the blows were deflected time and again. Wesley was so short in stature that many a blow aimed at him went over his head and struck one of the other rioters instead. Throughout the incident, Wesley remained perfectly calm and composed.

At various other times Wesley was struck in the chest, hit by stones, and punched in the mouth with such force that the blood gushed out. Wesley testified he felt no more pain than if he had been struck with a straw. His clothing was torn to shreds. Once the most profligate sinner in the area carried Wesley on his shoulders through a river to help him escape an angry mob. God saved this man, and five days later he became a Methodist society member.

At Falmouth, Wesley calmly and courageously faced a very dangerous mob and escaped uninjured. At Bolton, a wild mob tried to push him off the steps on which he stood. Each time an opponent tried to push Wesley off and stop the preaching, a stone aimed at Wesley struck and wounded the enemy instead. Another time, in the same town, a mob forced their way into the house where Wesley was staying. One of Wesley's men was rolled in the mud by the mob until he could hardly be recognized. But constantly, wherever Wesley or his men went, souls were saved and revival fires were lit.

In Ireland Wesley again faced angry mobs. At Cork, sticks and stones were thrown, but none hit him. An angry Roman Catholic woman blocked him, but a hard blow aimed at Wesley struck her and knocked her down flat. Wesley learned to look his opponents in the face, and by this many were calmed.

Almost every conceivable form of disturbance was tried in Wesley's open-air meetings. Drunk fiddlers and ballad singers were hired to disrupt. Drums were beaten, church bells rung, water let go out of a mill dam. At one place when Wesley announced his text, a Roman Catholic began to blow a horn beside him, but another person knocked him down and snatched away the horn.

As Wesley persisted, the tide turned. Mayors and magistrates began to welcome him and protect him and his followers. In many places the arrival of Wesley was like a public holiday, and he was greeted with welcome and respect.

WESLEY'S TRAVELS

Wesley was a constant traveler. In his Oxford days he often walked twenty-five miles a day. He also discovered he could read as he walked for up to ten or twelve miles at a time without discomfort. One year he walked 1,050 miles to preach in the churches around Oxford. Even into his old age he enjoyed walking.

Most of Wesley's travel was by horseback, and for years he averaged twelve to thirteen miles a day. He often read as he rode, and always he journeyed on, preaching the message of holiness and leaving a trail of revival fire.

Wesley records one instance when his horse was so lame that riding was difficult, and after seven miles Wesley himself had a headache and was tired. But when he looked to the Lord, he and his horse were both healed in the same instant. His horse had no further problem that day or the next.

Wesley traveled in wind, hail, driving sleet, piercing cold. He led his horse over such icy roads that it often fell down. At times he had to push through deep snow drifts. When he was told that the roads were impassable, Wesley once replied, "At least we walk twenty miles a day with our horses in our hands."[1]

Wesley's trips were carefully planned so that he could stop at as many places as possible and preach. Notices were sent ahead, and people from villages and towns around flocked to the points where he would stop. Only rarely (as when he held an eight-day campaign in Epworth church-yard) did he break his schedule.

One Friday afternoon Wesley began a journey of more than a 120 miles for a Sunday appointment. He traveled thirty miles of rough road that afternoon and spent the night. His horse was lame from the rough road. Wesley took the mail carriage the next morning, hoping that this would be quicker than his lame horse. Then he changed to another horse, and then to another mail carriage. A flooded road did not stop him; he found a man to lead him through. Wesley finally reached Epworth between 9:00 and 10:00 P.M. on Saturday. He noted in his journal, "After traveling more than ninety miles I was little more tired than when I rose in the morning."[2] Such travel was characteristic of Wesley.

Wesley thought it amazing that horses rarely stumbled while he was riding and reading. After 100,000 miles of such travel he could only remember two occasions. When he was sixty-nine he was injured and could not ride so comfortably. Friends took up an offering and got him a carriage when he was seventy. Wesley did not slow down, but now he could spend more time with his books while he traveled in his carriage.

When his carriage would break down, Wesley would borrow a horse and go on. On one trip when he was seventy-five, his carriage got through two swamps, but the third one was so bad a local man carried Wesley on his shoulders. A fourth swamp was even more difficult, and Wesley went on foot. Even in his eighties, Wesley battled bad weather, broken carriages, and lame horses to bring the Gospel message.

Wesley's contemporaries were amazed that he could continue such an arduous, unflagging itinerant ministry for more than fifty years. While he disciplined himself in diet and exercise, the only satisfactory explanation is the divine purpose Wesley was fulfilling and the divine presence in his life that strengthened him both spiritually and physically. In all it is estimated he traveled 226,000 miles in his ministry and preached 46,000 times.

WESLEY'S LAY PREACHERS FOLLOW IN HIS FOOTSTEPS

Wesley's preachers were godly, sacrificial, sanctified men, similar to Wesley himself. They traveled the circuits on horseback. Their saddlebags contained their few clothes and the Methodist books which they sold to the Methodist members. One of Wesley's preachers praised the Lord that his horse, which he purchased for five pounds, had carried him over 100,000 miles in his ministry. Another was less fortunate, and when his horse became sick he had to walk on foot 1,200 miles during winter and spring.

Wesley's preachers repeatedly faced mobs, just as he did. Some magistrates joined in the persecution and imprisoned one itinerant, calling him a vagrant. Two preachers were forcibly enlisted in the army. One was thrown again and again into a pond until he was unconscious. Then his clothes were covered with paint.

The circuit preachers were for years compelled to live in poverty. Often nothing was provided for their wives and children. Wesley's lay preachers loved him and were totally committed to him. They all had testimonies of powerful conversions, and they were prepared to live or die for the Lord's work. They shared the hardships and persecutions without complaint and won many souls to Christ. Wherever they went they took revival fire.

When one young lay preacher was imprisoned by a minister, who was also a magistrate, the young man preached through the jail window. People were so moved that they brought him bedding and food until he was set free. The young preacher eventually became a missionary to Ireland. Wesley did not know of any preacher who won so many souls to Christ in such a short time. The young man preached, studied, sacrificed, and poured out all his strength in soul-winning until he died of tuberculosis at the age of twenty-eight.

Wesley loved to gather his young lay preachers together and read lectures and books to them. He counted on the preachers carrying on the ministry. He quoted Paul: "Now I live, if you stand fast in the Lord" (1 Tim. 3:8).

Early in his life Wesley began a "shorthand diary," which eventually became a journal. In this he wrote how he spent every hour: his time of rising, his preaching, his studies before breakfast, all his day's activities. He wrote on the first page of each of these books, "I resolve, D.V. 1. To devote (to retirement and private prayer) an hour morning and evening—no pretense or excuse whatsoever. 2. To converse in the sight of God; no lightness; no jesting."[3]

For almost twenty years the work of sanctification in Britain seemed to come to a standstill. Then in 1760 it began again in Yorkshire, and then spread through the Methodist societies in most of England and Ireland, bringing new revival and growth. Wesley preached on the subject of sanctification in all the societies and was encouraged by God's fresh blessings on the people. It seemed to be the secret to maintaining continuous revival.

Methodism now spread rapidly. In August 1770 there were 29,406 members, 121 preachers, and 50 circuits. In America, the fiftieth circuit, there were 4 preachers and 100 Methodist chapels. Seven years later these numbers jumped to 34 preachers and nearly 7,000 members. Methodism was also making great inroads into Scotland and the West Indies.

Whitefield died on September 30, 1770, in America. The City Road Chapel in London was dedicated November 1, 1778, and became the "Cathedral" and central rallying point for Methodism. Wesley moved to the house next door, where he lived until his death.

WESLEY'S PREACHING

Wesley made every effort to preach simply so all could understand. After 1735, when he preached his first extemporaneous sermon, he never again took a sermon manuscript into the pulpit. There were greater orators, like Whitefield, but no preacher in the great evangelical revival preached with such power or produced such effect upon the conscience as Wesley. His words struck like a hammer and burned like fire (Jer. 23:29).

Speaking about God's anointing on his messages, Wesley said, "It is indeed the gift of God, and cannot be attained by all the efforts of nature and art united." He said at times that "God Himself made the application," and "Truly God preached to their hearts."[4]

At times Wesley was so anointed that he did not know how to stop, and after he did stop he began again, each time demonstrating even greater power than before. At such times, he spoke for as long as two or three hours. Of one occasion he wrote, "I was constrained to continue my discourse there nearly an hour longer than usual; God pouring out such a blessing, that I knew not how to leave off."[5]

Wesley published his sermons and Charles' hymns at cheap prices so that everyone could afford them. He also published many penny tracts.

Wesley corresponded with more people on spiritual matters than perhaps any other person in his century. He was always cheerful, no matter what he faced. At fifty-two years of age he said, "By the grace of God, I never fret; I repine at nothing; I am discontented with nothing. . . . I see God sitting upon His throne, and ruling all things well." When he was seventy-seven, Wesley wrote, "I do not remember to have felt lowness of spirits for one-quarter of an hour since I was born."[6]

Wealth held no temptation for Wesley. He spent his days among the poor and gave away almost all income that he received. In his longing to win the masses, he tried to do all the good he could in the wisest and best way so that he could reach as many as possible for Christ. Wesley was glad to learn from anyone and kept learning until the last day of his life.

Wesley seemed to see into men's souls, putting his finger on hidden sins. People felt as if Wesley was speaking to them alone. In his ministry, Wesley's speech was calm but full of power, certainty, and authority. Often the effect on the people was so overwhelming that they almost all bowed before the presence of God. Remarkable demonstrations of conviction of sin occurred in his ministry. People would suddenly be gripped with an awe of eternity and the solemnity of the Judgment. Wesley's very calmness seemed to bring a stronger sense of God's nearness, holiness, and sovereign power. Wesley did not seek this, but he accepted it as a solemn form of God's working.

Wesley planned his travels with great detail and almost military precision. He scheduled the places he would visit, the hour he would arrive, and the services he would hold. He lived like a soldier on a campaign, with no surplus baggage, ready at a moment's notice to march. Stormy weather, icy or flooded roads, angry mobs, great distance, or weariness could not stop him. So it was, day after day for more than fifty years of his ministry.

HIS FINAL WORDS

Wesley's last "field-preaching" was on October 6, 1790. One who was present said, "The Word was attended with mighty power, and the tears of the people flowed in torrents."[7] Wesley never lost his power. In those last years when Wesley walked through a street, people gazed on him with veneration. When they greeted him in a friendly way, he would respond, as his favorite apostle, John, had done: "Little children, love one another." His constant prayer was,

"Lord, let me not live to be useless!" In his last months at every place he visited he urged the people to "love as brethren, fear God, and honor the King."[8]

Wesley preached for the last time in his City Road Chapel on Tuesday, February 22, 1791. The following day he preached his last sermon at Leatherhead. On Friday he wrote his last letter to William Wilberforce, urging him to continue to take his stand against slavery. Wesley became increasingly weak and slept periodically. Three or four times he repeated, "We have boldness to enter into the Holiest by the blood of Jesus." He became so weak he asked for a pen so he could write, but was unable to do so. When asked what he would like to have written, Wesley replied, "Nothing, but that God is with us." In the afternoon he surprised his friends as he sang with vigor:

> "I'll praise my Maker while I've breath
> And when my voice is lost in death,
> Praise shall employ my nobler powers;
> My days of praise shall ne'er be past,
> While life, and thought, and being last,
> Or immortality endures."

Wesley's voice seemed to fail. He slept a bit and then asked for his friends to join in prayer. As they gathered around his bed, he grasped their hands and said, "Farewell, farewell." Wesley tried to say something more but was so weak they could not understand. When he realized this, he used all his remaining strength to cry out, "The best of all is, God is with us." He lifted up his arm in a token of victory and repeated one more time, "The best of all is, God is with us."

During the night he tried to repeat the forty-sixth Psalm several times, but he was too weak. They caught the words, "I'll praise—I'll praise." Wesley's niece and a few friends knelt around his bed. The last word they could hear him say was "Farewell." Joseph Bradford led in prayer. As he was saying, "Lift up your heads, O ye gates; and be ye lifted up, ye everlasting doors; and this heir of glory shall come in," without a groan or sigh Wesley passed away. The friends standing around his bed sang,

> "Waiting to receive thy Spirit,
> Lo! the Savior stands above,
> Shows the purchase of his merit,
> Reaches out the crown of love."

It was March 2, 1791, and John Wesley was eighty-eight years of age. The day before his funeral, his body was laid in City Road Chapel. People insisted that a heavenly smile lingered on his face. Some ten thousand people came to the chapel to see him. His tomb reads, "This great light arose (by the singular providence of God) to enlighten these nations. Reader, if thou art constrained to bless the instrument, give God the glory."[9]

The revival God began through John Wesley and his colleagues continued to spread in revival fire for some years on both sides of the Atlantic. When Wesley died there were more than 120,000 Methodists in his societies. Already the work was spreading rapidly in America and in the West Indies. Methodist missions began long before William Carey sailed for India and several years before all but one of the other famous missionary societies. One hundred and fifty years from the outpouring of the Spirit on New Year's Day 1739, the Methodists worldwide equaled in number the total population of England in Wesley's day.

CHAPTER TWELVE

Revival Fires
Follow Finney

One narrator of Christian biography has termed Charles G. Finney's memoirs "perhaps the most remarkable account of the manifestations of the Holy Spirit's power since apostolic days. It is crowded with accounts of spiritual outpourings which remind one of the Day of Pentecost."[1] One of Finney's closest friends, who was also his stenographer for some years, said of Finney, "The intensity and constancy of his ardour were surprising. The sacred fire seemed never to burn low."[2]

By 1832 Finney's revival movement had added several hundred thousand to the churches. His campaign in Rochester, New York, in 1842 seemed to prepare the way for the extensive revival of 1843–44. And his revival campaign in Rochester in 1856 prepared the way of the Lord for the mighty movement of revival that swept America in 1857–58. The people who were led to Christ directly or indirectly by Finney through his personal campaigns, writings, encouragements, and prayer probably brought a million people or more into the kingdom of God. While it is said that 70 percent of the converts even in Moody's meetings became backsliders, it is estimated that 85 percent of the professed converts in the Finney revivals remained true to the Lord.

The revivals of Finney's earlier ministry tended to occur in small-town churches and then spread to other nearby towns. Later in life, Finney directed his ministry to city churches or tabernacles. These revivals spread and blessed churches nearby and throughout the city. Almost always the revivals that began in a local church soon became community wide and brought in many invitations from nearby places.

From the time of his conversion and his infilling with the Spirit, Finney was a man ablaze for God with holy boldness, a lawyer's directness, and constant guidance and anointing by the Holy Spirit. Usually wherever Finney preached, people quickly became convicted of their sins, humbled themselves in repentance before God, and received the assurance of salvation. His revivals spread from town to town like a creeping vine, and wherever he went new spiritual life came to individuals, churches, and communities.

Charles G. Finney was born August 29, 1792, and heard almost no gospel preaching during his early years. At the age of twenty-six he joined a law office in the small town of Adams, New York. Here he was able to attend church services and prayer meetings regularly. He constantly analyzed the Christians' prayers and could not see that they were being answered.

The church members asked him if he did not want them to pray for him. He told them, "No. I suppose I need to be prayed for, for I am conscious that I am a sinner; but I do not see that it will do any good for you to pray for me, for you are continually asking, what you do not receive. You have been praying for revival of religion ever since I have been in Adams, and yet you have it not. You have been praying for the Holy Spirit to descend upon yourselves, and yet complaining of your leanness. . . . You have prayed enough since I have attended these meetings to have prayed the devil out of Adam, if there is any virtue in your prayers. But here you are praying on, and complaining still."[3]

On October 10, 1821, while praying alone in the woods outside the village, Finney experienced a powerful conversion. That evening in his small office he had a vision that he fell weeping at Jesus' feet. "I received a mighty baptism of the Holy Ghost. . . . Without expecting it, without ever having the thought in my mind that there was any such thing for me, without any recollection that I had ever heard the thing mentioned by any person in the world, at a moment entirely unexpected by me, the Holy Spirit descended upon me in a manner that seemed to go through me body and soul."[4]

The very next day Finney began witnessing to people. That evening, though no announcement had been made, he saw people from all over the village going to the place where prayer meetings were generally held. Word had spread through the whole village that Finney had been converted. Then he decided to go himself. When he got there the house was packed, but no one said anything. Then Finney arose. As he recounted his testimony, people were gripped by the Holy Spirit. The minister rose to his feet and confessed that he believed he had been a stumbling block in the way of the church. He asked Finney to lead in prayer. God anointed Finney as he prayed his first public prayer. From that time on they had a prayer meeting every evening. Revival had begun. It spread among all classes of people and extended out beyond the village in all directions.

PRAYER AND PREACHING

In his early walk with the Lord, Finney learned many lessons about prevailing prayer and prayer burdens. He gathered some of the young men of Adams in the early mornings before daylight for a daily prayer meeting. Finney began spending hours in prayer, often going to the woods to be alone with God. He began to add fasting to his prayer regimen. Just as Wesley had made rules for his Holy Club, so Finney proposed to the young people that they set aside three special times of prayer each day—at sunrise, noon, and sunset. God poured out a spirit of prayer upon the other young people as they prayed faithfully.

At Finney's second evening service at Evans Mills, he found the building filled to the rafters. Without introduction or song, he walked to the pulpit and quoted Isaiah 3:10–11, "Say ye to the righteous, that it shall be well with him: for they shall eat the fruit of their doings. Woe unto the wicked! It shall be ill with him: for the reward of his hands shall be given him" (KJV). People were immediately convicted by the Holy Spirit. Several times that night people sent to try to find where Finney was staying so they could get him to pray for them. Meetings continued in the schoolhouses, church buildings, and in a barroom of a notable convert.

Sinners became so convicted that they could not sleep. A nearby German church asked Finney to speak there. "The sword of the Lord slew them on the right hand and on the left. In a very few days it was found that the whole settlement was under conviction."[5] It was harvest time, but people threw down their implements in the field to come to a 1:00 P.M. service each day. The revival so blessed both the Presbyterian and the German Congregational churches that both soon built new stone church buildings.

During this revival campaign, the Presbyterian presbytery ordained Finney as an evangelist. Finney laid "great stress upon prayer as an indispensable condition of promoting the revival. . . . The means used were simply preaching, prayer, and conference meetings, much private prayer, much personal conversation, and meetings for the instruction of earnest inquirers."[6]

Finney took pains to preach simply and use only simple illustrations. He did this so that his listeners would not just remember the illustrations but would instead be convicted by the truth. He always spoke directly to the people. As a lawyer, he pleaded the case for Jesus Christ, to secure verdicts on the spot.

Finney said, "I visited from house to house, attended prayer meetings, and preached and labored every day and every night."[7] This was true month after month. Finney reported that the work of salvation was spreading in almost every direction. Before the year was over there were revival reports from eleven towns in the area.

RENEWAL IN THE SCHOOLHOUSES

Antwerp was thirteen miles from Evans Mills and had no church building. When Finney walked through the village one Saturday and heard the profanity, he spent much of the day in prayer. He had such a tremendous prayer burden that he spent Sunday morning praying in the woods until the time for the meeting in the schoolhouse. When he got there he found it packed with people. As Finney began to speak on John 3:16, he wept copiously. He told them that in Antwerp he felt he were on the verge of hell. The people were not offended. Several hours later Finney had a second meeting, and from then on he preached almost daily in the schoolhouse. A great portion of the 2,250 citizens of Antwerp were converted.

Finney was invited to a nearby village, and in the first service there the schoolhouse was full. There had never been a religious service in that village. Finney preached directly to the people. After about fifteen minutes, "the congregation began to fall from their seats; and they fell in every direction, and cried for mercy. If I had had a sword in each hand, I could not have cut them off their seats as fast as they fell. Indeed, nearly the whole congregation were either on their knees or prostrate, I should think, in less than two minutes from this first shock that fell upon them. Everyone prayed for himself, who was able to speak at all. I of course was obliged to stop preaching, for they no longer paid any attention."[8]

Finney told them, "You are not in hell yet. Now let me direct you to Christ." Everyone was calling out to God, and none could hear him. So Finney began to point people one by one to Christ until they had the witness of the Spirit to their salvation. That meeting went on all night and into the afternoon of the next day.

Back in Antwerp God worked in an almost identical service to the one just described, and revival spread to almost every part of the town.

MARRIAGE DOES NOT STOP REVIVAL

On October 5, 1824, Finney was married to his wife Lydia. He left her in order to bring her possessions from Evans Mills. He expected to be back in a week. The previous autumn Finney had preached several times in Perch River. A messenger came to him, begging him to preach one more time at Perch River because God was giving revival. Finney promised to be there on Tuesday night. God worked so powerfully that Finney promised another service Wednesday night, and then Thursday night and then longer. Some sixty to seventy people found the Lord and joined the Baptist church there.

Revival spread to a large town called Brownsville. The people there insisted that Finney spend the winter. Early in the spring Finney again set out to return to his wife. He had to stop and have his horse shod in Rayville. People recognized him and came running, insisting that he must preach one time there. So Finney announced a meeting for one o'clock. People crowded around him. The Holy Spirit came in power, and they begged Finney to stay overnight. He preached that night, and the revival fire kept burning. So he preached the next morning and had to stay that night since God was working so deeply. Finney asked a Christian brother to take his horse and sleigh and go for his wife. They had now been apart from each other for six months. Finney continued preaching in Rayville several more weeks, and most of the people were converted.

Then God led Finney to Gouverneur. He sent word to the people there that he was coming at God's direction and to prepare for the outpouring of the Lord's Spirit.

CHAPTER THIRTEEN

Revival Fire Spreads to Central New York

In August 1825, Finney journeyed to Oneida County in central New York. He preached at Western on a Thursday night, and the Lord brought some church leaders there to brokenness and repentance. God gave a prayer burden to Finney on Friday, and on Sunday, God came in power at the church services. Revival had begun, and Finney prevailed in prayer and spoke in several parts of the town.

The next week Finney met a Mrs. Harris, who had wrestled in prayer day and night. When she met Finney she said, "The Lord has come! This work will spread over all this region. A cloud of mercy overhangs us all; and we shall see such a work of grace as we have never yet seen." Finney said that Mrs. Harris's face had "a most unearthly, heavenly glow" that "was plainly from heaven." She had won a revival through prayer.[1]

After the revival fire had burned in Western for a while, Finney received a call from the town of Rome. In his third sermon at Rome, God gripped the people with such Holy Spirit conviction that Finney was afraid the people could not control their emotions. Finney led in prayer at the close of the meeting in a low, unemotional voice, trying to restrain the people, who had begun to weep and sigh. He urged them to control their feelings and to go home without speaking a word to anyone. The people obeyed, but their sighing and sobbing continued as they went down the street to their homes.

At daybreak the people began sending for Finney. He spent the morning going from house to house praying with the people. As he entered a house, he would find some kneeling, some prostrate on the floor. Neighbors would rush in. Finney could not keep up with the pleas for prayer, and he knew that he must change his methods.

Finney announced a meeting for inquirers at one o'clock. They came from every direction, some even running. Many were convicted by the Word that afternoon and by evening were already saved. In the evening service people were so overwhelmed by the Holy Spirit's conviction that Finney again dismissed the service and asked the people to go home for personal and family prayer.

Revival services went on for twenty nights, with a prayer meeting at one time of day, a meeting for inquirers at another time of day, and then services in the evening. The town radiated solemnity and awe. Ministers came from neighboring towns to see the revival. Conversions multiplied so rapidly that it was impossible to know the full story. Each night Finney would ask that all who had been converted that day come and stand in front of the pulpit. All were amazed at who and how many had been converted. Some people collapsed from conviction in the church services and some later in their homes.

Three men spent a day drinking and condemning the revival until one of them fell down dead. Nearly all of the adult population of Rome was brought to Christ: lawyers, merchants, physicians, and town leaders. The minister said, "So far as my congregation is concerned, the millennium is come already."[2] Everyone who came into the village felt an overwhelming sense of God's presence.

The sheriff of Utica, some twenty miles away, came on business. He had laughed and mocked at the reports of the revival. As his sleigh crossed the canal one mile outside of Rome, an awesome feeling of the presence of God gripped him. The nearer to the village he came, the more powerfully he sensed God's presence. The sheriff found the people in the business establishments so overcome with awe for God that they could hardly speak. To try to keep from weeping, the sheriff got up several times and went to the window. He hurried to complete his business and hastened back to Utica. Soon he was converted.

The revival spread to Wrights' Settlement, a village about three miles from Rome, and almost everyone there was converted. In each meeting Finney tried hard to restrain the people. Meetings were held with the greatest solemnity and order. The Spirit's work was so spontaneous, powerful, and overwhelming that for more than a year Finney held a daily sunrise prayer meeting that was well attended.

THE POWER OF PRAYER

Finney urged the people to pray to God earnestly and expectantly for "the immediate outpouring of His Holy Spirit." He told them that if they united in prayer, they would get God's answer quicker than a letter could come from Albany, the state's capital. Several men agreed to prove God in that way, and their prayer was answered just that quickly. Finney wrote, "Indeed the town was full of prayer. Go where you would, you heard the voice of prayer. Pass along the streets, and if two or three Christians happened to be together they were praying. Wherever they met they prayed. Wherever there was a sinner unconverted, especially if he manifested any opposition, you would find some two or three brothers or sisters agreeing to make him a particular subject of prayer; and it was very remarkable to see to what an extent God would answer prayer immediately."[3]

After some twenty days, Finney went to Utica to attend a funeral. He found a godly lady who had been prevailing in prayer almost incessantly for two days and nights. One of the Presbyterian pastors asked him to come back to Utica to speak. He returned almost at once. "The Word took immediate effect, and the place became filled with the manifest influence of the Holy Spirit. Our meetings were crowded every night, and the work spread and went on powerfully."[4]

THE HOLINESS ZONE

The sheriff of Utica, a new convert, was a bachelor and boarded in a hotel. He began to pray for the hotelkeeper. Soon the keeper, many of his family, and most of his boarders were converted. This hotel, the largest in town, became a center of holy influence in Utica. The stagecoaches always stopped there. A number of people who stopped for a meal or a night at the hotel were powerfully convicted and converted before they left the town. A divine influence seemed to pervade Utica and Rome during these revivals and turned the area into a zone of holiness. The same phenomenon was occurring along the whole eastern coast of the United States during the 1858 revival.

A merchant from Lowville arrived by stagecoach to do business but found that Utica "was all religion." Wherever he tried to do business, people witnessed to him. The merchant became so disgusted he decided to leave by the stagecoach late that night. Some of the boarders who were new converts heard his remark. They and the hotel keeper took him aside, prayed with him, and before the stagecoach arrived he was converted.

Instead of proceeding on his business trip, the merchant went home and began to witness. He won his family to the Lord and began to boldly witness in the town. God's Spirit came upon Lowville, and soon God caused a great revival there.

In the midst of the revival, the Oneida Presbytery met in Utica. An aged clergyman complained that everywhere he went in the town people talked about prayer and revival. He got up in the presbytery meeting and made a violent speech against the revival. That night many Christians prayed fervently that the revival not be hindered by the speech. In the morning this aged minister was found dead in his bed in the hotel.

News of the revival spread far and wide. In Utica itself over five hundred were won to the Lord. People came from considerable distances to see for themselves what was happening, and a number of them were also converted. God sent revival to villages on all sides of Utica.

Finney received an invitation to preach one night in the village of New York Mills. The building was crowded with people, especially young factory workers. God began to convict the people immediately. The next morning Finney was invited to tour the large cotton mill. He entered one room where the girls at the looms and spinning machines were light-heartedly laughing. As he walked toward the work area, one of the girls looked into Finney's eyes and began to tremble. Her shaking fingers broke the thread and the loom stopped. The girl next to her looked up to see why the loom had ceased. As she saw Finney's face, she also began to tremble and broke her thread. One after another, the looms stopped.

The owner heard the equipment stopping and came in to see what was going on. When he saw that the whole room was in tears, he told the superintendent to stop the mill, for it was more important for souls to be saved than for the mill to run. Up to this point Finney had not said one word. The workers assembled in a large room, and in a few days almost all the employees in the mill were saved. A Methodist church and then a Presbyterian church were eventually formed by the three thousand converts of this revival.

FINNEY'S VISION OF CHRIST

In the summer of 1826, Finney was invited to Auburn, New York. Some of the professors at the Auburn seminary were opposed to the revival and to his preaching since he had not been theologically trained. God gave Finney a vision, showing him that he would face opposition from the church but assuring him that God would triumph.

In this vision Christ drew so near to Finney while he was praying that his whole body trembled from head to foot. Finney had never been so awed and humbled before God. "Instead of feeling like fleeing, I seemed drawn nearer and nearer to God—seemed to draw nearer and nearer to that Presence that filled me with such unutterable awe and trembling." Then God lifted Finney up and assured him that He would be with him and that no opposition would prevail against him.[5]

Finney felt he must leave everything to God. God helped him become perfectly trustful, perfectly calm, and to have nothing but the most perfectly kindly feelings toward all the brethren that were misled and were arraying themselves against him. When it seemed that all the churches except the First Presbyterian Church where Finney was preaching had turned against him, he did not worry about it but carried on his revival meetings.

Early in the autumn of 1826 Finney was invited to Troy, New York, where God gave him an earnest spirit of prayer. Some people there bore prayer burdens for the salvation of particular individuals. A young lady from New Lebanon visited in Troy during the revival, was powerfully converted, and went back to New Lebanon to win a friend to Christ. The two of them began a ministry of intercession for revival in their community. They invited Finney to visit.

When Finney reached New Lebanon, "the Spirit of the Lord was poured out, and the revival soon went forward with great power. . . . Powerful conversions were multiplied."[6] An infidel doctor, a prominent and wealthy merchant, and a young lad who later became a noted evangelist were among the many conversions.

Finney was invited to nearby Stephentown, where only six people attended church services. As he began to preach, the place filled with people, and by the third service, the Spirit prevailed. A young lady had been praying day and night for revival in Stephentown. Hearing her weep and pray, the Holy Spirit powerfully burdened Finney also. The people were not only mightily convicted of their need for God, but strong and prominent men were smitten down or immobilized in their seats during the services. There were about 150 conversions, including almost all of the leading citizens of Stephentown.

Finney lists the "striking characteristics" of these revivals as "1. The prevalence of a mighty Spirit of prevailing prayer. 2. Overwhelming conviction of sin. 3. Sudden and powerful conversions to Christ. 4. Great love and abounding joy of the converts. 5. Intelligence and stability of the converts. 6. Their great earnestness, activity, and usefulness in their prayers and labors for others."[7]

CHAPTER FOURTEEN

Cities Ablaze

The Finneys were invited to Wilmington, Delaware, and arrived in December 1827. God sent revival blessing, and soon Finney began to commute two days each week to Philadelphia, forty miles away by riverboat. In 1828 he moved to Philadelphia and preached first in all of the churches. Then as crowds became too large, he held his meetings in the largest church in the city, which seated about three thousand. For about one year he preached in Philadelphia and experienced continual blessings.

SHANTY REVIVAL

In the spring of 1828 the revival spread from Philadelphia up the Delaware River toward northern Pennsylvania. Several thousand lumbermen made their home in this wooded region. They lived in huts and shanties, alone or with two or three others. The men logged the forests throughout the year, and when the snow melted in the spring, they floated the lumber down the river in rafts to be sold in Philadelphia. A number of these lumbermen attended the revival meetings in Philadelphia and were converted.

As these lumbermen returned back up the river, they began praying for their coworkers. God began to convert these lonely loggers; they would pray in their cabins, get saved, and go out to share their testimonies with other lumbermen. There were no ministers anywhere in the area at that time, and some men had never in their lives been inside a church building. The revival spread from shanty to shanty, and by the spring of 1831 over five thousand lumbermen had been converted in this region. It was a harvest without a church or resident evangelist.

In the winter of 1829–30, Finney went forty miles further to Reading, Pennsylvania. Again there were numerous conversions, many of them dramatic. Finney then moved on to Lancaster, where God sent almost instant revival. From there he went to Columbia and then to New York City. Souls were saved wherever Finney traveled.

Finney was then led to Rochester in central New York in September 1830, and he ministered there until March 1831. Here, for the first time, Finney began to make use of "the Anxious Seat" in the forward part of the church. People desiring salvation came there at the close of the service to be prayed with and counseled. God began to do a work of salvation, especially among the upper classes of society: merchants, physicians, and especially lawyers. Christians of various denominations united in the services.

A skeptic had a large, flourishing high school in Rochester. A number of the students attended the Finney meetings and became deeply convicted of their need for Christ. One morning after the meetings had continued for two weeks, the principal found so many students weeping over their sins in the classrooms that he sent for Finney to come and instruct them. Finney came, and the principal and almost every student were converted. More than forty of the male students and a number of the female students in time became ministers or missionaries.

One of the girls in that school became the wife of Titus Coan. The Coans went to Hawaii as missionaries, and seven years later they were leaders in the mighty revival that came in full tide to Hawaii. No doubt this was indirectly a result of the Finney revival in New York.

God used the revival to bring a profound moral change in the Rochester area. Every evening in the services a large number of people experienced rebirth.

PRAYER WARRIORS

A tremendous spirit of prayer pervaded the city. A minister, deeply convicted of his own sin, wept aloud as he walked down the street. This man was powerfully converted and became a prayer partner with Finney during these meetings. God gave the minister great faith that a mighty revival would take place. Other people slipped away from the services in order to pray.

Abel Clary was another of Finney's unusual prayer partners. He had been converted in the same revival in which Finney was converted years before. Clary was licensed to preach but carried such a heavy prayer burden for souls that he rarely could preach. When Finney went to Rochester, Abel Clary came without telling Finney. He never attended a service, but stayed in a Christian's home to pray for Rochester and the revival. After some weeks Finney discovered that Clary was there praying.

Clary was a silent man, but he often became so greatly burdened in prayer that he was unable to stand. He wrestled in prayer on his knees. Sometimes he could not even kneel but lay prostrate on the floor, pleading with the Lord for the salvation of souls.

God put similar heavy prayer burdens on several other men, and also on a large number of women. For ten years during the revivals in central New York, a deacon named Billious Pond carried a tremendous prayer burden and was welcomed by evangelists, pastors, and churches to come and pray. At the age of fifty-five Pond was ordained and then preached the gospel for forty more years.

"Father" Nash, a godly minister, came to Finney in several of his fields of labor and prevailed powerfully in prayer. At times Clary and Nash stayed together and spent many hours praying. In the Rochester area there were many instances of people agonizing in prevailing prayer for God's mighty power to work in salvation among the people. Clary and Nash later followed Finney to England and prayed for his ministry there.

The prosecuting attorney of the Rochester area was converted in the revival. He reported that in this fast-growing city, the population after the revival tripled but the crime rate decreased by two-thirds. Out of a population of ten thousand people, there were at least eight hundred conversions. Theaters were considered to be places of evil, and the Rochester theater went out of business. Seven years went by before another could be started, and more than twenty-five years passed before a theater could be permanently established. Converts of the revival became community leaders.

REVIVAL REPORTS

Some of the Rochester Christians wrote letters to their friends in several other states, telling how God was mightily working in the revival. God used these testimonies to bring revivals to these other places.

While continuing to lead the Rochester revival, Finney traveled briefly to surrounding towns. "Wherever I went the Word of God took immediate effect; and it seemed only necessary to present the law of God and the claims of Christ in such relations and proportions as were calculated to secure the conversion of men, and they would be converted by scores. The greatness of the work at Rochester at that time attracted so much of the attention of ministers and Christians throughout the state of New York, throughout New England, and in many parts of the United States, that the very fame of it was an efficient instrument in the hands of the Spirit of God in promoting the greatest revival of religion throughout the land that this country had ever witnessed."[1]

Years later Dr. Henry Ward Beecher, in conversation about this powerful revival and its results, remarked: "That was the greatest work of God, and the greatest revival of religion, that the world has ever seen in so short a time. One hundred thousand . . . were reported as having connected themselves with churches as a result of that great revival."[2] In the period between 1831 and 1835, more than two hundred thousand were converted.

According to the *Boston Recorder*, in the first four months of 1831, 362 places reported revivals. One hundred fifty of these were in the state of New York. God worked powerfully, and there was no scandal. Unity among all churches prevailed, and the opposition to Finney and his methods seemed to cease.

Finney grew fatigued. The doctors at Rochester were convinced he was dying of tuberculosis, but he insisted he was merely tired. He took a trip by stagecoach and stopped overnight at Auburn, intending to leave early the next morning. He was handed an earnest appeal to stay and lead them to Christ, signed by a long list of unconverted men who had opposed his ministry there in 1826. The first name was the ringleader of the opposition.

After prayer, Finney decided to stay on the condition that he only speak four times a week. God's Word immediately convicted people. Finney stayed six weeks, and some five hundred people were converted. The first one converted was the former ringleader of the opposition, and almost all of the others who had previously opposed him were won to Christ.

Rev. Abel Clary was present to pray for the souls of that place. "His desires were altogether too great to be expressed in words, and his groans could be heard all over the house." Finney considered this Auburn revival a holy wave of the revival in Rochester.[3]

Then came a call to Buffalo, New York, saying revival was beginning there. Buffalo was about sixty-five miles on the other side of Rochester. For one month Finney ministered with power in Buffalo. Here, too, the revival began among the higher classes. Then Finney went on to Providence, Rhode Island, and finally to Boston and New York. The Lord poured out His Spirit immediately.

Chatham Garden Theater in New York was leased and remodeled as a chapel to seat 2,500. On the opening Sunday in May 1832, up to three thousand people crowded in, with many unable to get inside. Cholera was at the time devastating New York City. At the height of the epidemic over one hundred per day were dying. Two-thirds of the population and many of the other ministers left the city. On September 28, Finney was installed as pastor of the new Chatham Street Chapel, but during the service he came down with cholera. He recovered slowly and was not able to preach again until the spring of 1833. He never fully recovered from his illness.

PERSONAL EVANGELISM TEAMS

Finney preached every evening for twenty days, and revival began immediately. Over five hundred were converted. Finney was too weak to continue to preach every night. There were so many converts that they started a daughter church. Finney taught his members to go two by two in bold personal evangelism. They traveled from house to house and waited at the entrances to theaters and drinking places to invite people to the services. Some members even picked up drunkards, took them to church, won them to Christ, and then returned them home sober and saved to the astonishment of their families.

Finney taught his members to scatter themselves among the large audience and watch carefully for people who were seized with conviction. They would then bring them into the prayer rooms and lead them to the Lord. In those days the upper galleries of most theaters were often used for prostitution. But now in these very galleries in the converted chapel, people were winning souls to Christ. Before Finney left New York, five daughter churches had been established. He urged his members not to fill the services with Christians from other churches but to bring in the unconverted so they could be saved.

AN ATMOSPHERE OF PRAYER

An eyewitness to the revivals wrote: "Probably no man, since the days of Whitefield, ever stirred the minds of men in this city so widely and deeply, in their relations to practical and personal religion, as this great and good man. Preaching and praying were his only weapons. He surrounded himself with an atmosphere of prayer, and a body of devoted praying and working Christians male and female such as New York had never before seen, and probably never since. His pulpit and church here were a center of holy and soul-converting influences, that were diffused in every direction, through the length and breadth of the land, and the impulse of his New York life and labors is still perpetuated and embodied in our churches and in various forms of Christian activity."[4]

Finney was strongly antislavery. He often referred to it in his prayers and preaching. His vast audiences nearly always included some slaveholders, and he refused to serve communion to them. Finney disagreed with his presbytery over inconsistencies of church discipline, so he resigned from the presbytery on March 13, 1836. Broadway Tabernacle was built to his design, and he became its pastor and formed a Congregational church.

Because Finney never fully recovered from his bout with cholera, he was forced to take a sea voyage in the Mediterranean. He was gone from January 20, 1834, to July

14. During his absence, he turned over the leadership of the Chatham Street Chapel to his assistant, John Ingersoll, urging him to moderation in confronting the slavery virus. However, Ingersoll did not follow Finney's instruction. When Finney returned he wept when he saw that the church which was crowded when he left now had only a few hundred people remaining. Soon after Finney returned, the scattered flock was regathered, the church revived, and the Holy Spirit again worked powerfully. Finney's comment was, "The Spirit of the Lord was poured out upon us, and we had a continuous precious revival as long as I continued as pastor of that church."[5]

A DAY OF PREVAILING PRAYER

While Finney was returning from his six-month sea voyage to regain his health, God gave him a day on the ship of tremendous blessing, renewal, and guidance. Finney realized his health was still not what it had been. He was burdened for revivals and distressed at the opposition of vocal Christians who objected to his form of revival ministry.

Finney spent most of one day in agonizing prayer, kneeling in a stateroom and walking the decks. He was so crushed by his prayer burden that he wrung his hands in agony. Finney had often experienced prayer burden but never so intense and so prolonged as on this day.

Finney spoke of it as "a day of unspeakable wrestling and agony in my soul." Just as night fell the Holy Spirit reassured him that all would come out well, "that the Lord would go forward with His work, and give me the strength to take any part in it that He desired. But I had not the least idea of what the course of providence would be.

"I have regarded all the revival work that I have since been able to accomplish, and all the results of preaching and publishing those lectures, as well as all else that I have been in any wise instrumental in accomplishing for the Zion of

God, as in a very important sense an answer to the prayers of that day. . . . Nobody but myself can appreciate the wonderful manner in which those agonizing throes of soul on that occasion have met with the divine response. Indeed, it was God the Holy Ghost making intercession in me. The prayer was not properly mine, but the prayer of the Holy Spirit. . . . He pressed my soul in prayer until I was enabled to prevail; and through infinite riches of grace in Christ Jesus I have been many years witnessing the wonderful results of that day of wrestling with God. In answer to that day's agony He has continued to give me the Spirit of prayer."[6]

A MANUAL OF REVIVAL

Upon Finney's arrival back in New York, the editor of a faltering publication, "The Evangelist," asked Finney to write a series of articles on revival. Finney prayed for a day or two and then promised to give a series of lectures on revival once a week. The editor was free to send a reporter to observe and write the articles. The lectures were reported in somewhat condensed form and later published in a book, *Finney's Lectures on Revivals*.

This book sold as fast as it could be printed: twelve thousand copies in the first six months. It was reprinted in England, France, and Germany, and many later editions were published in Britain and by various other publishers. *Finney's Lectures on Revivals* became a phenomenal bestseller. Men such as Godet, the famed Bible commentator, and David Livingstone, the missionary, both claim to have been greatly influenced by the book. It was used by God to light revival fires and fan revival flames in many parts of the United States and indeed the whole world for many years. Finney's book was undoubtedly God's preparation for the 1858 revivals across America and the British Isles.

CHAPTER FIFTEEN

Oberlin and Beyond

In 1834 the Reverend Asa Mahan founded the Oberlin Collegiate Institute in Oberlin, Ohio. It was renamed Oberlin College in 1850. Mahan and other leaders asked Finney repeatedly to come to Oberlin. Finney moved there in May 1835. He agreed to reside in New York from April to November each year and minister at the Broadway Tabernacle, and then live in Oberlin the rest of the year, ministering at the school and pastoring the church. The very first year nearly three hundred students arrived, and many more came the following year.

From Finney's first arrival at Oberlin, God began to give revival blessings in the school. "We not only prospered in our own souls as a church, but we had a continuous revival. It varied in its strength and power at different times; but we were at no time in a state that would not have been regarded as a revival state in any other place than this. Our students were converted by scores from year to year; and the Lord overshadowed us constantly with the cloud of His mercy. Gales of divine influence swept over us from year to year, leaving us His fruits among us abundantly of love, joy, peace, long-suffering, gentleness, goodness, faith."[1]

In 1842 Finney spent two months holding revival meetings in Boston and then two months in Providence,

Rhode Island. By then he felt completely exhausted. He rested a day or two in Boston, then traveled to Rochester to rest another day before he proceeded further. Judge Gardiner of the New York Court of Appeals and other judges handed him a request to hold special services for lawyers. Another evangelist held services for the general population.

God was working in the hearts of New York lawyers. One night Judge Gardiner asked Finney to pray for him by name. The judge immediately took the Anxious Seat before all the people. Seeing this, lawyers began flocking to the area of the Anxious Seat. The judge and many of the attorneys were wonderfully converted. Finney remained two months there in a powerful revival.

NEW BAPTISM

No sooner had Finney reached Oberlin than revival blessings began again there. In the fall of 1843 Finney returned to New York to the Second Free Congregational Church of New York, often called "The Sanctification Church" or "The Oberlin Church." It met in a leased theater that seated 1,500 people. Finney ministered there for about three months.

Finney returned by stagecoach to Oberlin. Wherever the stagecoach stopped, Finney heard of daily meetings for prayer or powerful revival. He wrote, "I found also to my great satisfaction that a continuous revival was prevailing throughout almost every town between here and New York." Finney had no clear estimate of how many were converted, but Albany alone reported over three thousand souls saved.[2]

In the winter of 1844, Finney testified to a fresh baptism of the Spirit. God's Word became all ablaze with light and alive with the life of God. Finney entered into a deeper sense of consecration than he had ever known. God flooded him with fresh love as he delighted in Jesus and reveled in the Song of Solomon. He had experienced these outpourings often before, but now liberty, buoyancy, and overflowing love seemed so abiding. Constantly, day after day, believers from different parts of the city came to his room to inquire and seek a higher Christian life.

REVIVAL MINISTRY IN ENGLAND

The illness and death of Mrs. Finney and his own lingering weakness kept Finney from active evangelistic ministry for a time. In November 1848, Finney married again. In September 1849, after many urgent invitations, he and Mrs. Finney sailed for England. God blessed his several weeks of ministry in Houghton. Then he ministered in Birmingham for about three months, seeing many conversions. Finney then spent several weeks in Worcester. Most of the non-Anglican churches were small and could not accommodate the large crowds.

Finney began to preach in the Tabernacle in London, the spot where Whitefield's tabernacle had been. The present tabernacle seated between three and four thousand. Finney continued to minister there for nine months, with services on Monday through Friday nights and twice on Sunday. Repeatedly he preached on prayer. The Sunday meetings were filled to capacity, and there were very large congregations on the week nights.

After several weeks of preaching, Finney felt that the Holy Spirit was leading him to give an invitation for salvation. He used a nearby hall, which seated 1,500 people and belonged to the church, as an inquiry room.

Finney said repeatedly that the inquiry meeting was not for Christians, nor was it for sinners who were not convicted of their sins. It was only for those unsaved who wanted to receive salvation immediately. The large inquiry room filled quickly. Night after night hundreds would arise to be prayed for, often nearly the whole congregation. People came from all parts of London, some walking several miles. People would stop Finney in the streets and testify how God had transformed their lives.

Thousands were converted during these months in England. A number of other ministers, including several Church of England ministers, changed their method of preaching to follow Finney's example and urged people to seek Christ and immediate salvation. One Anglican minister started twenty prayer meetings in different parts of his parish and won 1,500 people to Christ in his parish in a few months.

By the time Finney left London, there were four or five Anglican churches that had begun daily evangelistic services. Finney carried a tremendous prayer burden for London during this time. "I was scarcely ever more drawn out in prayer for any city or place than I was for London. Sometimes when I prayed in public especially, it seemed, with the multitudes before me, as I could not stop praying and that the Spirit of prayer would almost draw me out of myself in pleadings for the people and for the city at large." Finney spent no time sightseeing but sought to give himself only to "the express business of winning souls to Christ."[3]

Finney spoke much about confession and restitution as proofs of repentance. Almost every form of crime was confessed. Vast sums of money were given by people who wanted to make restitution for their sins.

After about five months in the polluted air of London, their incessant ministry affected both Mr. and Mrs. Finney. A Christian gave them funds and sent them to France for some weeks to recuperate and enjoy the solitude. Mrs. Finney's health improved greatly, but her husband's hoarseness largely remained. Finney, however, continued to minister through the winter until April 1851.

When the Finneys arrived back in Oberlin, God gave revival among the students all summer. In the autumn

Finney went to New York to visit his old congregation. But he found the pastor who had succeeded him there uncooperative. Only four hundred people still attended. The pastor refused to let the service be advertised with posters or handbills. Yet he permitted the building to be used by other organizations and was very independent in attitude. Finney felt under the circumstances it would not be possible to hold a general revival, so he went to Hartford, Connecticut, and began his ministry there the first of January 1852.

THE NECESSITY OF CONFESSION AND RESTITUTION

God gave revival blessing in Hartford, and there was a great spirit of prayer among the young converts. They began holding prayer meetings after the evening services, and nearly all of the new converts attended. Mrs. Finney established women's prayer meetings in the churches. The inquiry room meetings after the evening services were much blessed, and sometimes as many as four hundred people at one time were seeking the Lord. However, Finney's health became so weak that the Finneys had to return to Oberlin.

Wherever Finney went, he taught clearly that repentance involved confession and restitution. In many of his revivals the amount of monetary restitution totaled many thousands of dollars. The first winter that he ministered in Boston Finney preached two sermons one Sunday on Proverbs 28:13. For weeks afterward people of both sexes and all ages kept coming for spiritual advice. Many kinds of crime were confessed, and many restitutions were made.

The next winter Finney went to Syracuse, New York, for one Sunday. But when he saw the need, he consented to stay for another service the following Sunday. God worked among the leading members of the small Congregational church. They began to confess their needs, and as the revival momentum increased, the Presbyterians joined in. Mrs.

Finney conducted women's prayer meetings. Finney stayed all winter preaching from church to church. A new spirit of unity developed among the churches of Syracuse.

THIRD ROCHESTER REVIVAL

In the autumn of 1855, prayer warriors in Rochester, New York, were again prevailing for revival and sent urgently for Finney. At first he was reluctant to return again. But several judges of the Court of Appeals and of the State Supreme Court asked him to give another special series of lectures to lawyers on "The Moral Government of God." Finney began his series with 2 Corinthians 4:2.

Again, as in the other two revivals in Rochester, the Spirit moved from the higher classes of society and then spread generally to all citizens. Many attorneys were converted. The merchants often assigned half of their staff to attend the daytime services one day and the other half the next. The revival became the absorbing topic of conversation in banks, stores, public conveyances and along the streets. In each of Finney's previous revivals in Rochester, God had brought about large numbers of conversions, but this time there were more than ever. A special day of fasting and prayer for the colleges was held on February 28, 1856. Most of the students—eighty-five percent—were converted.

The revival spread in a remarkable way to the surrounding towns and villages. Reporters from two of the daily papers attended all the services and reported in detail the messages and sermons in their papers. People in other towns came by train to Rochester to attend. Morning prayer meetings began and continued for several years. These too were reported in the papers, and other towns began to have daily prayer meetings. It is quite possible that the newspaper reports of the meetings were influential in preparing the way for the 1858 revival of the United Prayer Meetings. These meetings seemed to spring up spontaneously in New

York City and then spread like wildfire across the country in the form of united noon prayer meetings. Finney continued ministering in the Rochester area throughout the winter and into the spring until his health forced him to leave.

In December of 1856 Finney again accepted an invitation to come to Boston for revival efforts. He preached mainly in Park Street Church. Immediately God began to save many. Finney continued to minister until April 19, when he returned to New York and then to Oberlin. An awakening began instantly among the students in the college. Finney considered his Boston meetings a part of the continuing revival movement that had spread from Rochester throughout New England, leading to the great revival that swept across America in 1858.

A NATIONAL REVIVAL

A daily prayer meeting resulting from the revivals had begun in Boston in 1840 and continued for ten years in Park Street Church. Then it broadened to include all Boston area churches and was moved to Old North Church. In September 1857, Jeremiah C. Lamphier began the Fulton Street prayer meeting in Old North Church. Within weeks noon prayer meetings began in churches across the nation with almost explosive rapidity. The meetings were led by laymen. At least one hundred thousand people were saved between January and April in 1858 in these meetings.

On March 8, a noon businessmen's prayer meeting was begun in Old North Church, Boston, in addition to the morning prayer meeting. Since the church was too small to accommodate the large crowds, a series of businessmen's prayer meetings began across Boston. Mrs. Finney held a ladies' prayer meeting daily in Park Street. It too was soon filled to capacity. Across the nation at least ten thousand cities and towns had noon prayer meetings and at least one million people were converted in the 1857–58 awakening.

This was a revival carried out primarily through prayer rather than through preaching. People everywhere prayed for their relatives and friends, and their confidence in God received a tremendous boost when so many of their prayers were answered.

BLESSINGS AGAIN IN BRITAIN

Finney returned to England in January 1859. He saw revival blessing come to several local churches but almost returned to America because of his poor health. Huntington, Edinburgh, and Aberdeen, Scotland, saw hundreds saved. Finney then journeyed to Bolton, England.

The second evening after they arrived, the Bolton revival began in the very home where the Finneys were staying. God convicted different ones in the home. They began weeping in prayer and were saved that very night. A national week of prayer had begun in England, and from the first night the meetings were crowded. When Finney gave the invitation, the vestry was thronged with inquirers.

They soon moved the meetings to a hall that could accommodate more people than the church. God poured out His Spirit on a crowded hall at each service. Finney preached twice on Sundays and four evenings during the week. This was all that his health could permit. Bolton was a Methodist center, and the Methodists cooperated fully in the revival. They had so many converts that they had to erect two new Methodist church buildings.

Finney encouraged others to canvass the entire city of Bolton two by two, praying in each home. Each night many inquirers found the Lord. People came from Manchester to attend the revival. Finney held a powerful meeting in a cotton mill, and sixty-two were converted. Finney was exhausted, but night after night the meetings continued, and often fifty to eighty people were converted. Finney preached on confession and restitution, and people obeyed God, often giving up hundreds of pounds. One person testified he made a restitution of £1,500.

Finney said of his time in Bolton that if they could only have found a building that could hold ten thousand, he believed it would have been filled. Mrs. Finney had held women's meetings in the daytime. During their year and a half in England, the Finneys became completely exhausted. Charles felt there could have been a great revival in Manchester, but he was too weak to stay. Returning to America, Finney went to Oberlin as soon as his strength permitted. The town had grown while he was gone, and there were many unconverted students in the college.

Finney plunged into the ministry with almost super-human strength. He often was in three services a day and met constantly with inquirers until nine o'clock at night. God began immediately to give gracious revival. After four months Finney came down with a chill and was physically unable to continue his ministry. Gradually the revival spirit diminished, although there were some conversions every week.

The college prayer meetings, both the general ones and the young men's prayer meetings, continued to be greatly used by God. Many of the students were themselves active in local revival campaigns. There was "more or less of a revival continually summer and winter from 1860 to 1866."[4] The revival reached its peak in 1866, a reminder of the great revivals of thirty years earlier. But in January 1866 Finney's health again broke. His second wife had died of tuberculosis in November 1863. In October 1865 Finney married a third time, this time to an Oberlin widow who was the assistant principal of the Oberlin College women's department.

From January 1867 until his death in 1875, Finney ministered as his health permitted. During the great Oberlin revival in 1866, Finney had remarked that he felt he could now say, "Lord, now lettest thou thy servant depart in peace" (Luke 2:29). In 1867 many people reported that Finney's preaching had never been more powerful. His strength, however, was quickly expended. He was forced to retire to his room or to bed for periods of time. Finney had been the instrument God continued to use in revival as long as strength permitted.

Finney had to give up his Oberlin pastorate in 1872, but he continued to teach in the seminary until July 1875, a few days before his death. He died of a heart attack August 16, 1875, two weeks before his eighty-third birthday. To the end he was humble, holy, prayerful, and a blessing to all.

CHAPTER SIXTEEN

Revival Prayer Ignites Revival Fire

In 1857–59 God began a movement of revival harvest in the United States that eventually swept across the British Isles, bringing spiritual rebirth to Northern Ireland, Wales, Scotland, and finally England. Dr. J. Edwin Orr, historian of revival movements, terms it the Fourth General Awakening.

All such widespread outpourings of the Spirit have their beginnings in a movement of prayer that is motivated, guided, and coordinated by the Holy Spirit. No human research can discover all the springs and streams of prayer that converge into such a mighty river of blessing. Prolonged and prevailing prayer has continued in many hearts, unseen by human eyes, but gathered into the current of the Spirit's preparation of the way of the Lord. We do not know all the ways the Holy Spirit prepared America and Britain for the 1857–58 revival, but we can recognize many of the people and events God used to bring about this great awakening.

THE INFLUENCE OF FINNEY

The instrument that God used perhaps most widely in the preparation was the life, ministry, and writings of Charles G. Finney. Some have considered him the greatest evangelist since the apostle Paul. Certainly no one person has so impacted the Christian world for revival as has Finney. Others have evangelized more people, listed more numerical results, and touched more parts of the world. But none has made a greater contribution to genuine revival or has been used by the Spirit to call more people to deep hunger and prevailing prayer.

Finney's book *Lectures on Revival* was born out of fasting, prayer, and his own rich experiences in revival ministry. The book influenced more Christians to pray for revival and expect spiritual outpourings than any book ever written. It was a best-seller of that day, with more than 250,000 copies in circulation at a time when the total population of the United States was considerably less than thirty million. While not all have agreed totally with Finney's theology of revival, praying Christians have been greatly blessed and influenced ever since. Probably this book and Finney's *Memoirs of Rev. Charles G. Finney* were used by God more than anything else in calling people to prepare the way of the Lord for the 1857–59 revival.

FINNEY'S NEW ENGLAND REVIVALS

During Finney's meetings in Syracuse in 1851, it seemed that almost the entire city was going to be converted. At least 100,000 conversions can be directly or indirectly related to these meetings.

For two years Finney was greatly used by God in local revivals in the Boston area and in New England. He preached mainly in Park Street Church, but scores of ministers and perhaps thousands of laymen came from distant parts of the United States to hear Finney during 1857. From Boston revival spread through New England, leading to the national awakening the following year. Revival had come the year before in Rochester, New York. The influence of those meetings spread to New York City itself, where the 1858 revival of the United Prayer Meetings began.

In the middle of the 1858–59 revival, a nationally distributed report described the renewal that was sweeping across New England. Soon many midwestern and western states began to experience a similar spiritual rebirth.

REVIVAL CONVENTIONS

The Presbyterians called a three-day convention of Presbyterian ministers from the synods of Pittsburgh, Allegheny, Wheeling, and Ohio. The meetings convened in Pittsburgh on December 1–3, 1856, and the focus was on revival: exploring the need for renewal, overcoming hindrances, and encouraging the pastors. Two hundred ministers and many laymen attended, and much of the time was given to prayer. The ministers went back to their churches to preach about revival on the first Sunday of January in 1857. The following Thursday was declared a day of humility, fasting, and prayer. Shortly afterward another convention on revival was held in Cincinnati with similar activities and results.

THE PALMER MINISTRY

Meanwhile, God had been using Dr. Walter Palmer, a New York physician, and his very talented wife, Phoebe, who was the chief speaker in revival campaigns and camp meetings in Ontario and Quebec in the fall of 1857. Hundreds were converted, and attendance ranged from five to six thousand. Mrs. Palmer held over three hundred such holiness camp meetings or revival crusades over a thirty-five-year period. Thousands were won to Christ, particularly during the summer months.

In the fall of 1857, a revival broke out in Hamilton, Ontario. This revival had all the characteristics of the revival movement that began weeks later in New York, except the Hamilton revival did not spawn the union prayer meetings. The renewal movement was widely reported in Christian periodicals and newspapers across America, especially in Methodist publications. Many Methodist pastors grew hungry for revival. At that time the Methodists were the largest and most evangelistic body of believers in America. Soon reports began to appear of local awakenings in various states across America.

JEREMIAH LAMPHIER IGNITES A FLAME

A quiet, zealous forty-six-year-old businessman in New York was appointed on July 1, 1857, as a missionary in downtown New York at the Dutch Church. Jeremiah Lamphier had been converted in 1842 in Broadway Tabernacle, Finney's church that was built in 1836.

Lamphier felt led by God to start a noon-time weekly prayer meeting in which business people could meet for prayer. Anyone could attend, for a few minutes or for the entire hour. Prayers were to be comparatively brief. Lamphier's group met on the third floor of the old North Dutch Reformed Church on Fulton Street in New York. Lamphier printed some handbills announcing the prayer meetings with the title, "How Often Should I Pray?" He left these in some offices and warehouses. He also put one on the door of the church on the street side.

The first day, September 23, 1857, Lamphier prayed alone for half an hour. But by the end of the hour, six men from at least four denominational backgrounds joined him. The next Wednesday there were twenty. On October 7 there were nearly forty. The meeting was so blessed that they decided to meet daily. One week later there were over one hundred present, including many unsaved who were convicted by the Holy Spirit of their sin.

Within one month pastors who had attended the noon prayer meetings in Fulton Street started morning prayer meetings in their own churches. Soon the places where the meetings were held were overcrowded. Men and women, young and old of all denominations met and prayed together without distinctions. The meetings abounded with love for Christ, love for fellow Christians, love for prayer, and love of witnessing. Those in attendance felt an awesome sense of God's presence. They prayed for specific people, expected answers, and obtained answers.

Newspapers began to report on the meetings and the unusual spirit of prayer that was evident. Within three months similar meetings had sprung up across America. Thousands began praying in these services and in their own homes. In New York, gospel tracts were distributed to those in attendance, with instructions that they pray over the tracts and then give them to someone God brought to mind.

The three rooms at the Fulton Street Church were filled beyond capacity, and hundreds had to go to other places. By early February a nearby Methodist Church was opened, and it immediately overflowed. The balconies were filled with ladies. By March 19 a theater opened for prayer, and half an hour before it was time to begin, people were turned away. Hundreds stood outside in the streets because they could not get inside. By the end of March over six thousand people met daily in prayer gatherings in New York City. Many churches added evening services for prayer. Soon there were 150 united prayer meetings each day across Manhattan and Brooklyn.

Meetings began in February in Philadelphia. Soon Jayne's Hall was overfilled, and meetings were held at noon each day in public halls, concert halls, fire stations, houses, and tents. The whole city exuded a spirit of prayer.

PRAYER MEETING FERVOR

Almost simultaneously noon prayer meetings sprang up all across America in Boston, Baltimore, Washington, D.C., Richmond, Charleston, Savannah, Mobile, New Orleans, Vicksburg, Memphis, St. Louis, Pittsburgh,

Cincinnati, Chicago, and in a multitude of other cities, towns, and in rural areas. By the end of the fourth month, prayer fervor burned intensely across the nation. It was an awesome but glorious demonstration of the sovereign working of the Holy Spirit and the eager obedience of God's people.

America had entered a new period of faith and prayer. Educated and uneducated, rich and poor, business leaders and common workmen—all prayed, believed, and received answers to prayer. Even the president of the United States, Franklin Pierce, attended many of the noon prayer meetings. This was not a revival of powerful preaching. This was a movement of earnest, powerful, prevailing prayer.

All people wanted was a place to pray. Sinners would come and ask for prayer. Someone would individually pray for them, and in minutes the newly saved person was rejoicing in Christ. Prayers would be asked by name for unconverted friends and loved ones from all over the country. In a day or two, testimonies would be given of how the prayers had already been answered. In some towns, nearly the entire population became saved.

Six months previous to Lamphier's prayer meeting boom, few would have gathered for a prayer service. But now a spirit of prayer occupied the land, as though the church had suddenly discovered its real power. The majority of the churches in most denominations experienced a new dimension of prayer. The *Presbyterian Magazine* reported that as of May there had been fifty thousand converts of the revival. In February, a New York Methodist magazine reported a total of eight thousand conversions in Methodist meetings in one week. The Louisville daily paper reported seventeen thousand Baptist conversions in three weeks during the month of March. And according to a June statement, the conversion figures stood at 96,216—and still counting.

CHAPTER SEVENTEEN

God's Glory
Over Land and Sea

The great awakening of 1857–59, which had begun in the cities, soon spread to towns, villages, and rural areas. It brought revivals to colleges and schools. For six to eight weeks during the height of the revival, some fifty thousand people were converted weekly. The average for two whole years was ten thousand new converts joining the churches each week.

The *Washington National Intelligencer* reported that in several New England towns not a single unconverted person could be found. State after state reported sweeping revival. In some places church bells daily summoned people at prayer times.

Among the daily prayer meetings reported were: 150 towns in Massachusetts, 200 in New York, 60 in New Jersey, 65 in Pennsylvania, 200 in Ohio, 150 in Indiana, 150 in Illinois, 50 in Missouri, and 60 in Iowa. Of the thirty million people living in the United States, nearly two million were won to Christ during the revival. The moral change was so great across the country that the Louisville, Kentucky, daily paper reported that the millennium had arrived.

The revival of 1857–59 boasted no organized movement,

structure, or "revival promoters." There was no coordination between the various prayer meetings. No revival evangelists apart from Finney operated in the New England area. It was not a movement planned by or guided by people.

It was a laymen's movement. Many pastors attended and were present whenever possible, but they did not lead the meeting. Bishops encouraged and attended the meetings but did not preside. Anyone could lead in brief, specific prayer, could request prayer for a friend, could start a verse of a hymn. It was a movement of Spirit-prompted, Spirit-guided prayer. People did not attend to see or be seen. They came to pray.

REVIVAL UNITY

The fourth great awakening was above all a revival of unity. Denominational backgrounds were forgotten. The spiritual unity of the body of Christ was never more beautifully evident or practically demonstrated. Everyone prayed for everyone else. All in attendance rejoiced over the answers to prayer shared one after another. People who had been prayed for by loved ones for years now surrendered their lives to Christ.

The first united prayer meeting in Kalamazoo, Michigan, saw people from five different denominations present. Four or five were saved that very first hour. Before the revival was over, there were nearly five hundred conversions in Kalamazoo.

A father asked the members of his group to pray for the salvation of his three sons in different parts of the country. The sons knew nothing of this, but within weeks letters came from each of them telling of new life in Christ. Another father asked prayer for a son who was then on board a ship in the Pacific Ocean. The son was converted at sea right about the time of the prayer meeting. A Columbus, Ohio, prayer group prayed for the public schools, and all but two of the youth in one high school were saved. A similar event took place in Toledo, Ohio. These are just brief examples of what was happening constantly all across the nation.

The accounts of the prayer meetings during those revival years describe how the people would quietly gather at the place of prayer promptly at the appointed hour. Whoever was leader for the meeting—a layman or a minister—arose and announced a hymn. They sang one or two verses with great joy, the leader prayed briefly, and then turned the service over to the members. Any person was free to speak or pray for no longer than five minutes. If the person took more than that time, a small bell was rung and it was someone else's turn.

Requests for prayer, often coming from distant places, were spoken or read. Often sinners arose and requested prayer for themselves. Members gave testimonies of answers to prayer, and the people praised the Lord. Brief exhortations on prayer or revival were allowed but limited to five minutes. Many testified of revival progress in various locations. Promptly at the closing of the hour the leader rose and pronounced the benediction, and the people quietly left the building. Occasionally someone might stay behind to pray with a spiritual seeker.

THE INVISIBLE CLOUD OF GOD'S PRESENCE

A canopy of holy and awesome revival influence—in reality the presence of the Holy Spirit—seemed to hang like an invisible cloud over many parts of the United States, especially over the eastern seaboard. At times this cloud of God's presence even seemed to extend out to sea. Those on ships approaching the east coast at times felt a solemn, holy influence, even one hundred miles away, without even knowing what was happening in America.

Revival began aboard one ship before it reached the coast. People on board began to feel the presence of God and a sense of their own sinfulness. The Holy Spirit convicted them, and they began to pray. As the ship neared the harbor, the captain signaled, "Send a minister." Another small commercial ship arrived in port with the captain, and every member of the crew converted in the last 150 miles. Ship after ship arrived with the same story: both passengers and crew were suddenly convicted of sin and turned to Christ before they reached the American coast.

The battleship North Carolina was anchored in New York harbor as a naval receiving ship. More than a thousand young men were on board. Four Christians agreed to meet together for prayer and knelt on the lower deck. The Spirit of God so filled their hearts with joy that they broke into song. Ungodly men on the top deck heard the singing, looked down, and saw the boys kneeling. They began running down the stairs, mocking and jeering. The convicting power of the Holy Spirit so gripped them that by the time they reached the bottom deck they fell on their knees and began crying for mercy.

Strong men who were deep in sin were broken down by the Spirit's power and knelt humbly in penitence and faith. Night after night the sailors prayed, and hundreds were converted on the ship. Ministers were sent for, and they came out from shore to help in the gracious work of the Spirit. The battleship became a mighty center of revival. Converts of the movement, completing their periods of training, were sent out to other navy ships. Wherever they went revival fires were kindled in other naval vessels.

IN HOMES, SHOPS, FIELDS, AND CHURCHES

Reports came in of hundreds being converted in prayer meetings, private homes, workshops, and fields. Often the doors of businesses held signs reading, "Closed. Will reopen at the close of the prayer meeting." Five prayer meetings took place daily in Washington, D.C. Five thousand or so attended daily services in the Academy of Music Hall.

In Philadelphia, Jayne's Hall removed partitions and added space for six thousand people to attend daily meetings. At this time George Duffield wrote the hymn "Stand Up, Stand Up for Jesus." For months multitudes of churches opened every evening for prayer, and some of them had from three to five services of prayer each day. All were filled. The services consisted of simple prayer, confession, exhortation, and singing. But it was "so earnest, so solemn, the silence . . . so awful, the singing . . . so over-powering" that the meetings were unforgettable.[1] A canvas tent was erected for outdoor meetings, and it immediately filled with people. In four months' time, a total of 150,000 people attended the ministry in the tent, with many conversions. Philadelphia churches reported five thousand converts.

The Presbyterians in Northern Ireland heard of the awakening in Philadelphia and sent fraternal delegates. These delegates returned to their homeland and reported what they had seen, and the revival broke out in Ireland, spreading across the British Isles.

REVIVAL IN THE ARMY

Because of the bitter tensions of the Civil War and the slavery issue, for a time it seemed that the southern states would not be as powerfully influenced by the revival as the northern ones had been. Others dispute this assumption. An unusually powerful revival broke out among the southern troops stationed around Richmond, Virginia, in the autumn of 1861. It began in the hospitals among the wounded men and then spread into the camps as these men returned to active duty. Prayer meetings were organized and hundreds converted. The movement spread rapidly throughout the army, reaching the troops of Tennessee and Arkansas.

Revival was encouraged by Generals Robert E. Lee and Thomas J. "Stonewall" Jackson, who were well known as devout Christians. By the mid-summer of 1863 the revival had spread through all the Confederate armies, and thousands of men had been converted. Chaplains and lay missionaries went out among the troops, preaching and distributing tracts and dealing personally with hungry hearts. By the end of the war at least 150,000 soldiers had been converted, and more than a third of all of the southern troops had become praying men. The revival among the southern troops was primarily a revival of prayer, as the earlier revival in the North had been. While the best estimates are that 6.6 percent of the entire population of the United States was converted during the revival, the percentage among the southern troops was 21 percent.

CHAPTER EIGHTEEN

Across the Sea to Ulster

God blessed America with sweeping revival in 1857. It was often called the revival of the United Prayer Meetings. When this news reached the British Isles, especially Northern Ireland, many ministers and deeply spiritual Christians felt renewed hunger and earnestness in prayer that God would move in Ireland in the same gracious way.

So widespread was the interest in the American revival that the Presbyterian Synod of Ireland, at the general assembly in Dublin in 1858, set apart two sessions for conferences and addresses on the subject of revival. The two thousand people present listened with intense interest. The assembly appointed two of their leading ministers, Dr. William Gibson, who became the moderator the next year, and Rev. William McClure to go to New York to attend the Fulton Street prayer meeting, investigate the revival, and bring back a report.

When the two men returned, their report deepened the hunger for revival throughout Northern Ireland. They testified publicly on several occasions to what they had witnessed across the Atlantic. As the Irish Christians prayed, hungered, and believed, God visited them with the outpouring of His Spirit, and revival spread from place to place. The year of 1859 became known as God's year of grace across the nation of Ireland. The sample accounts in this and the following two chapters illustrate the mighty working of the Holy Spirit in this small country.

THE FIRST IRISH PRAYER MEETINGS

In September 1857, four young Irishmen had begun a weekly prayer meeting in Connor, County Antrim, in a small rural schoolhouse near Kells. This revival meeting began the same week as the revival prayer meeting in Fulton Street, New York, fountainhead of the revival in the United States. On January 1, 1858, the first person in the Kells meeting was converted, and after that every week at least one more conversion occurred. By the end of 1858 the Kells group had an average attendance of fifty. They permitted no unsaved person to attend, as their prayer meeting was focused on an outpouring of the Holy Spirit in revival. They were greatly influenced by three books: George Müller's *Life of Trust*, *The Life of Murray McCheyne*, and Finney's *Lectures on Revival*. Soon other general prayer meetings began in homes. By the end of 1858 about a hundred prayer meetings took place each week in the district.

Two of the converts from the Connor District accepted an invitation to the town of Ahoghill to hold a revival meeting. On March 14, 1859, such a crowd gathered that they filled the largest church, until they feared the galleries would collapse. So they poured out into the street, and some three thousand people of all denominations—Presbyterian, Anglican, Methodist, and Roman Catholic—were gripped by the Holy Spirit and stood as if paralyzed. A chilling rain fell on them, but people knelt in the mud of the streets and prayed. A number of people were so smitten down by the Holy Spirit that they lay prostrate on the ground. These prostrations occurred repeatedly thereafter throughout the revival.

Professor William Gibson, who the next year was elected the moderator of the synod, gave this description:

"At these meetings many convictions have taken place. From one up to ten and twelve have been arrested by the Spirit of God through the word and prayer of these honored brethren. Even strong men have staggered and fallen down under the wounds of their conscience. Great bodily weakness ensues. The whole frame trembles. Oh! It is a heart-rending sight to witness. With ringing of hands, streams of tears, and a look of unutterable anguish, they confess their sins in tones of unmistakable sincerity, and appeal to the Lord for mercy with a cry of piercing earnestness. . . . I have heard the cry as I have never heard it before, 'Lord Jesus, have mercy upon my sinful soul; Lord Jesus, come to my burning heart; Lord, pardon my sins; Oh, come and lift me from these flames of hell!'

"These convictions vary in different individuals, both in strength and duration. While some obtain peace and believing soon after their conviction, others do not attain it for several days."[1]

Revival fire broke out and spread throughout the district. Every night meetings for prayer, praise, reading of the Scripture, and exhortations were held, even during the busiest seasons. Meetings were held in kitchens, barns, churches, schoolhouses, fields, and on roadsides. There were all-night sessions of prayer and weeping. People forsook their farm work and crowded into the meetings, gripped by the Spirit of God.

LIKE A PRAIRIE FIRE

The revival spread quickly across Ulster (Northern Ireland). Reports of intense conviction of sin and glorious conversions arrived almost hourly. In Ballymena in mid-April, a thirty-year-old man suddenly fell on his knees in the street, crying out in agony as if someone had attacked him. People came running from all directions, expecting to find a victim of crime. For ten minutes he called out, "Unclean! Unclean!

God be merciful to me a sinner!" The awesome fear of God fell upon the people.

One after another were gloriously saved in homes and in schoolhouses. People opened the windows so that those outside and around the buildings could hear the prayer and praise inside. Careless sinners broke down and wept like children. Drunkards were awed into solemn silence. Often people did not go to bed for two or three nights. Passersby heard people crying aloud for mercy inside their houses, calling out to God in prayer, or singing hymns and songs.

Business almost came to a standstill. Workmen, carpenters, shoemakers, and others in trade spent nearly every minute in meetings the first week. Day and night they prayed with people stricken by the Holy Spirit with conviction for their sins.

From all directions people called for ministers. New believers had to instruct and comfort the seeking sinners. Prayer meetings in private homes were held at all hours of the day and night. Every night Presbyterian churches overflowed. It was not unusual to see praying thousands filling a gravel pit or a graveyard. Many faces were filled with pain as people realized what sinners they were. The faces of the new converts beamed with such joy that the newly saved were easily identified.

The revival spread to nearby communities, and every area experienced mighty outpourings of the Holy Spirit. In one large gathering in the open, as one of the converts began to pray, people fell to the ground crying bitterly, confessing their sins. Others went to a nearby graveyard and fell on the graves, weeping and sobbing over their sin. When a message was given, many people fell on the ground before the speaker. The meeting continued all through the night.

At Boroughshane workers in a spinning factory were seized by the Holy Spirit's conviction of sin. Within an hour more than twenty people were lying prostrate, and the factory had to be closed for two days while people prayed. Several thousand gathered in the open before the Presbyterian church, and services lasted late into the night. Notorious profligates were converted.

In May dozens of people of all temperaments and characters were convicted of their sins, prostrated themselves before God, and received His forgiveness, their faces shining with an indescribable glory. "Very many of them received a marvelous fluency and power of prayer. A hatred of sin, a love for the Savior, a zeal for His cause, and affection for one another, and an anxiety about perishing sinners, took possession of their hearts, and literally ruled and governed their actions."[2] At least one thousand were converted.

In one district every housewife was converted, and these women formed a women's prayer meeting. Similar women's meetings were used by the Lord in other places. In the general prayer meetings, frequently God's presence so swept over the people that every person was moved to weeping, praying, and rejoicing. People felt as if the Lord had breathed upon them. "They were first affected with awe and fear—then they were bathed in tears—then filled with love unspeakable." Such times came even during ordinary Sunday services.

Prayer meetings were so crowded that temporary chairs filled the aisles, and other people had to stand throughout the service. Young and old of all denominations, even Roman Catholics, were eager to attend. Winter and summer the tide of interest remained high. Family worship flourished. Drunkenness, swearing, quarreling, and fighting diminished. Many carried Bibles wherever they went, even stopping their work in the fields or stopping as they walked along the road to read more of God's Word. An area fair ended in a prayer meeting with five thousand attending.

FROM TOWN TO TOWN

The revival burst suddenly upon Ballymena. The whole town was stirred, and crying and prayers filled the streets and almost every house. Many were so convicted by the Holy Spirit that they could not sleep for several nights.

At least twice a week large mid-day prayer meetings were held in fields and town halls. At these meetings people from all denominations united in prayer. Some five thousand met in a quarry. Laymen exhorted the gathering with special power and anointing from the Holy Spirit. Repeatedly people were smitten to the ground by the convicting power of the Holy Spirit.

Children of ten and twelve were wonderfully saved and prayed with great power for unsaved adults. A Presbyterian minister, returning from a meeting of the synod, walked through the streets and heard people inside the houses on both sides of the street weeping and calling on God for mercy.

Young businessmen took leaves of absence from their jobs and gave themselves to prayer and the revival. Prayer meetings were held in homes and at all hours of the day and night. For some weeks noon-time united prayer meetings were held in the town hall and attended by the ministers and members of all churches. Hearing of the revival, people came from England, Scotland, and other parts of Ireland just to see the work of God.

As the revival spread to other towns and villages, reports came of whole families being visited by God. At Ballyrashane fifteen hundred assembled in the open air, and about fifty became so convicted that they fell to the ground.

In Derry united meetings were held every evening in the Victoria Market. A Church of England minister, reporting on the revival, emphasized that all denominations were affected, and that young men of the worst character, after being saved, prayed powerful prayers superior to any minister's.

About two thousand people attended the "monster" prayer meeting at Cloughmills. Many Roman Catholics were saved. At Ballymoney one hundred prayer meetings in the town and district kept the revival fires burning. At Portrush a united prayer meeting drew two thousand from the surrounding area. Then daily union prayer meetings began. A throng of six thousand attended a prayer meeting at Dunmills, four miles outside of Portrush. Many were prostrate before God.

At Ballycarry, after revival broke, meetings continued forty-two nights. Often prayer with inquirers continued until daybreak. In almost every meeting people were stricken. Many were stricken while alone praying in their own homes. Weeknight prayer meetings, led by laymen, had attendance of one thousand and more. People seemed to have a wonderful gift of prayer.

At Dundrod the revival spread "with the rapidity of a prairie fire." After a short message by the Presbyterian pastor, first one and then another rose to testify. The Holy Spirit moved upon the people. "Here and there throughout the church, parties rose and went out laboring under deep conviction, and immediately the graveyard is filled with groups singing and praying around the prostrate bodies of men and women. Some are in a trance, others crying for mercy. Some are still falling into the arms of friends and sinking as into a swoon. Some stagger a distance, and drop on their knees to pray. . . . and a few rush to the gates, and fly in terror from the scene."[3] God's Spirit worked until evening among both women and men. For ten days the revival continued in power.

Revival fire came to Carrickfergus during the observance of the Lord's Supper. Revival spread to the salt mines, and great prayer meetings were held hundreds of feet underground. The Congregational minister of Straid told of the deep spirit of prayer that flowed through the area and brought a genuine revival. "Profanity, Sabbath profanation, and drunkenness are set aside. Many public houses (taverns) are closed, a cock-pit has become a preaching station and families, where nothing but vice in its worst forms could be seen, have been brought to love and adore the Lord."[4]

CHAPTER NINETEEN

The Belfast Connection

News of revival in outlying towns had stirred Belfast, but the actual revival there began in June 1859 at a public gathering at Linen Hall Street Presbyterian Church. Crowds began to gather nightly in Episcopal, Presbyterian, Wesleyan, Independent, and Baptist churches. Night and day revived laymen visited convicted people in their homes and prayed with them. Revival spread powerfully among the young people.

Then a united weekly prayer meeting began in the music hall. At the first service almost one hundred ministers from the various denominations were present. The lord mayor of Belfast presided. In the second service, the Anglican bishop, assisted by the moderator of the Presbyterian church and the president of the Methodist church, led the prayers. The building overflowed, and hundreds could not get inside.

THE BELFAST "MONSTER" MEETING

On June 29, 1859, a "monster" open-air union prayer meeting was held in Botanic Gardens, Belfast, with an estimated forty thousand people filling every available space. Children sat in the branches of the trees. Many who could

145

not hear distinctly formed separate meetings of five hundred to a thousand each on the edge of the massive crowd.

The moderator of the general assembly of the Presbyterian church led the service. He said, "We are especially met to do homage to the Holy Ghost, whose convincing and converting power have been so strikingly manifested among us for these several months. Let us not resist the Holy Spirit, nor grieve Him, but ask unceasingly, earnestly and expectingly, that He will descend upon us this day as He did on the Day of Pentecost, in answer to the many prayers offered up, and to be offered, and that many sons and daughters may this day be born to the Lord Almighty."[1] In the smaller meetings, people were struck down under deep conviction of sin. Many wept silently and others cried out for mercy. Groups of boys and girls, a number of them the children of poverty, prayed in separate groups on the edges of the crowd.

Evening services from then on were held daily in many local churches. The Great Georges Street Presbyterian Church was so crowded the following night that one service was conducted inside and one or two simultaneously on the outside. During the service many cried out to God for mercy. These people were taken into the church garden or the pastor's house, where lay leaders prayed with them, exhorted them, and, in some instances, sang and praised the Lord. It was impossible to dismiss the service, and some did not leave the gathering until 5:00 A.M. Great Georges Street Church alone reported eight hundred who came to Christ during the revival. In many places there were so many converts that the churches could not hold them all.

GLORIOUS TRANSFORMATIONS

A well-known Presbyterian minister told how the pains of hell came upon people as they felt convicted by the Spirit. Their cries changed to angelic rapture and outpourings of

Christian love as the Spirit witnessed to their conversion. "Oh! I wish I could tell you of Jesus' love; I would take all sinners in my arms, if I could, and lay them at His feet." All the church services were crowded, and thousands attended open-air services.[2]

Conversions crossed all boundary lines of society. Learned men, wealthy merchants, lords and ladies wept under the same deep conviction of sin that affected illiterate farmers and craftspeople.

Often revival came to churches before the services even had a chance to begin. A Christian merchant, uninvited, felt compelled to tell a church what he had seen God do in revival that week. By the time he had spoken ten minutes, people began to be smitten down. The glory of the Lord so filled the church that many began to weep, and that night fifty were saved.

In the same church a few weeks later God's Spirit moved on a service, and more than a hundred were saved before the night was over. As people left the service they so overflowed with the joy of the Lord that they sang along the Belfast streets and village roads in the early morning hours as they walked home. Twenty prayer meetings were started and continued by the people of this church, and about four hundred were converted.

Before the week was over, revival had spread to large numbers of strong young men and women from among the farming population. On some days the schools shut down as revival spread among the children in the classrooms. One school of about eighty saw half of the children converted in one day. Then the children began to pray for the salvation of friends and loved ones. Strong men wept as they heard the children pray.

In July there was another open-air gathering of about fifteen thousand. The ministers prayed with burdened sinners until two and three o'clock in the morning.

GENERAL ASSEMBLY ADJOURNED

When the general assembly of the Irish Presbyterian Church met in July, minister after minister arose and told how the Holy Spirit was poured out on his congregation. All the ministers wanted to hurry back to their congregations, where they were needed by their people as the revival continued to spread from church to church. Revival fire burned so mightily that the assembly adjourned, agreeing to complete its business three months later.

In August another union prayer meeting was held in Belfast with twenty thousand attending. Ministers of all denominations were again present, and numbers of people came from Scotland.

All over Belfast prayer meetings were held for both adults and children. Bible studies sprang up like flowers in the spring. Holy reverence, Christian joy, and a spirit of prayer hung over the city. One church reported forty weekly prayer meetings among their congregation.

BELFAST REBORN

The revival in Belfast was tremendously used of the Lord. Prostitution as a way of life began to fade as many of the prostitutes were saved. Litigation decreased and savings deposits in banks increased. Political demonstrations temporarily ceased. Employees in a printing office were so convicted of their sins and driven to prayer that the firm had to close temporarily. Several factories closed their doors for a time because the employees, convicted of their sins and seeking God's mercy, could not work.

From Belfast the revival spread in all directions. In many places crowded services, conviction of sin, and public or private prayer continued into the night or early morning. Unusual anointing and power in prayer, even on the new converts, was reported again and again.

Among the most impressive results of the revival were the tremendous freedom, eloquence in prayer, and anointing of the Spirit manifested by the new converts. Prayer took on an added dimension as people became more fluent, bold, and expressive of their concern for the salvation of others. Under God's guidance, prayer lives matured, and outstanding examples of answers to prayer were reported everywhere.

People sang in groups as they walked home from the services, even late at night. Singing bands became a common sight in many parts of the country. People often marched four or five abreast as they sang. At times the bands were so blessed and zealous that they would walk the roads singing until dawn. Some bands boasted thirty or more members.

A report from Coleraine said that for three weeks it had been one continual Pentecost. Hundreds of people were convicted of sin, and in cottage after cottage, groups were gathered to pray, read the Bible, and sing psalms and hymns. A new town hall had been built in Coleraine, and the mayor had scheduled a ball to celebrate its opening. But the spirit of repentance was so widespread that the new hall had to be used for prayer. The courthouse in another part of town was filled also. Ministers prayed with penitent ones hour after hour until they were completely exhausted. Pastors even ministered to crowds in the streets, exhorting and praying with people repenting of their sins.

Rev. W. Arthur describes the amazing awakening God sent to a large school in Coleraine. "In it a boy was observed under deep impressions. The master, seeing that the little fellow was not fit to work, called him to him and advised him to go home, and call upon the Lord in private. With him he sent an older boy, who had found peace the day before.

"On their way they saw an empty house, and went in there to pray together. The two school fellows continued in prayer in the empty house until he who was weary and

heavy-laden felt his soul blessed with sacred peace. Rejoicing in this new and strange blessedness, the little fellow said,
'I must go back and tell Mr. . . .' The boy, who a little while
ago, had been too sorrowful to do his work, soon entered
the school with a beaming face and going up to the master
said in his simple way, 'Oh, sir, I am so happy; I have the
Lord Jesus in my heart.'"

The report continues, "The attention of the whole
school was attracted. Boy after boy slipped out of the room.
After a while, the master stood upon something which
enabled him to look over the wall of the playground. There
he saw a number of his boys ranged around the wall on their
knees in earnest prayer, every one apart. The scene overcame
him. Presently he turned to the pupil who had already been
a comforter to the one school fellow, and said, 'Do you
think you can go and pray with those boys?'

"He went out and kneeling down among them, began
to implore the Lord to forgive their sins, for the sake of Him
who had borne them all upon the cross. Their silent grief
soon broke into a bitter cry. As this reached the ears of the
boys in the room, it seemed to pierce their hearts; as by one
consent they cast themselves upon their knees and began to
cry for mercy.

"The girls' school was above, and the cry no sooner
penetrated to their room, than apparently well knowing
what mourning it was, and hearing in it a call to themselves,
they too fell upon their knees and wept. Strange disorder for
school master and mistress to have to control! The united
cry reached the adjoining streets, and soon every spot on the
premises was filled with sinners seeking God."[3]

CHAPTER TWENTY

The Irish Year of Grace

In 1859, the whole country of Northern Ireland seemed studded with prayer meetings, and the face of Irish society had changed. From the Presbyterian church in the village of Ballycarry, considered the cradle of Irish Presbyterianism, came a report of three hundred conversions in a short period of time, half of them being stricken down. All of these conversions, and indeed the vast majority of conversions across Ulster, were genuine and lasting. There were no backsliders. In Ballycarry the Sunday school quadrupled, and one Bible class contained 150 new members.

The church was filled: pews, aisles, vestibule, and pulpit stairs. "And then such prayers!" The prayers of the women in their meetings were "peculiarly beautiful, spiritual, and sublime." Formerly timid young ladies now had eyes "sparkling with delight." While the pastor was gone on a trip, two hundred more were added to the church, and the work was progressing "with marvelous power."[1]

More Roman Catholics experienced new birth during the revival than in the previous half century. Many received threats and some were brutally beaten for their faith, but most Catholic converts remained steadfast. Several made comments such as, "I would rather have my body to be burned than to worship saints any more."

From the town of Derry came the report of great awakening. There were daily united prayer meetings in churches and in the corporation hall where the people were led in prayer by various ministers. At 7:00 P.M. each day in the Corn Market, prayer meetings were attended by five hundred to five thousand. When these united meetings were closed, the people adjourned to the churches and prayed till 10:00 P.M. Seldom were the ministers able to leave their vestries until midnight or later.

How did this Derry awakening begin? Four young men, converts from Connor, gave their testimony in a crowded service in the First Presbyterian Church. Several thousand were present. Suddenly a number of people began to call out to God for mercy.

That night many of the people could not sleep. Some wept in their homes for hours. Others cursed and swore in anger. Monday night again there was a united service in the First Presbyterian Church. The building was overcrowded, but the ministers spoke calmly. "The meeting felt still as a grave; the stillness was fearful. Those who were present will never forget it. At length the silence was broken by unearthly cries, uttered simultaneously by several in different parts of the church." In a few minutes the vestry was filled with people "who lay in mental agony and absolute bodily prostration."[2]

Here is one account from among the hundreds in that service. A well-educated merchant of high morality suddenly saw hell opened before his eyes, and an irresistible power seemed to force him headlong into it. He looked around and said to himself, "I know where I am. This is the church where I usually worship. I am under a delusion." But as he looked down, there was hell!

He arose from his seat and seized the back of the pew in front of him. The smoke from hell seemed to rise in his face. He shuddered and his heart cried out, "My sins! My sins! I am lost!" He staggered out of the building and went home. "Had anyone asked me, where are you going? I would have answered, in calm despair, I am going to hell."

Upon reaching his room, for several hours he called out to God for mercy. Then God's promises came to his mind. He joyously seized them, and "a heavenly radiance" spread over his soul. He arose a Christian. He raced out into the night across town and knocked on his business partner's door. When the door opened, he called out, "I have found Christ and have come to tell you!" They prayed together, and three days later his partner was converted.[3]

PROSTRATED BY CONVICTION

An Episcopal clergyman wrote that over a six-week period there had been fifty cases of prostration in his Sunday worship services, and that some 250 of the people in his parish had been converted. Another Episcopal minister reported that of the five thousand people in his parish there was scarcely a family in which one or more members had not been soundly converted.

A Presbyterian minister assigned to tour the Assembly churches on behalf of home missions reported concerning the revival: "I soon found that the half was not told me. At some of the meetings which I attended, there were instances of bodily prostration. It was truly dreadful to see some of these. To hear at intervals the agonizing cries for mercy, and to see the terror depicted on every feature of the countenance was truly awful. But how delightful it was to observe the sin-stricken souls resting on the Savior. . . . Words can convey no idea of the heavenly joy that beams from the eye, or of the calm assurance deposited on the countenance" when they found Christ.

It was his opinion that God was using the prostrations to draw attention to the Spirit's work. He found the physical manifestations decreasing, but the cases of "conviction of sin and conversion unto God" increasing rapidly. Revival was reaching new districts, "carrying with it floods of enriching blessing. . . . Thousands of God's people have been literally revived and refreshed by it."[4]

In many places the revival reports told of the transformed faces of the newly saved. From Derry came the account of a girl who felt as if she were in hell for three hours while she was prostrated under conviction. "Her face during this time gave one the idea of a lost soul." She then fell into a kind of trance and her face was completely changed. "The radiance of glory overspread it, and for four hours she seemed to be in the regions of the blessed." She was given special visions during that time but was never heard to describe them. She continued steadfast in faith, "an example of humility and love, and all the other graces of the Spirit."[5]

In some instances those prostrated while seemingly oblivious to all else showed wonderfully anointed memory. One pastor told of a girl who lay with fixed eyes turned to heaven for four hours. She quoted over a hundred Scriptures all related and applied to her own case. She repeated sermons and exhortations that the pastor had preached over previous months, quoting large sections of these verbatim. Afterward the pastor questioned her, but she could not remember the sermons or quote those Scripture passages accurately as she had done when gripped by the Holy Spirit.

A thirty-year-old man at Ballymoney, born deaf and mute, was working in a peat bog when the Holy Spirit so convicted him of his sin that he started to his sister's house, where he lived. He was so smitten that he lost nearly all his strength and had to lie down twice before he reached home. He prayed all night until breakfast the next morning. Suddenly he felt God's saving grace, leaped up into the air and clasped his arms as though holding some person to his heart. His face beamed with delight and radiated love and gratitude.

Another man, going home from the market where he

had sold his produce, was walking along the road counting his money. Suddenly he was struck by such conviction that he fell on the ground, like Saul of Tarsus, and his money was scattered on the road.

Even Roman Catholics sitting in their chapels during Mass were stricken down. The priests sold them holy water to keep away "the revival devil."

Revival started in the village of Maghera by the fireside in a farmhouse. A visitor began to describe revival scenes he had seen in another county. Suddenly a servant boy who was listening in felt convicted. Moments later a servant girl and then the brother of the visitor lay prostrate with conviction. None of these people had shown any religious interest before. Word spread through the village, and neighbors gathered and spent the night in prayer and singing.

Early in the morning they sent for the minister. Before the day was over, the news had spread throughout the whole area. The revival fire spread, and new converts started prayer meetings and revived Sunday schools that had ceased. Young men began daily morning prayer meetings that were still continuing six months later.

The revival in Armagh was reminiscent of the way in which the Holy Spirit worked in the school in Coleraine. One of the Armagh ministers in his own church began to lead in prayer, and such a powerful anointing came upon him that he poured forth a torrent of prayers for a whole hour. God began a mighty movement of the Spirit throughout his congregation. After two united prayer meetings, a third unannounced meeting began, but united intercession was impossible. Each pew was like a separate prayer meeting. In some groups, people prayed with those who were prostrated by agonizing conviction. In others, new converts rejoiced in the Lord. Hundreds were saved in these three nights. They telegraphed the pastor to come from the general assembly he had been attending. He returned at once and took charge on the fourth night.

REVIVAL TRAINS

As a result of the revival, Northern Ireland became known for a time as the most peaceful province in the British Empire. A great revival gathering was held in Armagh, and twenty thousand attended. Special trains ran from Belfast and other cities to bring people to the revival gathering. The people crowded to capacity in the train cars, sang hymns along the way, and passed out tracts when the train stopped at a station.

In Belfast and across the country, wherever revival was present, ministers were busy day and night praying in homes and in churches after the services. Many became exceedingly weary, yet rejoiced in it all. Said one minister, "Oh! What a heaven to minister to a revived people!" At least one minister was thought to have died from exhaustion and overwork.

An Episcopal minister described the physical manifestations as being of two kinds. The vast majority responded with tears and trembling. The rest were completely prostrated. The minister said the latter were treated with prudence and caution. Evil effects were guarded against, and "we see clearly the plainest and happiest results in countless cases." God used this "striking down" to arrest the attention of the worst sinners of the population and to bring them face to face with the reality of God and eternity.[6]

Another minister said of the prostrations, "They were sent by God to serve a special end, and when that purpose was served, they ceased. They were sent—in my mind—fully as much for the benefit of others, as for those who were the subjects of them. Every prostration I firmly believe was a sermon, a thrilling appeal to the profligate and a solemn warning to those who were at ease in Zion."[7] Undoubtedly they were God's best means to awaken some people.

The minister at Boveva wrote about Sunday, June 12. "Oh, with what power and majesty Jehovah walked among us. Zechariah 12:10 was wonderfully fulfilled to us." The crowd at the Boveva church became so large that they had to conduct the worship outside. "A more solemn assembly never met on earth. During the service the tears and suppressed sobs of many showed that it was no ordinary occasion—that it was the day of God's power—that the spirit of power was dealing personally with men's souls. When the benediction was pronounced, a few retired, but the great majority lingered—stood, in fact, as if held in a vice or bound with a chain.

"In a moment, as if struck with a thunderbolt, about a hundred persons were prostrated on their knees sending forth a wail from hearts bruised, broken, and overwhelmed with horror, such as will never be forgotten, and which, perhaps, for solemnity and awe, will never be surpassed until the Judgment Day. . . . For hours these stricken, smitten, bleeding souls remained on their knees unconscious of everything but their own guilt and danger and need of a Savior, pleading and praying with an intensity and fervor which surpasses all description."[8]

The Wednesday church service in Boveva was appointed for prayer. The church was overcrowded long before it was time to begin the service. "The awful sadness in every countenance bespoke the deep earnestness within; even the most ungodly were overawed, and wore a solemn sadness on their faces. Had a pestilence swept over the neighborhood, leaving one dead in every house, greater awe would not have been produced."[9] Again and again the service was dismissed, but the people refused to leave.

Ministers did not encourage emotional demonstration. Far from it! "For several Sabbaths the services of the sanctuary had to give way to the sobs and cries of pierced souls; and though every lawful effort was made to suppress all excitement, yet the agony and sorrow within were too great to be repressed, and frequently the audible cry broke forth for mercy."[10]

An ignorant, illiterate, and irreligious woman visited a house where people had been emotionally converted the day before. Now in her own home she lay prostrate on her bed, telling of her sinful life, how Satan had sought to destroy her, but how Christ had saved her. She quoted many texts of Scripture, which surprised everyone because she could not read and had not been to church for years.

In Castlederg the congregational service had begun singing the first two lines of a hymn, when suddenly a strong man fell to the floor. He was removed from the service. Instantly there was an amazing manifestation of the divine presence. "The whole house was filled with the glory of the Lord; the singing had to cease; there was nothing through the house but sobbing and sighing, some calling for mercy, others rejoicing in the sin-pardoning God. The Lord was present in mighty power. The sense was such that no mortal could describe. After hours, the minister could not get the congregation to leave, even after he had pronounced the benediction six times.

"Eventually some left singing, others crying to God for mercy left with friends. Some were smitten down on the road home crying for mercy. Through the night hours one by one several found peace. They immediately began to point others who were still convicted by their sins to Christ."[11]

A LASTING GRACE

Among the wonderful changes resulting from the revival that were reported across the country were decreases in drunkenness, crime, prostitution, profanity, quarreling, fights, cock-fighting, feuds, fraud, dishonesty, and family bickering. There arose a great new interest in education, sacred music, the Bible, personal cleanliness, and even in eliminating poverty. People seemed more courteous and considerate. In one district the year before the revival, there were twenty-six paupers, but when revival came there were only four.

All across Northern Ireland ministers were eager to write or tell about the amazing work of the Lord in their own churches and communities. Months after the revival had passed, many pastors testified that every person they knew who was truly converted during the revival, regardless of his or her previous life or background, carried on faithfully in the Lord.

It is not surprising that in the early days of the revival, many ministers had questions in their minds about some of the physical manifestations of conversion experiences. Yet nearly all came to a profound awareness that these manifestations were proof of the presence and ministry of the Holy Spirit.

One such cautious minister reported that at first he was somewhat suspicious of the revival movement. But "the Spirit of God came down upon his people and on the neighborhood around, with such sudden and awful power, that he was bowed to the dust in adoration and astonishment! His church became the scene of glorious manifestations."[12] He told of the spiritual resurrection of whole families and of great moral and social change in the district.

In 1840 in the "Evidence of Revivals" furnished by ministers of the Church of Scotland, Rev. Robert Murray McCheyne testified, "I have myself frequently seen the preaching of the Word attended with such power, that the feelings of the people could not be restrained. I have heard individuals cry aloud as if pierced through with a dart," and when "tender gospel invitations" have been given, "every sentence has been responded to by the bitterest agony. At such times I have seen persons so overcome that they could not walk or stand alone."[13]

Professor William Gibson, who the next year was elected moderator, wrote that the prostrations "served to my certain knowledge, very much the purpose of the 'rushing, mighty wind' preceding the outpouring of the Holy Spirit on the Day of Pentecost. They roused the slumbering mass; they startled whole streets; they called special attention to the deep conviction of the person affected; they awed and awakened the minds of many whom curiosity had brought to 'come and see'; and they were overruled to send many back to their homes and churches to think of their own lives, to cry to God for their own souls, and to look to Christ for pardon and acceptance as they had never looked before."[14]

CHAPTER TWENTY-ONE

The 1859 Prayer Revival in Wales

Wales has experienced revival on a local scale a number of times throughout its history. There was blessing in 1739, "the great revival" in 1762, and further visitations of God in 1791, 1817, 1840, and 1848.

By the middle of the nineteenth century, many godly Welsh Christians felt the need of a new powerful awakening. Many prayed privately, at times of family worship, and in congregational services, "Will you not revive us again, that your people may rejoice in you?" (Ps. 85:6). When revival came in 1859, it was, like the 1857–58 revival in America, a revival of united prayer.

God used two ministers to ignite the revival flame in 1859. Rev. Humphrey Jones, a twenty-seven-year-old Methodist, had been greatly influenced by the writings of Charles Finney while he was ministering in the United States. Jones returned to Wales, and for six months he was greatly used of God. He preached at Tre'r-ddol for five weeks, and God anointed his messages mornings, afternoons, and evenings.

Beginning at 5:00 A.M. every day, even in the busiest days of harvest, the chapel at Tre'r-ddol was crowded. People lined the roads for a half mile in all directions. Young and old came and, in a very orderly way, prayed, praised, and worshiped. Prayer meetings were held each night. In this small community a few were converted each night— seventy-six in all. The same revival manifestations followed Jones from village to village until mid-October. Then a pastor named David Morgan was transformed by the Lord.

Rev. David Morgan, a Calvinistic Methodist minister, was deeply challenged by Jones. After much prayer for three nights, he awoke at 4:00 A.M. and had a profound religious experience. The two ministers labored together in ministry from October until December. From then on, Jones faded out of the picture and Morgan was the one mightily used by God. By Christmas two hundred had been converted.

REVIVAL FOLLOWS MORGAN

By March 1859 revival fires burned in a number of villages. The Holy Spirit was reaping the harvest of years of faithful Welsh preaching and recent years of praying. Wherever Morgan went the Holy Spirit was poured out and scores of people were converted.

At Trevecca College a communion service lasted for four hours as students worshiped, sang hymns over and over again, and then sat hushed in silence before God. Tears flowed as they sensed the nearness of God's presence. Finally the service closed, and the young men sat together sharing quietly with each other. Many felt that this was what Pentecost must have been like. Students said in the words of Genesis 28:17, "How awesome is this place! This is none other than the house of God; this is the gate of heaven."[1]

The revival fire and blessings spread from church to church among all denominations, into outlying villages and other counties. A tremendous work of God spread through the men working in the huge state quarries. Revival spread like a belt of fire encircling the mountains.

Hundreds came to God in the counties of Cardigen and Camarthan in South Wales. They sensed a deep, profound, and awfully solemn work of God. Notorious sinners flocked to the church by hundreds. In one town three hundred joined the Church of England and four hundred the Calvinistic Methodist Church. Many ministers throughout the area were revived. People left the churches weeping but could proceed no farther and came back into the churches to commit themselves to the Lord.

Within two months more than twenty churches had added one to two hundred to their memberships. The Church of England, Independents, Baptists, Wesleyans, Calvinistic Methodists—all were reaping harvest. Over three thousand new believers joined the Calvinistic Methodists alone. The fire kept spreading. Children ten to fourteen years of age held prayer meetings of their own and prayed fervently. Something extraordinary had seized the mass of the people. All were amazed, many rejoiced, and sinners felt a terror from God. Older Christians reported having seen more of God in 1859, the year of revival, than they had ever known. One report said only half a dozen people in their entire valley did not profess to be saved.

One village reported that all the churches there had new believers, chiefly young people. Another town reported scores saved, including the greatest drunkards of the area. News from yet another place reported that the Holy Spirit had been poured out and blasphemers were humbly seeking God. Revival was almost universal in that area.

UNITED PRAYER MEETINGS

God poured out His Spirit most unusually on united prayer meetings, though all prayer meetings were greatly blessed. One minister wrote that at his meeting, the Spirit came suddenly like a rushing mighty wind, and in three months some two hundred had come to the Lord.

The churches of four counties held a day of prayer, and from then on the prayer meetings experienced new life as members prayed for the outpouring of God's Spirit. In February 1859, "It pleased Jehovah to pour down His Spirit from on high, as on the day of Pentecost. Then anxious inquirers came forward in dozens."[2] Daily prayer meetings began and continued for months.

Churches were overcrowded, and there were new converts daily. The heavenly fire continued to burn. All the denominations united in the prayer sessions. A minister reporting on the event had received 650 new members in his own church. People were gripped by God's Spirit at their jobs, and they cried to God for mercy. Nominal church members were born again and began to praise God. Whole congregations shouted hallelujahs. Rev. William Griffiths reported that now and again he saw new believers leap for joy. The new converts organized various prayer groups. They prayed for friends and relatives by name and held on until these people also yielded to Christ.

"Thousands, since the commencement of this revival, have been converted and brought home to God. . . . This period must surely be the dawn of the glorious Millennium."[3]

THE POWER OF PRAYER

From the "iron districts" of Wales, Rev. W. Edwards wrote, "The revival came after a year's longing, praying, and laboring for it. . . . This revival is distinguished by solemnity of feeling and great earnestness in prayer. There is something in it which leads the people to make every effort to gain others."[4]

At Aberdare some twelve hundred were added to the Independent denomination alone in six months' time. Ministers prayed and preached as they never did before. In Brecknochshire revival began with singing in a home prayer meeting. The people left the meeting singing with joy and peace, bubbling like an overflowing fountain as they walked home. As they neared the village, others heard them, and the revival spread like wildfire. Children began to pray and sing for hours. Children and youth held prayer meetings from house to house. Revival continued to spread, and people came from a distance to see it and then took the fire to their own areas. A letter said, "Every day is a Sabbath now. The people cannot think of anything but to feed their cattle and attend the prayer meetings."[5]

At place after place across Wales the churches held special days of prayer as requested by the Welsh missionaries in India. God used these days of prayer to prepare the way for revival. In many places revival began that very day of prayer. In a remarkable way drunkenness disappeared.

A spirit of prayer prevailed for four months at one Baptist church. The members decided to begin prayer meetings every night, and pled in the words of Isaiah 64:1, "Oh, that you would rend the heavens and come down." Then the three local denominations began united prayer services, rotating from church to church. They felt as though the glory of the Lord was passing by, and they were in the cleft of the rock (Ex. 33:22). But soon, at another united service, the Holy Spirit descended upon them "as the gentle zephyr, till it filled the whole place. So powerful was the influence that none of us could speak for some minutes. We all gave vent to our feelings in floods of joyful tears."[6]

"This revival is altogether a REVIVAL OF THE SPIRIT OF PRAYER; it takes its embodied form in CHRISTIAN UNITY," read an 1860 report on the revival (emphasized words are from the original text of the report). This wonderful unity in prayer was evident in a mountainous district in North Wales. Three young men came to work on Monday morning at the slate quarry under such conviction for sin that at times they wept as they worked. The next day after lunch all five hundred workmen in the quarry went to the top of the hill and held a prayer meeting. Nearly all prayed, wept, and sobbed. The next day they left their work again and returned to the hill to pray. They also met each evening in the church. On Saturday the men went back to their surrounding churches and spread the revival fire.

At eight o'clock Sunday morning another prayer meeting was held. The workers and their families prayed and wept, wept and prayed until they were exhausted. At noon all the congregations and churches met on the top of the hill near the quarry to pray. The prayer meetings continued the following week. All denominations were affected, and the greater part of the population was saved and became church members.

This revival began in October, and revival fires were still burning in January. There was prayer and more prayer. Other slate quarries reported similar revivals. Often they began with the most profligate sinners who would fall on their knees one after another and pray for five or ten minutes. Others would hear, and soon they were on their knees weeping and praying also. At times five or six people would be on their knees in various places, each praying at the same time and seemingly oblivious of the others.

FROM YOUNGEST TO OLDEST

The children formerly cursed and swore as they played, following the example of their parents at home. Now they held prayer meetings, sang, read the Bible, and prayed for hours. Young men fifteen to twenty years of age went to private homes after the public service and held their own prayer meetings there.

One minister wrote that though he was accustomed to prayer meetings from his first years of ministry, he had never heard such amazing prayer. "The earnestness, humility, sense of their own weakness, the clear perception of Christ as their only refuge, and of the Spirit's influence as their support, guide, and consolation is beyond anything I have ever witnessed before. . . . Never, since the commencement of my ministry, have I seen men so earnest. They seem to take the kingdom of heaven by force."[7]

Another minister wrote, "Nothing has caused me so much surprise as to hear these men engage in prayer. They pray so scripturally and earnestly that I am constrained to believe that they are taught by the Spirit of God."[8]

There were cases of men so convicted of their sins as they walked down the street that they began to call on God for mercy as they walked. People were amazed and astonished at the prayers of the children. In the town of Bala the students and tutors in both colleges were gripped by the revival. Prayer meetings continued to be held in every house in the town except three or four. Even inns and public houses were used for mighty prayer meetings.

In Llandinorwig, revival began the same Sunday night in several different places of worship. The whole neighborhood was in a blaze. Prayer meetings were held in the open air and in the churches. In many places God specially used the prayer of young people. At Bangor a most powerful movement of the Spirit among children was reported. They met to pray everywhere, in houses, schoolrooms, and along the roads. They were full of the spirit of prayer as they prayed for all classes and ages of people.

From Anglesea came reports of sinners prevailing before God with irresistible power as they pled for forgiveness through "the blood of the atonement." At times it seemed it was raining tears. Converts prayed with great prayer burden for the salvation of others. A reporter told of "remarkable prayer meetings and that prayer and praise was heard at the midnight hour in the roads, woods, and outhouses."[9]

At the public school in one community, as the headmaster opened the day session with prayer, the Holy Spirit came so intensely and fully that he and the children continued in prayer and praise until noon. Neighbors heard and gathered outside, deeply moved by the prayers of children for unsaved parents and family members.

Revivals began among the coal miners. One county reported revivals in more than forty mines, with much prayer and weeping. The Spirit of prayer was poured out on the Christian churches. Such power prevailed in the prayer meetings that people attended who had never participated before. Night after night the prayer meetings continued, and it was almost impossible to close them before midnight. Union prayer meetings were especially powerful.

One sinner saved in a late prayer meeting so changed in appearance that when he arrived home, his wife asked, "What is the matter?" "I am arrested," he answered. She began to swear and asked him, "Who arrested you?" He meekly answered, "Oh, never swear again; it is Jesus who has arrested me."[10] The two wept together.

In place after place drunkenness decreased and drinking establishments sat empty. Bibles and New Testaments sold rapidly. The cursing and swearing in the coal mines nearly disappeared. One village reported that young people who used to walk the streets now attended prayer meetings. This town held six separate prayer meetings: boys from six to twelve, boys ten to fifteen, young men, girls from eight to fifteen, young women, and another for adults of all ages.

Another district reported countless scenes resembling the Day of Pentecost. Services often continued until midnight, and people by the dozens went home to weep and pray till dawn. A prayer meeting held in one quarry had four thousand people present. After two o'clock and six o'clock prayer meetings in another place, people sang and praised in the fields until midnight. It was raining heavily, yet hundreds were drawn to the sound of prayer and singing. The Spirit of

God poured out as heavily as the rain. Many cried aloud to God, and others fell as though dead.

A NATION BORN IN A DAY

Reports of the mighty revival in Wales said it was a "most powerful awakening," "heavenly fire," and "the finger of God." "Truly, this is the greatest outpouring of His Spirit . . . ever experienced by our nation and country." It was as marvelous as if a nation had been born in a day (Isa. 66:8). "It is questionable whether anything more powerful has been felt in America, Ireland, or Wales."[11]

Tension between the denominations disappeared, replaced by a new and blessed unity. The prayer lives of multitudes of people were transformed. Until cold weather forced them to stop, many new converts and other Christians spent whole nights outside among the mountains in prayer.

The spirit of revival in Wales was communicated, not so much by preaching, as by prayer. Prayer meetings multiplied everywhere: in homes, churches, by the roadside, in quarries, and in mines. At one mine everyone was saved except one sinner for whom the rest were praying.

Prayer meetings became the principle means of awakening churches. As soon as people were saved, they became mighty prayer warriors. The power of children's prayers astonished everyone. It was a prayer revival from first to last.

A report in a church magazine stated, "I have never witnessed anything like that which I now see daily. You hear of nothing but the revival. Ungodly people quake and tremble. . . . I have seen a large congregation in this neighborhood, containing at the time many scores of hardened ungodly people, bathed in tears, and as incapable of leaving the place at the close of the public service as if their feet had been nailed to the floor of the chapel. . . . Some of the most ungodly men seemed to be entirely bewildered; they could hardly find their way home that night. Blessed be God! Many of them found their way to the blood of the Cross. I thank God I have lived to see the year 1859. God in His grace, has done more within the past two weeks in this part of the country than had been accomplished for an age previously."[12]

CHAPTER TWENTY-TWO

Revival Fires
in South Africa

By 1859 the revival fire had spread to Northern Ireland, where about 10 percent of the population was converted. Then the prayer-revival movement of the Holy Spirit spread to Wales, Scotland, and England, and another million new believers were added to the churches throughout the British Isles.

As the news of the Spirit's working reached a number of European countries, spiritual hunger and earnest prayer increased and prepared the way for new spiritual blessing. In the colonies of South Africa, Australia, and wherever Europeans had settled, the ripples of revival began to appear.

One of the outgrowths of the American and British revivals was a renewed interest in missions. Old missionary societies were revived, and new ones like the China Inland Mission were born. Spurgeon built his Tabernacle in 1859. Moody soon developed an international ministry. Within a decade a thirty-year revival began in Germany. Revival fire began to burn in India, South Africa, Indonesia, and in the West Indies among the British and European populations, resulting in newly empowered evangelism and folk movements among the castes and tribes.

SOUTH AFRICAN REVIVAL

For some years Rev. Andrew Murray, Sr., longed and prayed for revival in South Africa. Every Friday night he spent several hours in prayer. The revivals of 1858 in the United States and 1859 in Northern Ireland were reported in the Dutch Reformed journals. A little book on "The Power of Prayer" was published. Individuals and prayer groups in various places across South Africa began to pray specifically for revival.

In April 1860, a conference attended by 374 was convened at Worcester, South Africa. Representatives of twenty congregations — sixteen Dutch Reformed, plus Methodist and Presbyterian leaders — gathered together. The main topic was revival. Andrew Murray, Sr., was moved to tears and had to stop speaking. His son, Andrew Murray, Jr., prayed with such power that some say the conference marked the beginning of the revival.

Fifty days after the Worcester conference, revival fires began to burn. In Montague, near Worcester, a prayer revival began in the Methodist church. Prayer meetings were held every night and on Monday, Wednesday, and Friday mornings, sometimes as early as 3:00 A.M. People who had never prayed before began to pray. One evening God anointed a young girl to pray. Young and old began to cry to God for mercy and continued until midnight. As Dutch Reformed people left their prayer meetings, they crowded into the Methodist church.

For weeks the village of Montague experienced great conviction of sin. Strong men cried to God in anguish. Six prayer meetings were going on throughout the village. The report reached Worcester, and prayer meetings began there as well. Whole families, both European and native African, were humbled before God.

THUNDER FROM HEAVEN

One Sunday evening, during the youth fellowship meeting, an African servant girl arose and asked permission to sing a verse and pray. The Holy Spirit fell upon the group as she prayed. In the distance there came a sound like approaching thunder. It surrounded the hall, and the building began to shake. Instantly everyone burst into prayer. The assistant minister knelt at the table.

Andrew Murray had been speaking in the main sanctuary to the service there. He was notified and came running. Murray called in a loud voice, "I am your minister, sent from God. Silence!"[1] No one noticed as all continued calling out loudly to God for forgiveness. Murray asked his assistant to sing a hymn, but the praying continued undiminished.

All week long the prayer meetings were held. Each service began with profound silence. "But as soon as several prayers had arisen the place was shaken as before and the whole company of people engaged in simultaneous petition to the throne of grace."[2] The meetings often continued until 3:00 A.M., and as the people reluctantly dispersed, they went singing their way down the streets.

Services were moved to a larger building because of the crowds. On Saturday, Andrew Murray led the prayer meeting, preaching from the Bible. He prayed and then invited others to do so. Again the mysterious sound of thunder approached from a distance, coming nearer until it enveloped the building. Everyone broke out in simultaneous prayer.

Murray walked up and down the aisle trying to quiet the people, but a stranger in the service tiptoed up to him and whispered, "Be careful what you do, for it is the Spirit of God that is at work here." Murray learned to accept the revival praying. As many as twenty found the Lord in one service. Mrs. Murray wrote, "We do feel and realize the power and presence of God so mightily. His Spirit is indeed poured out on us."[3]

REVIVAL SPREADS

The South African revival then scattered like buckshot and spread to other areas. At Wellington a Christian had prayed for weeks for revival and had organized prayer meetings. God worked so mightily that the church consistory declared that God had accomplished more in a few weeks than in all the previous history of the church.

One pastor reported something of "the glory of the church in the first century."[4] Prayer meetings multiplied. Many Christians met each week in prayer groups of three to four. Some churches could not hold all who came to worship. Spiritual awakening came to places up to two hundred miles away.

In another center people were suddenly and instantly gripped by the Holy Spirit. Four times a week a prayer meeting was held, which often lasted all day. On Sunday meetings were held everywhere. In another district, a shaking awake was reported with hundreds converted until the minister reported less than fifty unconverted were left in the district.

In Heidelberg, Cape Colony, the first revival occurred in 1860, a second in 1868, a third in the 1870s, a fourth in 1884, and a fifth movement of the Spirit in 1889. Congregation after congregation experienced repeated revivals for half a century.

Fifty young men from Andrew Murray's congregation felt called into the ministry, and the revival launched Andrew Murray, Jr., into a worldwide ministry of speaking and writing. The Dutch Reformed denomination decided to devote the ten days between Ascension and Pentecost each year to evangelistic preaching and prayer for revival. Not only were the Dutch Reformed moved by revival, but God sent real awakening to English-speaking churches also.

Although there was no telegraphic communication between North America and South Africa, at the same time revival moved across the USA in 1857–58, revival began in the Bantu tribe and among the European churches at Grahamstown.

Actually, revival began among the Zulu and Bantu before it reached the Dutch Reformed church. Tribal people flocked to the mission stations on the frontier. Congregations overflowed and hundreds were baptized. In Natal on the east coast there was a Zulu revival awakening that touched nearly all mission stations manned by American missionaries.

On Sunday evening, May 22, 1859, at the close of a service, the Spirit came upon the Zulus with such power that they prayed all night. The news spread far and wide among the Zulus, and so did the work of God all that year. The Zulu revival produced extraordinary praying, tremendous conviction of sin, immediate conversions, and vigorous evangelistic outreach.

Some two hundred miles west in Botswana revival came to different tribes in a different language. Daily prayer meetings, morning and afternoon, went on for weeks.

WILLIAM TAYLOR'S "INSTANT" REVIVALS

God extended the 1858 revival around the world through the ministry of William Taylor, a fire-baptized American Methodist evangelist and later bishop of Africa. Few people have ever made the world their parish as Taylor did.

Taylor was converted in 1841 at the age of twenty. He began Methodist ministry the following year as an itinerant preacher. Taylor evangelized in California during the Gold Rush and then returned to the eastern United States and

Canada during the 1858 revival. God called him to international ministry and gave him fruitful evangelism wherever he preached.

Taylor was continually on the move, but God worked quickly, and the local churches almost instantly experienced revival wherever he went. In South Africa God began with a movement of the Spirit and numerous conversions among the English-speaking churches. There were many conversions but no special breakthrough. The first real revival movement began among the Xhosa-speaking people. Here Taylor's interpreter was Charles Pamla, a young African chief.

Taylor preached to the believers in a day service on the verse, "Ye shall receive power after that the Holy Spirit is come upon you," and in the evening to outsiders on "Turn ye from your evil ways, for why will ye die?" Pamla was an especially gifted interpreter. A hush from God fell upon the people, and in the after-meeting two hundred were deeply moved to repentance. Taylor and his helpers prayed with them until midnight.

At sunrise everyone returned for praise and prayer. In five days an unprecedented three hundred had found Christ's salvation. At the next location, a thousand tribesmen crowded the service. Again Taylor's message to the believers was "Ye shall receive power." At the close, Taylor held silent prayer and then invited seekers forward. At least three hundred fell upon their knees calling out to God. Then the noise died down to quiet sighs and groans.

The local missionary reported that with sparkling eyes and "countenances beaming with joy unspeakable," they burst into praise. He writes, "What a day! I know not how to record it, I have never witnessed anything that so reminded me of the scenes of Pentecost."[5]

Taylor moved on to another center, and hundreds of Xhosa people and many Hottentots were converted. A mighty spirit of prayer came on them. Taylor preached six times, and that day more than 250 came to the Lord. He moved on from center to center and tribe to tribe. Reports tell of indescribable scenes, hundreds of converts, spreading revival, and an outpouring of the Holy Spirit. Church membership increased 400 percent in one circuit and 350 percent in another, with many in discipleship programs and on probationary membership. The Xhosas gave Taylor a name meaning "The Blazing Firebrand."[6]

In the Grahamstown district, missionaries reported that the whole land was being blessed. "In every place the Word of God is the power of God unto salvation."[7] Reports from the various mission stations told of three hundred, five hundred, and in one place eight hundred conversions among the Bantu. In addition, more than six hundred Englishmen were converted.

At Fort Beaufort, Taylor himself reported, "The awful presence and melting power of the Holy Spirit on this occasion surpassed anything I have ever witnessed before."[8] At Healdtown several hundred in the chapel fell on their knees crying, sobbing, and groaning over their sins. In two days more than three hundred were converted.

Taylor traveled from place to place, seldom staying more than a week in a circuit. His converts were of every age from ten to sixty, both married and unmarried, and from all social ranks. In two years the Methodists increased 40 percent in membership, and many Presbyterians and Dutch Reformed churches were also blessed.

Taylor's ministry had lasting impact. J. Edwin Orr summarized: "Missionaries and national pastors experienced a baptism of the Holy Spirit and went everywhere preaching repentance and faith, pardon and purity, to illiterate and semi-illiterate tribesmen."[9]

CHAPTER TWENTY-THREE

Prayer Preparation

Long before 1904, God began preparing for the world-wide revival that burst into flames at the turn of the century. Dr. J. Edwin Orr, the historian of revival, considers the mighty movements of God's Spirit in revival during the first decade of the 1900s as the most extensive revival movement of all time. Revival fires burned more brightly in some nations than in others, but the spiritual fires glowed to God's glory in Europe, North America, Australia, South Africa, Korea, China, and Latin America. More than five million people in these nations were won to Christ in the first two years of this revival.

IT STARTS WITH PRAYER

Not until all God's records are opened in heaven, as God's people stand before His judgment throne to receive their eternal rewards, will we know the hours of prayer that were invested by His intercessors as they prayed for revival. Only God knows the amazing extent of the Holy Spirit's work in guiding prayer warriors to pray for the revival we now record.

Where did the 1904 series of mighty revivals and harvests begin? Historians usually refer to the revival that began in the village of Loughor in south Wales as the flash point of revival. Evan Roberts was God's instrument in the launching of the 1904 revival. Roberts began in 1891 as a boy of thirteen to hunger, thirst, and pray for two major requests: (1) for God to fill him with His Spirit, and (2) for God to send revival to Wales. Roberts made perhaps the largest investment in God's prayer bank for the revival God was longing to send. And perhaps that is why God began the international wave of revivals in Wales—through Evan Roberts.

Even before the turn of the century, Saturday night prayer meetings for worldwide revival were being held at Moody Bible Institute in Chicago and at the annual Keswick Conventions in Britain. Missionary prayer meetings, local church prayer meetings, and personal emphasis on prayer for revival occurred in India, the Far East, Africa, America, Britain, and Latin America. Few of the most faithful intercessors had ever seen widespread revival personally. But the Spirit was moving and calling thousands of God's children to pray for revival even though they did not fully realize how many others shared the same vision and prayer burden.

Thirteen Welsh people attended the 1896 convention for the deepening of Christian life at Keswick in England. These thirteen prayed together and asked God to start a similar convention in Wales. After seven years their prayers were answered, and the first Llandrindod Wells Convention met in 1903.

Several young Welsh ministers had become conscious of the need for God's visitation. They began to preach on repentance, restitution and reconciliation, the lordship of Jesus, sanctification, and total surrender to the Holy Spirit. Fires of revival burned in a number of places.

In early 1903 four young Welshmen began to pray together every night for revival. Others heard about it and joined them. Soon their fervor reached the whole local church, and many were moved with a spirit of prayer and a new passion for souls. In an unbelievably short time the whole neighborhood was ablaze with the divine fire. As many as six meetings were held some Sundays, and one Sunday thirty new people found the Lord. For six months the nightly prayer continued.

Another pastor reported that for five months God visited his church. Young people thirsted deeply for a more holy life. The pastor convened special Sunday evening services. "The Holy Spirit came down and took possession of that meeting and overwhelmed us with power from on high. . . . I could hardly speak, so manifest was the presence of God." For several Sunday evenings God repeated the same awesome manifestation. After several weeks, the pastor reported: "Ever since souls have been saved every day. The church has entered upon the blessing of Pentecost. . . . Now I have a new church with a large number of men and women filled with the Holy Spirit, and who are used to win souls."[1]

Flames of local revival fire began to burn in a number of other places in south and central Wales as a result of special revival conventions. Pioneering spirit-filled evangelists from several denominations began to be used by God.

In a local convention in September 1904, a number of young people, including Evan Roberts, experienced a new working of the Holy Spirit. They referred to this humbling before the Lord and total surrender and submission as "bending." It led to a special outpouring and infilling of the Spirit. Now began the amazing revival flames that swept across Wales and into distant parts of the world. In Wales it was led particularly by young people, although people of all ages were caught up in the mighty movement of the Spirit.

AN EVER-WIDENING CIRCLE

Earlier and smaller kindlings of revival fire and harvest preceded the Wales outpouring of the Spirit. In Australia, from 1890–1901, some forty ministers and laymen met each Saturday afternoon to pray for revival. Out of this came "circles of prayer," and by 1901 there were more than two thousand of these, with about forty thousand people praying. In 1902, Dr. R. A. Torrey led fruitful evangelistic campaigns in Australia and New Zealand, and these produced revival-like scenes. In Japan, a 1900 prayer movement developed into periods of evangelism and awakening.

In July 1902, news of the prayer circles in Australia reached the Keswick Convention. Home prayer circles for worldwide revival began in England and spread to other nations. Thousands prayed in their homes for "an outpouring of the Holy Spirit."

In 1901, Pandita Ramabai began special prayer for the widows and famine refugees in her mission at Mukti, south of Bombay. In December and January, 1,200 of these women were converted and baptized, and in July 1902, 600 more were converted in a three-week revival. When Ramabai heard of the Torrey revivals in Australia in 1903, she asked Australian Christians to start prayer circles to pray for her work in India. She herself organized prayer circles of ten girls each in her Mukti center. When Ramabai heard of the revival in Wales, she began praying even more earnestly with her girls. Revival came to India on June 30, 1905.

Meanwhile, for several years God had been leading groups of two or three in various parts of Wales to pray regularly, sometime daily, for revival. In January 1903, an aged, esteemed Welsh minister sent out a call for Christians to pray in the words of Isaiah 64:1: "Oh that Thou wouldest rend the heavens, that thou wouldest come down" (KJV).

Within weeks, several ministers banded together for prayer. In another place four young men gathered each night to pray for revival. And in two months scores were meeting nightly for prayer on a mountainside. God's faithful intercessors were preparing the way of the Lord for mighty international revivals.

CHAPTER TWENTY-FOUR

The Vision of Evan Roberts

In February 1904, blessing fell on a meeting in New Quay in south Wales, as a timid girl in tears stood and said, "Oh, I love Jesus Christ with all my heart!" In a midnight prayer meeting in August 1904 at the second "Welsh Keswick," everyone together asked God "to raise up someone to usher in the revival."[1]

In late September, nightly services began to be held in one Welsh church by several young men who had surrendered themselves to God and been filled with the Spirit. By the end of the year, 120 had been saved. In another church, revival blessing fell on November 20, and nightly services began. Yet another church held ten weeks of nightly prayer meetings, and a number were saved. By the end of 1904, 150 had received salvation.

Although the revivals in south Wales are perhaps better known, the Holy Spirit so divinely synchronized His use of prepared hearts, that on the same days of the same week the fires of revival burst into flame in both north and south Wales.

In the north, revival centered in Rhos and spread from there to many villages in north Wales. The minister most instrumental in the northern revival was one of the young ministers who had been filled with the Spirit the year before. In the south it was Evan Roberts who became the best-known figure of the Welsh revival.

In all parts of Wales the scenes were similar. Churches of all denominations were drawn together by the Spirit of God and almost forgot their denominational distinctions. Prayer meetings were so crowded that church buildings could not hold them. Some prayer meetings lasted as long as eight hours. The meetings were characterized by unbroken prayer and singing.

THE LORD'S PRESENCE EVERYWHERE

Throughout the country there was an overwhelming sense of the presence of God. It seemed to be universal and inescapable. Not only in churches and prayer meetings, but on the streets, on the trains, in homes, and in taverns people were gripped by the Spirit. Rich and poor, old and young— all were moved by God.

One of those present during the days of spiritual renewal looked back twenty-five years later and felt utterly incapable of describing adequately the work of the Lord. He summarized his impression: "It was the universal, inescapable sense of the presence of God."[2]

According to the Rev. R. B. Jones, "A sense of the Lord's presence was everywhere. It pervaded, nay, it created the spiritual atmosphere. It mattered not where one went, the consciousness of the reality and nearness of God followed. Felt, of course, in the Revival gatherings, it was by no means confined to them; it was also felt in the homes, on the streets, in the mines and factories, in the schools, yea, and even in the theatres and drinking-saloons. The strange result was that wherever people gathered became a place of awe, and places of amusement and carousal were practically emptied.

"Many were the instances of men entering public-houses, ordering drinks, and then turning on their heels leaving them on the counters untouched. The sense of the Lord's presence was such as practically to paralyse the arm that would raise the cup to the lips. Football teams and the like were disbanded; their members finding greater joy in testimony to the Lord's grace than in games. The mine pit-bottoms and galleries became places of praise and prayer, where the miners gathered to worship ere they dispersed to their several stalls. Even the children of the Day-schools came under the gracious power of God. Stories could be told of how they would gather in any place they could, where they would sing and pray in most impressive fashion."[3]

Indeed the cloud of God's presence hung low over much of Wales for months. The land was covered by a canopy of prayer, and people everywhere hungered for more of God's presence and power.

Rev. R. B. Jones describes the greatest meeting he ever attended. It was months later on the island of Anglesey, just off the coast of northwest Wales, where he had been ministering in revival services for several weeks. In the large, crowded chapel, Jones preached on Isaiah 6. When he spoke about sin in the light of God's holiness, the whole audience was so deeply convicted, they felt almost crushed with despair. Could God ever forgive and cleanse?

Then Jones spoke of the altar and the burning coals Isaiah saw. He explained to them how God could touch their unclean lives with a cleansing coal from the altar (Isa. 6:6–7). Jones confessed he had no words to describe how God came upon the people. "As one man, first with a sigh of relief, and then, with a delirious shout of joy, the whole huge audience sprang to their feet. . . . The whole place at that moment was so awful with the glory of God—one uses the word 'awful' deliberately; the holy presence of God was so manifested that the speaker himself was overwhelmed; the pulpit where he stood was so filled with the light of God that he had to withdraw!"[4]

A MIGHTY WORK OF THE SPIRIT

In September 1904, Seth Joshua, evangelist for the Forward Movement of the Calvinist Methodists, began revival meetings in New Quay. Then he went to Newcastle-Emlyn to visit a preparatory school for students studying for the ministry. Among the students was Evan Roberts, who had quit his job two weeks before and come to prepare for the ministry.

Evan Roberts had been spiritually responsive his entire life. As a child he loved the Lord, memorized hymns, read his Bible, and prayed. He held church services for the neighborhood children and "preached" to them. Roberts always hungered to do more for Jesus. He attended every church service—on Sunday and five nights each week.

At the age of twelve, Evan went to work in the coal mine, as most boys did. But from the age of thirteen he prayed continually for God to fill him with His Holy Spirit and to send revival to Wales. As he worked in the mine, Roberts kept praying, singing, and repeating Bible verses. In the evening at home he would read the Bible for hours. He would pray silently but often groan with deep holy desire. Often Roberts preferred to pray rather than to eat his meal, and he frequently rose in the middle of the night to entreat God for revival.

On Thursday morning, October 27, Seth Joshua took about twenty young people, Roberts among them, from Newcastle-Emlyn to Blaenanerch to attend his meetings. On the way they sang:

> It is coming; it is coming;
> The power of the Holy Ghost.
> I receive it; I receive it;
> The power of the Holy Ghost.

The following day, in the 7:00 A.M. service, Seth Joshua closed by praying, "Lord . . . bend us." The Holy Spirit said to Evan, "That is what you need." Evan walked out of the door praying, "Lord, bend me!" During the nine o'clock service that morning, the Holy Spirit came on him mightily, and he fell on his knees crying out, "Bend me, bend me, bend me! Oh! Oh! Oh! Oh! Oh!" Tears streamed from his eyes and perspiration poured down his face. After thirteen years of praying, Evan was at last filled with the Spirit. Soon his thirteen-year prayer for revival was also to be answered. "I felt ablaze with a desire to go through the length and breadth of Wales to tell of the Savior," he said.[5]

ROBERTS' VISION OF REVIVAL

Roberts began to pray for 100,000 souls, and God gave him the assurance that 100,000 would be won to Christ. He testified, "The divine fire has taken hold of us."[6] Roberts felt the necessity of full obedience to the leading of the Holy Spirit. He envisaged taking a team of young people with him in evangelism across Wales. He kept urging the people to surrender fully to the Holy Spirit and to obey Him.

God came upon Evan mightily as he prayed. One night he could not sleep. "The room was full of the Holy Spirit. The outpouring was so overpowering that I had . . . to plead with God to stay His hand!"[7]

God gave His servant visions those days during prayer time. In one vision Roberts saw the vast fiery pit of hell surrounded by a wall with one door. He saw a surging mass of people as far on the horizon as he could see coming toward the pit. He pled with God to shut hell's door for one year. In another vision Roberts saw Satan in a hedge, deriding and laughing in defiance at him. Then he saw a glorious white figure with a flaming sword held high. The sword struck the figure of Satan, who instantly disappeared. Roberts knew Christ was going to defeat Satan.

In another vision Roberts saw a brilliant moon and an arm stretched out to the world. He saw the vision again, and this time the hand held a piece of paper on which was written "100,000."

On Sunday night, October 30, as he sat in the service at Newcastle-Emlyn, Roberts had one more vision. He saw the school room in his own village and his young friends and companions sitting in rows before him. He saw himself speaking to them. He heard God's voice saying, "Go and speak to these people." At last Roberts said yes to God, and instantly the vision vanished and the whole chapel seemed filled with light and glory. In the Sunday service Roberts' friends noticed that his face was shining. In the youth prayer meeting, tears streamed from his eyes as he prayed repeatedly, "Glorify Thy Son."

That week God gave Evan such a prayer burden for his home area at Loughoron that he asked his principal's permission to go home for one week's meetings with the young people. Obtaining permission, he immediately went home, where his family could not understand why he had come. He talked of being blessed and of being baptized and filled with the Spirit. When he thought of the need in Wales, he would burst into tears. When he thought of God's promise of revival and souls, he would laugh for joy. His family wondered: Had Evan become mentally ill?

CHAPTER TWENTY-FIVE

Songs of Revival in South Wales

Evan received his pastor's permission to have a youth meeting with the young people on Monday night, October 31, immediately following the regular Monday night prayer meeting at Moriah Chapel. Seventeen youth stayed for the service. Evan told them how God had been working in New Quay and at Newcastle-Emlyn. He shared his burden and his vision for Wales, and he asked each person to confess Christ as his personal Savior. By the end of that rather difficult two-hour meeting, each one had done so.

On Tuesday six more young people openly confessed Christ in a three-hour service of prayer, exhortation, and personal testimony. Several told of how real Christ had become to them the night before. God's presence and power increased, and by the end of the week one service had lasted until 6:00 A.M.

Wednesday night two services were held: one in the nearby Congregational Church in Gorseinon and the other back at Moriah. People listened spellbound as Roberts told of the mighty coming revival and 100,000 new believers that God had promised to save. God gave such tremendous blessing and joy that the service lasted for eight hours. Roberts reported that twenty more confessed Christ.

Roberts wrote, "Now I have to work under the guidance of the Holy Spirit among every denomination. . . . Three things show that God is with us. 1. Enormous congregations. 2. Unity between the denominations. 3. The baptism of the Holy Spirit."[1]

Thursday night twenty more confessed Christ. Friday night the attendance was larger than ever. Saturday night four were baptized with the Holy Spirit. (Note: This was not a demonstration of tongues-speaking, but a reception of the fullness of the Spirit's presence and power.) A minister confirmed that when some people were filled with the Spirit, their faces seemed actually transfigured.

Roberts taught the people to pray, "Send the Holy Spirit now, for Jesus Christ's sake." Throughout the revival period he repeatedly emphasized four points: (1) confess openly and fully any unconfessed sin; (2) put away from your life anything doubtful; (3) obey promptly anything the Spirit tells you to say and do; (4) confess Christ openly.

THE PRESENCE OF THE SPIRIT

The first week of revival under Evan Roberts culminated in a powerful Sunday evening service. Here is Roberts' description of the events. By midnight the whole congregation was "overwhelmed with tears. . . . Then the people came down from the gallery, and sat close to one another. 'Now,' said I, 'we must believe that the Spirit will come; not think He will come; not hope He will come; but firmly believe that He will come.' Then I read the promises of God, and pointed out how definite they were. (Remember, I am doing all under the guidance of the Holy Spirit, and praise be to him.) After this, the Spirit said that everyone was to pray. Pray now, not confess, not sing, not give experience, but pray and believe, and wait. And this is the prayer, 'Send the Spirit now, for Jesus Christ's sake.'

"The people were sitting, and only closed their eyes. The prayer began with me. Then it went from seat to seat—boys and girls—young men and maidens. Some asking in silence, some aloud, some coldly, some with warmth, some formally, some in tears, some with difficulty, some adding to it, boys and girls, strong voices, then tender voices. Oh, wonderful! I never thought of such an effect. I felt the place beginning to be filled, and before the prayer had gone half way through the chapel, I could hear some brother weeping, sobbing, and saying, 'Oh, dear! dear! well! well!' 'Oh, dear! dear!' On went the prayer, the feeling becoming more intense; the place being filled more and more (with the Spirit's presence)."[2]

The sixty or more remaining at this time now gathered around the revivalist, many almost overcome with awe. Some called out, "No more, Lord Jesus, or I die!" Others cried for mercy, weeping, singing, praising, and lying prostrate on the floor in agony of conviction for their sin. Eventually they closed the meeting, and Roberts got to bed at 3:15 A.M. By now simultaneous revival had also come to Gorseinon, with praying, weeping, and singing such as people had never known before.

THE SOUNDS OF PENTECOST

By Monday night of the second week, the church was crowded and almost everyone was moved to tears. People began to cry aloud in prayer. Many present insisted they heard a powerful sound in the distance, and then it seemed God's presence entered and filled the building. Many prayed in great distress of soul or with prayer burden for others. Roberts again asked the people to pray, "Send the Holy Spirit now, for Jesus Christ's sake." He called this "direct prayer," and he asked each person one after another to stand and recite the prayer.

Roberts repeated the prayer chain two or three times until God's Spirit came irresistibly upon the people. There were tears and agonizing prayer interspersed with singing. For the first time, a hymn about the ocean of Calvary's love was sung. This became "the revival hymn" during the succeeding months. It was impossible to close the service until 3:00 A.M.

In 1964 two of the first five converts of this revival took me to Moriah church and described how God came among them. Henry Penry pointed out to me where he was sitting when the fire fell. Roberts had told the people to pray—not to confess, not to sing, not to testify—but just to pray, believe, and wait. The sense of God's presence and of His divine blessing became more and more powerfully experienced.

On the tenth night the group moved again to a larger building. Workmen, as soon as they got out of the mines, ran in their work clothes for fear there would be no room for them inside the building. News reporters were present, and every day in the paper there were thrilling accounts of the revival. So the story spread far and wide across Wales and to many other parts of the world.

The meeting went on in power. Many people were "bent" in humble submission beneath God's powerful hand. Some were on their knees for so long in prayer agony that they could not utter a word. Some fell as if smitten to the ground. Others prayed powerfully for notorious sinners and drunkards, and many reconciliations were made between enemies.

On Friday night the crowd was larger than ever, with Baptists, Congregationalists, Calvinists, and Methodists present. The service lasted for five hours. Roberts again asked everyone present to repeat the "chain" prayer, "Send the Holy Spirit now for Jesus Christ's sake." Then he started again in the front row and had everyone repeat, "Send the Holy Spirit now more powerfully for Jesus Christ's sake."

Scores fell on their knees so deeply convicted of their sins that they were unable to utter a syllable. Others cried pitifully for God's mercy. Then a minister prayed for a long time. Roberts himself prayed with such soul burden for the people and for national revival that the perspiration poured from his brow. Soon he called out, "What of heaven if it is so good here!" An offering for foreign missions was taken, and some gave their last penny.

REVIVAL BEGETS EVANGELISM

On Saturday two young women held an open-air evangelistic meeting during the day, while others went to a gypsy camp and won many to the Lord. Many homes in the area held all-day prayer meetings. Girls held open-air services outside of drinking establishments. When the drinkers came outside, they became gripped by the Holy Spirit and were saved. Revival fire began to spread as people read the newspaper reports and came to see for themselves.

At meeting time there were such crowds that simultaneous services were held in two churches. A well-known singer was so overcome that he stood up in the balcony and began to sing "Saved by Grace." The people sang it over and over. At 2:00 A.M. Sunday, both churches were still so crowded that people could not push in or out. People lost all sense of time and had no desire to eat or to go home. One service lasted until 6:00 A.M.

"Above all a sense of the presence and holiness of God pervaded every area of human experience, at home, at work, in shops and public houses. Eternity seemed inescapably near and real," Efion Evans wrote. "At the end of the second week it was evident that the plans of the revivalist had been superseded by the initiative of the Spirit, and the hopes of

Evan Roberts had been overshadowed by the power of God."[3]

By now revival blessings were falling in other parts of Wales as well. God used a number of other young people and evangelists. It seemed wherever special meetings began, the holy fire of the Spirit fell. From Carmarthen it was reported that "flood gates of blessing" were opened. On the last day of a conference, "hardly a quarter of an hour passed without a number of people, young and old, men and women, in one part or another of Water Street Chapel praying themselves or others from the bondage of sin to the liberty of the Gospel."[4]

From Ammanford came the report, "A heavenly nearness to God was felt by all present. . . . The weeping was general throughout the congregation." Seth Joshua arrived, and in his diary he notes, "I have wrestled for personal baptism of the Spirit and for a national revival. It has come and I rejoice." When he arrived, he found "a wonderful fire burning here. The ground is very prepared, thank God." A day later Joshua wrote, "This has been one of the most remarkable days of my life."[5]

Bookshops sold out of Bibles. Coal mines were transformed from places of blasphemous oaths to places ringing with praise to God. Homes were filled with joy and singing. Notorious blasphemers and profane sinners were transformed and in open-air meetings quoted Scripture and testified with Spirit-anointed fluency.

REVIVAL LEAPS TO LONDON

A firsthand report of the revival in South Wales reached London, and revival fire began to blaze in Welsh churches there. Of two hundred converts in one church, half had been drunkards. Six Welsh students held a campaign in another Welsh church in London and saw 720 conversions.

Evan Roberts made four revival campaign journeys to London: (1) November 13, 1904, to March 1, 1905; (2) March 29, 1905, to April 17, 1905; (3) June 6, 1905, to July 7, 1905; and (4) December 6, 1905, to January 14, 1906.

On Roberts' first journey, five young ladies from his Gorseinon congregation accompanied him as his evangelistic team. They sang solos, duets, led in prayer, testified, and in many other ways shared his prayer burden. From time to time other young people of Roberts' acquaintance joined his team for a period. Roberts usually stayed in each locality for about three days, but occasionally he moved on after only a day. Sometimes some of the other young helpers stayed behind and carried on meetings for several more services. Evan's brother, Dan Roberts; his close friend, Sydney Evans; and Miss Annie Davies, "the Nightingale voice singer," were among them.

The days were filled with services, up to three or four each day: a 7:30 A.M. prayer meeting, a 10:00 A.M. service, a 2:00 P.M. service, and the final meeting at 7:00 P.M. The final service often lasted into the night or early morning.

At times in the afternoons and evenings, chapels were filled and hundreds stood outside. Some walked the streets at night singing hymns until morning. Often Evan appeared at the mine pit head at 5:00 A.M., shaking hands with the men as they emerged from the night shift and inviting them to the 7:30 prayer meeting if they were not too tired.

At times when one church was filled, hundreds would go to another nearby church and have a blessed service there also. People traveled from many miles away to attend Roberts' meetings. Hearts were set afire, and the people returned to their own towns and villages across Britain, carrying revival fire with them and starting meetings in their own villages.

People who came to the market in towns where Roberts was holding a service often were gripped by the

Spirit and forgot their business. Salesmen left their business samples and became absorbed in the meetings.

At times, even after Roberts had moved on to the next place, such blessing lingered that churches continued to be crowded night after night. Skeptics, backsliders, the self-righteous, and the hopeless drunkards—all found salvation. A noted agnostic was converted and went from place to place pointing sinners to Jesus.

NEW LIFE THROUGH MUSIC

Roberts did not try to control the services but urged people to obey the Lord. Lay men and women led in prayer with such anointing and eloquence that ministers were amazed. Sinners broke down and wept. Someone would start a hymn, which would be joined in by all. Often ministers joined in and led in prayer. As person after person surrendered to the Lord, the conversion was announced. Then praises ascended to God, and the meeting continued on. At times people paraded the streets all night long singing hymns. Often when the service in one church was crowded out, the overflow went to another church and started a simultaneous service there. At times three or more services continued at the same time in the same town.

Roberts continually evaluated spiritual progress during meetings, pausing to ask, "How many have just now received the Lord and confess Him as their Savior?" Often eight to twenty-two or even more people rose and confessed Christ for the first time. Those in the service were electrified by what God was doing.

People coming to the revival by train sang and prayed on the way to the station, on the platform, and in the train. Groups walking over the mountains to their villages held prayer meetings along the way, and their singing could be heard from afar. English-speakers and Welsh-speakers interspersed and blended together in song and prayer. In many towns the coal mines closed temporarily so the miners could attend the services.

While the most intense excitement and enthusiasm followed Roberts wherever he went, revival fires burned simultaneously in dozens of other places. Reports of conversions, open-air meetings, processions, and overflowing churches came from all directions. God was moving across the nation. Ministers and news reporters came from England and Scotland to see for themselves the amazing reality of the revival.

After only a month of revival, many lives had been transformed, drunkards and gamblers delivered from their vices, family feuds healed, debts paid, drinking establishments emptied, and cultural values changed. Dozens of churches and chapels were filled every night.

Denominational differences were forgotten, and huge singing processions were led along the streets. Some days all compartments on the trains were filled with people singing the hymns of the church. At times if the train stopped and people saw a crowd around some church, they would leave the train and join the services. The revival meetings moved from village to village. There were great times of powerful singing and powerful praying. Many ministers seen in the services had come from far and wide to be blessed in the meetings. "There are no advertisements, no brass bands, no posters, no huge tents. All the paraphernalia of the got-up job are conspicuous by their absence."[6]

Evan Roberts spoke "simply, unaffectedly, earnestly, now and then, but he makes no sermons, and preaching is emphatically not the rule of this revival. . . . The revival is born along by the billowing waves of sacred songs. . . . It is the singing, not the preaching that is the instrument which is most efficacious in striking the hearts of men."[7]

A daily newspaper reported: "The meetings . . . were absolutely without any human direction or leadership. 'We must obey the Spirit' is the watchword of Evan Roberts.

Three-fourths of the meeting consists of singing. No one uses a hymnbook. No one gives out a hymn. . . . People pray and sing; give testimonies; exhort as the Spirit moves them. . . . I have seen nothing like it."[8]

CHAPTER TWENTY-SIX

The Spreading Flame

Almost simultaneously with the revival under Roberts in south Wales, the work of the Spirit began in north Wales. One village was so transformed that the drinking houses were practically emptied and swearing was rarely heard. Children met frequently for prayer and even used school properties for prayer for revival. By December 9 a newspaper there reported, "The religious revival appears to be rapidly spreading throughout North Wales. Meetings are held practically at every town, and great enthusiasm prevails. Even in the granite quarries, workmen are holding prayer meetings of the most impressive character every dinner hour."[1]

GOD'S WORKERS IN THE NORTH

In the meantime God raised up Evan Lloyd Jones, a twenty-year-old teacher in north Wales. Joseph Jenkins and two young women from the southern town of New Quay were attending a meeting in north Wales. Jones went into the pulpit and appealed to the young people to receive a new anointing of the Holy Spirit. Many prayed and received God's powerful answer. The whole church seemed filled with the glory of God.

From that time on, Jones appeared clothed with an

irresistible spiritual authority. His face on occasion "shone with such brilliance that they became oblivious of all else in the meeting."[2] Some tried to leave the service but Jones' glory and authority gripped them. Jones preached up and down the coast of Wales. David Lloyd-George, politician and later prime minister, said the effect of the revival was like a tornado sweeping over the nation.

In another town in north Wales, a middle-aged farmer's wife, Mrs. Mary Jones, was suddenly raised up by the Holy Spirit. A faithful prayer warrior, she was anointed mightily by the Holy Spirit as she interceded in a public meeting. Mary Jones soon developed a tremendous home visitation ministry. God guided her in which homes to visit and frequently told her how many she would lead to Him. She led at least seventy to the Lord in her village. Once the power of the Spirit came so mightily upon her that she pleaded, "O Lord, stay Your hand until I put on immortality."[3]

God sent a four-month revival to Rhos that brought 2,267 souls to Christ. Congregations were melted to tears. Many prayed simultaneously. A ruthless gang of thirteen notorious sinners were all powerfully saved. Prayer meetings were held in coal mines. Family feuds were settled, and the temperance cause was strengthened. New converts routinely led processions of believers, even children, through the streets, witnessing to everyone they saw. God's sovereign power stretched like a blanket over both northern and southern Wales.

The press in many nations, even Roman Catholic countries like France, Italy, and Portugal, reported the Wales revival extensively and even included photos. Visitors came from Russia, France, Germany, the United States, and all over the British Isles to see God's power at work. Prayer requests came in from many nations, and the Welsh Christians believed that God would spread the revival fire throughout the world. God did, even in India, Korea, North China, and Latin America.

ROBERTS UNITES WALES

Meanwhile, Evan Roberts' ministry continued to flourish throughout all of Wales. He constantly depended on the guidance of the Spirit in accepting invitations, attending services, and even participating in services he attended. He did not go to Cardiff, where thousands were waiting, because he felt checked by the Spirit. He wanted to be in the background and leave all the glory to Christ.

In some areas the meetings were sparsely attended at first, but since Roberts knew God had sent him, he persevered. Soon there were many powerful conversions in these places. Roberts would walk along the aisles radiant with joy. At times he wrestled in agonizing prayer, even during services he was attending.

Evan Roberts visited the mine pit heads to greet the night shift men as they left the mine. He would shake hands with each one and invite them to the meetings. Most came. Strong men sobbed as the Holy Spirit convicted them of their sin. The transformed miners added both volume and power to the singing and fervency to the praying.

Some of the mightiest revival scenes took place in the first two months. The revival swept like a sea wave from valley to valley. Often revival began even before Evan Roberts arrived. A newspaper reporter visited one mine and at seventy yards from the bottom of the shaft found a group of eighty miners listening to a workman read Matthew 6 by a dim lantern light. Then the men sang, shouted amens, and one miner after another led in prayer until it was time to begin work. At times two hundred, three hundred, or even five hundred were converted before Evan Roberts arrived at a given place.

SPIRIT-LED WORSHIP

A London journalist who attended the meetings was amazed at the way the services continued almost without human leadership or direction. Singing, Scripture reading, prayer, testimonies of converts, and brief exhortations by various people followed one after another as the Spirit led. Three-fourths of the meeting was taken up by singing the great hymns of the church; although a thousand or two might be in attendance, order reigned. If someone exhorted at too great a length, someone else would start a hymn. Evan Roberts urged continually, "Obey the Spirit," and the Spirit kept the meeting peaceful and orderly.

As time went on, Roberts became more and more convinced of the priority of prayer over all else, even over singing. He said, "We may sing all night without saving. It is prayer that tells, that saves, and that brings heaven down among us. Pray, friends, pray."[4]

Evan Roberts did not preach against gambling, dishonesty, drunkenness, injustice, or immorality. He pointed people to Christ the Savior. Yet the social impact of the revival was profound, and many of these sins for a period almost disappeared from Wales.

Roberts ministered for two months in north Wales. He was used by God there, yet not so spectacularly as in south Wales, since Evan Lloyd Jones and Mary Jones, among others, already had vital ministries in the north. Repeatedly Roberts expressed his concern over three things: (1) that all the glory be given to God, (2) that the people pray, and (3) that all obey God.

Many Christians elsewhere, hearing about the revival in south Wales, were led by the Spirit to hunger for revival in their own towns. In most of these towns, revival began with prayer meetings led by young people. Prayer continued until the Spirit was poured out. Sometimes these prayer meetings were started by individuals, sometimes by church leaders, and sometimes even by the entire presbytery. Smaller visitations of revival fire appeared in various other parts of the British Isles.

THE SECRET OF REVIVAL

"Bend the church and save the world," was Evan Roberts' battle cry. When asked the secret of the revival, he replied, "I have no secret, ask and ye shall receive." Again he said several years later, "It is certainly beyond my power to instigate a fresh revival, for revival can alone be given by the Holy Spirit of God when the conditions are fulfilled."[5]

Were the results of the 1904 revival permanent? Thank God, most were. Some six years after the revival, 80 percent of the converts were still members of the church they joined at the time of the revival. But that does not mean that the other 20 percent were all backsliders. Many became members of independent mission halls or transferred membership to some of the other denominations that arose.

In Gorseinon itself I have ministered on several occasions to Christians in the mission hall. This building was founded by the first five converts of the revival. When these men testified in their home church that before the revival they had never been born again, they were excommunicated and so built the mission hall. It was a joy to hear firsthand accounts from those faithful worshipers of how God worked during the time of the 1904 revival.

By the autumn of 1905, Roberts' ministry and influence waned. He felt physically exhausted and suffered a breakdown. In April 1906 he retired to rest and recuperate in the home of Mr. and Mrs. Penn-Lewis in England. For some years Roberts and Mrs. Penn-Lewis combined their efforts. From 1907 on he gave himself almost exclusively to the ministry of intercession.

In October 1932 Roberts wrote, "My work is confined to prayer, and it is to such that I have devoted myself for the last twenty-five years. . . . I work as hard at prayer as if I had undertaken any other form of religious work. . . . By preaching I would reach the limited few—by and through prayer I can reach the whole of mankind for God."[6] In 1928 he returned to Gorseinon for a short time and fellowshiped with a prayer group of some thirty members. God used him to heal the sick and cast out demons. Many were converted as a result of specific prayers offered for them by the group.

Evan Roberts was very much aware of the conflict with evil spirits and Satan, as is indicated by the book he coauthored with Mrs. Penn-Lewis, entitled *War on the Saints*. Roberts continued to emphasize the importance of being filled with the Spirit. On the few occasions when he spoke at some service, it was clear that he carried a continual prayer burden for another great revival. From 1930 until his death in 1951, Roberts lived in Cardiff, in south Wales.

In Gorseinon, Evan Roberts' friends told me that occasionally he would come back and sit quietly in one of the local services. In 1964 his last surviving relative, Mrs. Dan Roberts, widow of his brother, gave me a page from the surviving fragment of the Welsh Bible Evan always carried to the coal mine when he was a miner. The Bible had been damaged in an explosion in the mine at Loughor on January 5, 1897. I protested, but she insisted on giving me the page. "You are giving your life for that for which my brother-in-law gave his entire life," she said. (I edited a monthly publication called "Revival Magazine" for some years.) I felt assured that until his death, Evan Roberts' life work was to intercede for the work of the Holy Spirit and real revival. His prayers, like those of Jesus, Paul, Wesley, Whitefield, Brainerd, Praying Hyde and a host of others, will continue to live on until the final harvest is gathered in.

CHAPTER TWENTY-SEVEN

1901–10:
The Revival Decade

The wind of the Holy Spirit carried the revival fire from nation to nation as the wonderful news of the revival in Wales reached prayer groups in many parts of the world. Christians began to believe that the renewal they had prayed for might well be on its way. Praise God, as the news of His mighty work in Wales reached them, Christians and Christian leaders in other places renewed and multiplied their efforts to seek the Lord until He answered. Holy hunger and thirst were deepened. Holy zeal was fanned into flame, and encouragement and expectancy filled many hearts.

The decade following the Welsh revival saw spiritual victories multiplied and fresh and powerful outpourings of the Spirit in place after place. Let us now note some of these highlights. Heaven's bulletin boards must have creaked with the weight of all the new names that were added to the Book of Life during this period. Praises surely were shouted around Christ's throne as parents, pastors, and multitudes of hidden prayer warriors eagerly awaited the next revival bulletins. At last their prayers were being answered in thrilling rapidity.

ENGLAND AND SCOTLAND

England experienced scattered revival blessings, but there was not a general revival there. One parish church had an amazing rebirth, and 950 new converts were confirmed. Thirty English bishops endorsed the revival, and the Archbishop of Canterbury called for a nationwide day of prayer. Protestant denominations gained 10 percent in four years. Revival also moved across Scotland and Ireland but to a lesser degree than in Wales.

SCANDINAVIA AND EUROPE

Bishop Berggrav called the revival in Norway the greatest in his experience. The flames leaped to places in Sweden, Finland, and Denmark. The Lutherans called it the greatest movement of the Spirit since the Vikings were evangelized. A movement of prayer and confession flamed in Germany, France, and in other European nations.

SOUTH AFRICA

Among the first scenes of revival, even before the outpouring of the Spirit in Wales, were the mighty revivals in the prisoner-of-war camps in 1902 and 1903 after the Boer War. One camp was in Ceylon and the other in Bermuda. Prisoners experienced deep conviction of sin, confession, repentance, and lasting conversions, and at least two hundred volunteered for missionary service while they were still prisoners. Later revival came to South Africa itself, and in three years the Methodist church increased by 30 percent. There was a similar blessing among the Afrikaans Dutch Reformed churches.

INDIA, KOREA, AND CHINA

India was mightily blessed with revival in many of the areas where missionaries worked. These are described in detail in chapters 29–33. The Christian population

increased 70 percent in 1905 and 1906. Protestant growth
was double that of the Roman Catholic Church and sixteen
times the growth of the Hindus. Burma Baptists had been
averaging two hundred converts a year, but in 1905, 3,113
were baptized.

The revival flame that leaped from Wales to northeast
India then leaped to Mukti south of Bombay, where Pandita
Ramabai was ministering. The flames then leaped across
India to Korea. There were three waves: 1903, 1905, and the
main wave of revival in 1907 (chapter 34). After the visit of
Jonathan Goforth to Korea, revival spread to northern
China in 1908–1909. The China revival is told in chapters
35–36.

INDONESIA

In Indonesia the number of evangelicals escalated from
100,000 to 300,000 during the decade of the revival. This was
the result of "People Movements"—when tribal groups forsake their old religion en masse. These responses occurred in
various areas of the Indonesian islands. For example, on the
island of Nias, there was revival in 1908 followed by a People Movement. The number of believers doubled in five
years, and the island became two-thirds Christian.

A few years later God sent a movement of deep conviction of sin to the same island. Prayer sessions were held.
People came individually, by families, and by groups, often
weeping, trembling, and wanting to confess all kinds of sins.
Conviction led to salvation and great rejoicing, and again a
People Movement followed. Hardened pagans came confessing theft and even murder. Many were convicted by
dreams and visions. Wave after wave of revival swept over
the island. This seven-year revival movement was called
"The Great Repentance."

JAPAN

Japan's revival was characterized by large prayer conferences. In Tokyo, a movement of prayer in October 1900 was followed by "taikyo dendo" (aggressive evangelism) in May–June 1901. The Tokyo revival was also called the Forward Movement. Over 11,000 attended prayer meetings in local places in the afternoons, and the Gospel was preached to 84,247 in the evenings. Thousands professed to receive Christ. Missionaries of all denominations cooperated, and by mid-1901 they called it "Pentecost in Japan." Suburban churches grew the most. Protestants grew from about 40,000 to 65,000 in twelve months, and by 1910 the number of Japanese Christians had doubled to 75,000.

SOUTH AMERICA

God sent revival blessings to Brazil and Chile, but the revival as a whole had comparatively little effect on most of Latin America. In Brazil, the Baptists experienced the equivalent of twenty-five years of growth in three years, from 1905 to 1907. Between 1903 and 1910 in Latin America and the Caribbean islands, there was 180 percent growth of Christian communicant members.

AUSTRALIA AND NEW ZEALAND

In 1901 in Sydney, three months were devoted to prayer for revival and evangelism. For the next ten years or more, Australia experienced times of intensified prayer and extensive evangelism and harvest. For seven weeks in Melbourne, up to forty thousand people met for prayer in two thousand homes. The central meetings were held in the town hall, with simultaneous meetings in tents and halls in fifty suburban districts. A simultaneous campaign was held in Sydney with evangelists Dr. R. A. Torrey, W. Edgar Geil, and D. C. Davidson from the United States, and James Lyall from Scotland, assisted by a number of Australian evangelists.

In 1902 a second series of simultaneous campaigns was held across Australia. Later the same team of evangelists was used by God in New Zealand. A second wave of revival evangelism reached New Zealand in 1905. The movement of the Spirit was spontaneous, and many scenes like the revival in Wales were reported. When the news of the Welsh revival reached Australia in 1904–1905, there were renewed calls to prayer, daily mass prayer meetings, and other smaller prayer sessions. At times people were gripped by the power of God. Revival spread to some of the New Hebrides and Solomon Islands as well.

In 1909 Dr. J. Wilbur Chapman and Charles Alexander were busy in Australia, and simultaneous missions were carried out in Melbourne, Sydney, Ballarat, and Bendigo. Later there were second campaigns in Melbourne and Sydney. In 1913 revival climaxed with the campaigns of Dr. Chapman in New Zealand. These were preceded by massive prayer participation: ten thousand intercessors praying daily in Auckland itself.

These were years of tremendous blessing, extensive evangelism, and almost revival-like conditions in the South Pacific. Certainly there was God-blessed harvest. In seven years the Baptists increased 50 percent and the Methodists 60 percent. After World War I it took forty-five years to add another 60 percent. During these first ten years, there were unusual harvest results in New Guinea and throughout the Pacific Island groups. Revival and harvest movements continued well into the next decade.

CHAPTER TWENTY-EIGHT

Harvest in America

News of the revival in Wales was of great interest to the Christians and Christian press in America, but especially so to the Welsh-speaking churches in Pennsylvania. Revival fire began to fall in December 1904, only weeks after the outpouring in Wales. Revival blessings and conversions were reported in towns and cities across the state. Within four months, the Methodists alone reported ten thousand conversions in Philadelphia. The converts received into churches exceeded those of the Moody-Sankey meetings the previous century.

STATE BY STATE

Revival spread quickly from Pennsylvania to New Jersey. In Atlantic City, not more than fifty unconverted people were reported to be remaining in a population of sixty thousand. Newark reported, "Pentecost was literally repeated . . . spacious churches crowded to overflowing, and great processions passing through the streets."[1]

In Schenectady, New York, all evangelical denominations joined in prayer and evangelistic rallies, and the revival movement continued for months. The secular press published two columns daily on topics like "The Power of Prayer," "The Fires of Pentecost," and "Yesterday's

Conversions." Zealous women formed teams and witnessed from saloon to saloon.

In Troy, New York, twenty-six churches reported revival blessings. In New York City, churches were crowded as never before, and 364 were received into membership in one church in one Sunday morning service. The Baptist Temple of Brooklyn experienced great revival. Five hundred waited for individual prayer and counseling from the pastor.

Although there were no large evangelistic campaigns, New England churches reported the greatest outpouring of God's power since 1858. More people were added to the churches in April 1905 than during any one month for years. Town after town in Connecticut experienced the movement of God's Spirit, and churches in Rhode Island, Massachusetts, and Maine were stirred. Drunkards were transformed. In summer conferences from Northfield, Massachusetts, to Winona Lake, Indiana, God's Spirit worked in special ways.

About a thousand businessmen met in Atlanta to pray for an outpouring of the Holy Spirit. On November 2, in an unprecedented way, stores, factories, and offices closed at noon for prayer. The Supreme Court and even saloons closed so people could attend prayer meetings.

In simultaneous meetings in Louisville, Kentucky, there were fifteen hundred inquirers, and one thousand joined the churches at once. Soon the press reported "the most remarkable revival ever known,"[2] with four thousand recorded conversions in the city. Fifty-eight leading business firms closed at noon for prayer meetings. In Danville, Kentucky, all businesses closed, and management and employees attended services as a body. In Paducah, Kentucky, Southern Baptists reported that God sent "a great Pentecostal revival"[3] that lasted for five months. One church alone added one thousand new members.

Many of the states in the South reported united prayer, evangelism, and blessing. In Florida, revival meetings multiplied and were termed "part of the mighty movement the world over." Rev. Mordecai F. Ham, who later led Billy Graham to Christ, was greatly used throughout Florida. Across the South white and black people alike experienced rebirth. Again the Methodists and Baptists were the churches that reaped the greatest harvest. Houston reported "a tidal wave" of revival; not only were churches crowded, but the gambling houses closed as well.[4]

In Ohio and Michigan, there were reports such as "a spirit of extraordinary prayer" falling on a congregation for two hours, "Fifty churches stirred," "An awakening unheard of for years," and "The unction of the Spirit outpoured." Lansing reported 1,100 converted, with the Methodists alone adding 740 members. The Albion district added 1000, and Big Rapids gained 500.

In state after state throughout the Midwest, the Methodists and Baptists reported conversions, baptisms, and victories. Indianapolis held prayer meetings for revival in all the churches. In Chicago, noonday prayer meetings were held. Hundreds were added to the local churches in the city and suburbs. Ministers and lay workers met together for prayer. A great wave of revival touched many churches in Minneapolis. In one Minnesota town one-sixth of the population professed conversion.

Out west, a campaign in Denver went on for weeks. The mayor declared a day of prayer and requested all stores to close. The Colorado legislature postponed business so the congressmen could attend the prayer meetings. Every school was closed. In Los Angeles one hundred churches cooperated in a simultaneous campaign, and over four thousand inquirers were registered. One night four thousand singing people marched through the streets to the Grand Opera House in torrents of rain. They gathered drunkards, brawlers, blatant scoffers, and prostitutes for a mighty gospel service.

In Portland, Oregon, business almost came to a standstill for three hours each day from eleven until two o'clock. More than two hundred major stores signed an agreement to close so that their customers and employees could attend prayer meetings. There was a general awakening throughout the Pacific Northwest.

CHURCH GROWTH

The largest Protestant denomination in the United States at that time was the Methodist church, which included one-third of all Protestant church members. One of their editors summarized, "A great revival is sweeping the United States. Its power is felt in every nook and corner of our broad land. The Holy Spirit is convicting people. . . . There is manifested a new degree of spiritual power in the churches. Pastors are crying out to God for help. . . . The regular prayer meetings and public services seem to be surcharged with convicting power, so that cries of penitence and prayers for mercy have been heard in places unused to such demonstrations. . . . It is a real revival."[5]

The Methodists added thirty-five thousand new members per year for four years during the revival period. A few years later they had a nationwide campaign to gain two million new Methodists, but only a few were added to their rolls. Revival does what human programs and campaigns, even though well intended, cannot do. Presbyterians reported 1905 to be the most remarkable year of evangelism they had ever witnessed.

The Baptists were America's next largest denomination, claiming not quite a third of the Protestant population. A national Baptist journal reported, "The tidings of revival come from every side. . . . There is a remarkable responsiveness."[6] In Missouri they baptized ten thousand, and in Oklahoma five thousand. Colorado Baptist churches grew by 10 percent and Oregon Baptists by 12 percent. Black membership doubled in several southern states. Among Southern Baptist believers, baptisms increased 25 percent in one year.

The empowering results of revival were also felt on university and college campuses. Student prayer groups and Bible studies multiplied. Several thousand students volunteered for missions. At Asbury College a few male students, including E. Stanley Jones, were holding a prayer meeting in a dormitory room when the Holy Spirit descended upon them. The next day the Spirit was poured out upon the regular chapel service in Asbury and intercession took over. The revival spread through the college and town and continued for days. This was the first of several mighty collegiate revivals that occurred at Asbury College over a sixty-year period.

CHAPTER TWENTY-NINE

Revival at Ramabai's Mukti

The Holy Spirit burdened many people around the world with special prayer for revival in the latter part of the nineteenth century and the first years of the twentieth.

In 1891 Rev. R. J. Ward, an Englishman who had been in the ministry and missionary work for twenty-seven years, experienced renewal at the Keswick Convention in England. He returned to Madras, in southern India, ablaze for God and hungry for revival. Spiritual hunger began to deepen all across India among missionaries, Christian workers, and others as they longed for a mighty revival through the Holy Spirit.

Books on the Holy Spirit began to have wide circulation in India. Beginning in 1895, the first Saturday of the month was set apart in Bombay for prayer. Interdenominational conventions for the deepening of spiritual life were held at Mussoorie in north India and Ootacamund in south India. These meetings, widely attended by missionaries and Christian workers, focused attention on the infilling of the Spirit and how to receive it.

In 1897 the leaders of the Student Volunteer Movement called for a day of prayer across India, encouraging all to pray for a great awakening. In 1898 Rev. R. J. Ward called for another day to be set apart as a day of intercession. From that time on it became an annual event. By 1902 Ward had begun a movement of prayer for missionaries of all denominations, and soon more than eight hundred were praying for an outpouring of the Holy Spirit.

In 1892 an American Presbyterian missionary sailed for India, received a new infilling of the Holy Spirit, and soon formed a prayer fellowship for God's work and revival across north India. This was John Hyde, who in time became known as Praying Hyde.

By the end of the century prayer circulars were being sent from India to Britain, America, and Australia to mobilize intercession for India. For eleven years each Saturday afternoon ministers and laymen in Melbourne, Australia, banded together to pray for revival there and around the world.

After the 1899 week of prayer at the Moody Bible Institute and Moody Church in Chicago, regular Saturday evening prayer meetings for worldwide revival continued. Some three hundred or more were present at each session, the prayer at times continuing all night. Moody himself longed to see real revival before he died in 1899. His influence was so great that prayer meetings spread from nation to nation, in India, East Asia, Africa, and Latin America.

In the 1902 Keswick Convention in England, five thousand Christians agreed to form home prayer circles for the outpouring of God's Spirit worldwide. Praying bands began all across India and spread to distant parts of the world. There was a revival of Bible study in many mission stations in India. Indian Christians displayed a new spirit of faith, obedience, and self-sacrifice.

A WOMAN OF GOD

Pandita Ramabai, a brilliant and famous Hindu social reformer, became a nominal Christian but in 1891 was wonderfully converted. She had built a center for Indian widows, and she bore a special burden for the younger widows and orphans, many of whom came to the center as famine victims. In 1898 while visiting the Keswick Convention, Ramabai pled with the four thousand gathered there to pray for evangelization and revival in India. In 1901 she had some two thousand girls in her institution, which she called Mukti (salvation-deliverance), near Pune south of Bombay.

Ramabai felt strongly the need for revival among her young widows in India and throughout the whole world. For more than five years Ramabai challenged her friends in her magazine, the *Mukti Prayer Bell*. From 1899 on she spent much time in fasting and prayer. In September 1901 she began a special prayer meeting for the outpouring of the Spirit. There was much blessing in December and January, and twelve hundred of her Mukti girls were baptized. All professed to have accepted Christ, and many were truly born again. In July 1902 God sent to Mukti three weeks of real revival, and some six hundred were saved. In 1903 Ramabai heard of revival blessings in Australia connected with the Torrey-Alexander campaign. So she sent her daughter to Australia to enlist prayer for India among the hundreds of newly formed prayer circles.

In December 1904 Ramabai received word of the revival God had just sent to Wales, and her hunger for an outpouring of the Spirit deepened. She started prayer circles of ten girls each, urging them to pray for the salvation of all nominal Christians in India and for the outpouring of the Spirit in India and across the world. At first there were seventy in her prayer circles there. She sent out a call for other prayer circles to be formed among friends and supporters, giving each a list of ten unsaved girls or women for whom to pray. Within six months there were 550 at Mukti who met twice a day to pray for revival.

REVIVAL AT MUKTI

While these groups were longing and praying for revival in western India, God was doing a simultaneous work in northeast India in the Khasi hills of Assam. Ramabai got word of the early outpourings of the Spirit in Assam and the evangelistic witnessing that followed. She asked for volunteers from among her Mukti girls to give up their secular studies and go out into the villages to preach the Gospel. Thirty young women volunteered and met daily to pray for the endowment of the Holy Spirit. After some days of praying, on June 29, 1905, the Holy Spirit came upon a larger group of the girls, with weeping, confession of sins, and prayers for empowerment.

One of the thirty volunteers was so set aflame spiritually that the other girls saw a vision of fire engulfing and surrounding her. One of the other girls ran across the room to grab a pail of water to throw on her, only to discover that the fire, though visible, was not literal. It was the fire of the Spirit as seen in Old Testament times and at Pentecost.

The next day, June 30, while Ramabai taught from John 8, the Spirit came in power. All the women and girls began to weep, confess their sins, and pray for an endowment of the Holy Spirit. Girls became stricken down under conviction of sin while studying, attending the industrial school, or at work. Lessons were suspended, and all Mukti began seeking God. Two young girls were so gripped with the power of the Spirit that they prayed for hours and hours, until their faces literally shone with a heavenly light.

As soon as the girls had fully repented and received the assurance of forgiveness, they began to pray for sanctification and baptism by the Holy Spirit. They searched their hearts before God until He showed them their inner impurities. Many girls had visions of the "body of sin" within themselves. They testified that the Holy Spirit came into them with holy burning, which they called a baptism of fire, that was almost unbearable. The girls then became flooded with peace and joy until their faces radiated God's glory.

"One little girl of twelve is constantly laughing—her face, plain, even ugly, is beautiful and radiant. She does not know it. She is occupied with Jesus. You think you have looked on an angel face. Some claim to have seen the Lord—one, a blind girl. All speak of His coming again. One sang hymns, composing them as she sang—lovely hymns to Indian tunes."[1]

June 30, 1905, is the day revival truly began in India. It spread across the country to Pune, Bombay, Yeotmal, Manmad, Hoshangabad, Ratnagiri, Dhond, Allahabad, Aurangabad, and towns in Gujarat.

WAVES OF PRAYER

Another account from the Mukti revival states: "It is the marvelous spirit of prayer that has been most evident. Waves of prayer go over the meetings like rolling thunder; hundreds pray audibly together. Sometimes after ten or twenty minutes it dies away and only a few voices are heard, then it will rise again and increase in intensity; on other occasions it goes on for hours.

"During these seasons there are usually some confessing their sins, often with bitter weeping which is painful to hear. The conflict seems so great that they are almost beside themselves. It reminds one of the narratives in the Gospels about our Lord casting out evil spirits, and truly evil spirits are being cast out. There is much one cannot understand at first, but one grows by His grace into the work and learns to distinguish by the outward signs as well as by the Spirit's inward teaching the false from the true. Satan counterfeits all that the Lord does, and is working hard to hinder and spoil the work of God, but he is a conquered foe!"[2]

At first Ramabai did not want the story of the revival told, fearing that publicity would hinder the work of the Spirit. However, the Holy Spirit convicted her that she needed to get the word out so others could be encouraged and blessed. Two weeks later Ramabai took a band of her Spirit-filled Mukti helpers and began a series of meetings in Pune to reach the Indian Christians. Daily meetings were attended by Indians, Europeans, and British soldiers, including both Christians and non-Christians. Ramabai exalted the cross of Christ. The greatest visible results from the meetings came to pupils in orphanages and schools in Pune who were permitted to attend. Famine orphans had been taken in by these institutions, and the Holy Spirit worked mightily among them.

Then Ramabai's praying bands were sent to other places to minister to famine orphans. They visited schools and mission stations of different denominations, and in many places a deep revival work resulted. In Mukti itself special time was spent daily in Bible study. Those who visited Mukti remarked that they had never been in any place where there was so much time given to Bible study and prayer.

About seven hundred of the Mukti residents felt called to go out witnessing, and so they gave themselves to prayer and study of God's Word. These women and girls began visiting nearby villages, where they would sing, read the Bible, and pray with the townspeople. Every day a group of sixty would go out, taking turns. Each volunteer was able to have her turn for evangelism every twelfth day. The day began with a long prayer meeting. Those who did not go out on that particular day continued to pray especially for those who did.

Missionaries came from all parts of India to see the revival and hear its account themselves. Many were tremendously revived by the experience and testified to receiving themselves a new "baptism of fire." Indian Christians also came to Mukti to receive new blessing.

A well-known missionary in another part of India working with "the Brethren" had been in the country for sixteen years. After spending seventeen days at Mukti observing the revival, he wrote, "There was hunger, real pain of hunger, for a share in this visitation of God; shame, bitter shame, at the ignorance, after long years of Christian life, of what this travailing in prayer, prevailing in prayer, being lost in prayer meant, as it was seen here in many mere children; then there was wonder, praiseful wonder, at the marvels of grace.

"Little girls were lost for hours in the transport of loving Jesus and praising Him; young Christians were counting it a rare privilege to spend many successive hours of intercessory prayer for strangers never seen or known. . . . In one meeting we were seventeen hours together; the following day more than fifteen hours passed before the meeting broke up with great joy; and such songs of praise as hoarse and broken voices could utter. The work goes on. It is now eleven months since the blessing began, and yet while we were at Mukti we daily saw souls seeking and finding, coming out into blessing so full and definite as often to be almost more than could be borne, filling the mouth with laughter and the life with gladness.

"We are full of praise that we have been allowed to live to hear such sounds in India. Souls in agony, with bitter wailing and moving entreaty seeking the Lord. Hearts overflowing with joy in Jesus abandoned to the luxury of praising Him, sitting on the ground or kneeling, lost to all that goes on around, with clasped hands and upturned faces aglow with love, in the midst of a crowd but apart with Him, exchanging the holiest confidences of affection. This is worship, the worship the Father seeks for, and it is one of the loveliest sights one can conceive out of heaven. When some hundreds are carried away and can only sing 'Hallelujah, Hallelujah to the Lamb' until unable to sing any more, God is surely getting His own, and His heart is refreshed."[3]

Dr. Nicol MacNicol, the scholarly biographer of Ramabai, reports that those who seemed to have such emotional blessing at the time of the revival were still living steadfast, godly lives twenty years later.

CHAPTER THIRTY

Prayer Transforms Central and Northern India

In August 1905, through the Mukti girls' prayer bands, the fire of revival swept toward central India to the Free Methodist Mission in Yeotmal. The mission closed its schools to intercede for revival. Next, revival fire leaped to the Methodist churches in Bombay, and then to churches and schools of other denominations. Revival then came to the central part of India to the English Friends Mission in Hoshangabad. There was confession of sin and restitution. In January of 1906 blessing extended to other Friends' centers in the area.

In the Maharati area at Khudawandpur, news of the Mukti revival stirred the boys' orphanage. When a blind boy was converted, many at the orphanage scoffed. A missionary there spent the whole night in prayer. In the morning the missionary gave a message in the Marathi language from Isaiah 28:14: "Therefore hear the word of the LORD, you scoffers." Deep conviction by the Holy Spirit fell upon the hearers, and for five or six days missionaries and Indians humbled themselves before God in deep repentance. Revival then spread to the neighboring orphanages in Bhaisdehi and Chikalda.

Bands of Mukti girls traveled from place to place across Maharashtra. In November 1905 one band arrived at Ratnigiri on the coast of Maharashtra. They continued in prayer for several weeks. Soon others joined them, and the doors opened for revival. A spirit of confession reigned, and for a whole week Christians and non-Christians alike confessed sin and received new victory in Christ. All sang songs of holy joy and began a renewed outreach to the non-Christians around them.

The Mukti praying bands continued to visit towns and villages throughout central India. In place after place the revival fire fell with extraordinary conviction of sin, confession, restitution, reconciliation, restoration, prayer, and new aggressive evangelism by Christians.

The Church Missionary Society of the Church of England at Aurangabad asked for a Mukti praying band to come. Revival came to the local church and to fifty preachers gathered from eleven churches. A girl from Bombay was visiting in Aurangabad and took revival flames back with her to her school.

In 1906 revival came to the Gujarat work of the Christian and Missionary Alliance. God began revival during a Sunday prayer meeting. Orphan boys, renewed by the Spirit, led spontaneous prayer meetings even at midnight. There were days and nights of prayer, repentance, confession, and restitution, and a wave of evangelism surged out into the surrounding villages for some months.

A MAN OF PRAYER

From the time that Rev. John Hyde was filled with the Spirit shortly after arriving in India in 1892, he began to put a special emphasis upon prayer in his life. The Punjab area where Hyde was stationed was practically barren of conversions. Hyde immediately began praying for revival. But it was twelve years before he saw an answer to his prayer.

Hyde kept on depositing prayer in the bank of heaven. In 1896 he felt God granted his request to be "a real Israel, a wrestler with God, a prince prevailing."[1]

The Presbyterian mission united in prayer every Sunday for the outpouring of the Holy Spirit upon them. By 1899 Hyde was beginning to spend whole nights in prayer. He felt strongly that prayer was the only hope for results in India. Wherever he spoke his deepest concern was to communicate the need for all those involved in missionary work to be filled and empowered by the Holy Spirit.

In April 1904 Hyde and several other missionaries laid the foundation for the Punjab Prayer Union. Its purpose was to pray for revival and harvest in the Punjab and India. Each member of the Prayer Union was asked to answer these questions:

1. Are you praying for quickening in your own life, in the life of your fellow-workers, and in the church?
2. Are you longing for greater power of the Holy Spirit in your own life and work, and are you convinced that you cannot go on without this power?
3. Will you pray that you may not be ashamed of Jesus?
4. Do you believe that prayer is the great means for securing this spiritual awakening?
5. Will you set apart one-half hour each day as soon after noon as possible to pray for this awakening, and are you willing to pray till the awakening comes?[2]

THE SIALKOT CONVENTION

A general call went out through India for all Christian workers to gather in late August 1904 at Sialkot in the Punjab at the United Presbyterian Mission center. For one month before the convention began, John Hyde, R. M'Cheyne Paterson, and George Turner spent days and nights in prayer. At the convention itself there were two prayer rooms, one for women and one for men, and once the convention began the prayer rooms were never vacant. Hyde was there almost constantly. Many Indians also joined in the prayer rooms, some of them spending whole nights in prayer.

Each time Hyde attended a Sialkot convention, he virtually never slept, spending most of his time in the prayer room. In that very first convention the spirit of revival began, and there was humble confession of sin, making things right with God and man, and new liberty in Christ Jesus. In the 1905 convention, John Hyde was in the prayer room day and night. It was his mount of transfiguration.

Revival had begun. Missionaries who up to that time had been "good" missionaries now became powerful missionaries. Often Hyde fasted until his bodily strength gave out. God laid upon the hearts of the people the burden of a world battered and bound in sin.

Often during this and later conventions, Hyde and Paterson, after praying all night, would spend the day in fasting. In one service, Praying Hyde stood before the people and spoke three words in Urdu and in English: "O Heavenly Father." A great tide of blessing swept over the service. Hearts were melted, open confession of defeats and sin broke forth, and many people received new victories.

God sent revival to a Presbyterian girls' school where Mary Campbell ministered. The Holy Spirit brought confession of sins and real repentance. Then the revival spirit touched the theological seminary. Visitors from the Sialkot Convention came to Ludhiana, and God brought revival to the boys' school there.

By 1906 there were 1,300 people present at the Sialkot Convention, including 70 missionaries. Day and night intercession was made. God began to send revival to other districts of the American Presbyterian Mission. The Fatehpur and Fatehgarh areas, between November 1905 and November 1906, reported many professions of faith and many receiving the Holy Spirit.

ECHOES OF SIALKOT

Touches of revival blessing were reported at the Church of Scotland camp at Kathala in the Punjab. Reports describe a 1906 People Movement in the Punjab with fifteen hundred inquirers, an awakening at Jammu in Kashmir, a revival in Dehra Dun, in Landour, and at Almora in the foothills of the Himalayas.

In October 1905, after two years of much prayer, revival came to the Church Missionary Society congregation in Meerut, in the densely populated northern state of Uttar Pradesh. Revival began in February 1906 in the Methodist Girls' School in Moradabad. The girls in one school prayed for the boys in another school, and many of the boys were converted while lying in their beds in their dormitories. Bishop Warne of the Methodist church reported that two hundred young people made a covenant to enter the Christian ministry.

A Hindi Methodist church in Allahabad was in a desperate spiritual condition. They asked for prayers from some of the prayer bands. Suddenly in a midweek prayer meeting there came a deep conviction of sin upon all present. The Indian pastor was unable to close the meeting. He announced special meetings and these continued for weeks. The church was reported to be completely transformed: old troubles settled, enemies reconciled, and evangelism extended. At the following district conference the revival spread to other Methodist congregations and mission stations.

Walker of Tinnevelly held meetings in Agra in 1906 with tremendous blessing. In Calcutta, Rev. D. H. Lee gathered a group together for a day of fasting and prayer on February 9, 1906. Five days later revival came. The house was filled with people praying, sobbing, and confessing their sins. There were many wonderful conversions. Some young Bengali men formed an evangelistic band and toured the villages.

Revival came to the Church Missionary Society district of Nuddea in Bengal and to the Santal country in Bengal. A missionary reported that at Mihijam, Jamtara, and Karmatur there was revival beyond anything he had seen in eighteen years of missionary service. The London Missionary Society reported many revivals in Bengal, including the cities of Calcutta and Moorshidabad.

While missionaries were heavily involved in the revival across northern India, the leaders of the revival were almost always the Indian people themselves. Following each revival there were large People Movements into the churches. The Presbyterians baptized eleven thousand people in four years. In Fatehgarh in 1904 there were twelve hundred Christians and in 1909 there were six thousand. The number of Christians in the Punjab quadrupled from 37,695 to 163,994. During the decade of revival in India, the Christian population increased by 69.9 percent, which was sixteen times the amount of increase in the Hindu community.

Three hundred people attended the first Sialkot Convention; at the second convention, attendance topped thirteen hundred plus seventy missionaries. The Sialkot Conventions continued annually for decades following. Here and there echoes of revival were heard in distant parts of northern India. Revival touched Jammu in Kashmir, Dehra Dun, Almora, Mussoorie, Meerut, Lucknow, Moradabad, and Allahabad. The number of Indian evangelists and workers doubled between 1900 and 1905 and doubled again between 1905 and 1910.

CHAPTER THIRTY-ONE

A Year of Blessing
for Southern India

As news of the revivals in the north filtered down to the state of Tamilnad in 1905, many in the large city of Madras and all across Tamilnad began praying for an out-pouring of the Holy Spirit. A missionary conference issued a call to prayer and stated that the revival had already begun. The Indian pastor at Zion Anglican Church in Madras reported, "I am passing through a new spiritual experience. I cannot explain it in words. I dread the very idea of telling anyone about the great and wonderful things that God's Holy Spirit is commencing to do through what is known as 'the revival.' "[1] Meetings were held each night and morning in Memorial Hall. The same outpouring of the Spirit was sensed in several parts of Madras.

At Coimbatore the Christian Brethren missionaries held their annual conference, which was attended by people from various parts of India. At the Sunday morning "Break-ing of Bread" the Holy Spirit came upon several "in mighty power, causing them to sob and cry out in pain for the sins of the church."[2] God gave a spirit of humiliation and con-fession. Wrongs were righted, questionable behavior aban-doned, and estranged brothers reconciled. The service went on until four o'clock in the afternoon. Many sinners were convicted that evening. Believers gathered and continued humbling themselves before God and confessing sins. The communion service was delayed until three o'clock the next morning, and all rejoiced in a new sense of God's forgiveness.

Handley Bird, a well-known Brethren missionary, wrote: "God has come to Coimbatore and we are like them that dream. Our mouth is literally filled with laughter, our tongue with singing."[3] At times the soul agony and sobbing of the brokenhearted were more than some people could stand. Praises for deliverance and amazing requests for prayer were occurring at the same time. Bird was reminded of Ezra 3:13: "No one could distinguish the sound of the shouts of joy from the sound of weeping, because the people made so much noise. And the sound was heard far away."[4] Such a meeting had not been a common occurrence among the Christian Brethren. Yet in the revival of 1905 God worked mightily.

The revival in another Brethren station was reported by Florence Bird. "One girl (Rupli) was in a trance, quite unconscious, the Lord speaking through her in the first person, for example, 'As I have saved my child Rupli, so will I save you.' The use of the Word was wonderful, wonderful. Passage after passage would be quoted, chapter after chapter asked to be read. There were confessions, weepings, songs of victory, cryings, callings on God for others. . . . The agony in prayer was terrible to witness."[5]

In Madurai Dr. John P. Jones, missionary of another denomination, said that they never expected Indian people to experience spiritual conviction as deeply as people did in other countries. "This revival wave opened our eyes to our error in this matter, for never before were wilder scenes of agony and of despair under this deep conviction witnessed among any people than in India." Jones reported that at

Pasumalai, meetings were held for hours and Christians wept under deep conviction of sin, leading to blessings untold "by those who entered into the fullness of the Christian life."[6] Practically every student in the theological seminary experienced renewal.

The London Missionary Society reported from Nagercoil that young men who had been a terror and disgrace were now completely transformed and living holy lives. Revival came to the Danish Lutheran Mission. The Reformed Mission, led by famed Dr. Ida Scudder, also reported revival with "a great breaking down under conviction of sin, and the usual accompaniments of manifestations of the Spirit."[7] The Wesleyan Methodists reported revival from Chitoor that resulted in a passion to read the Bible and pray. Revival came to the Tamil church in the Kolar goldfields.

Amy Carmichael, along with many others, had been praying and longing for a new visitation of the Holy Spirit all over India such as had come to Wales and to the Khasi Hills. On October 22, 1906, "Jesus came to Dohnavur." At the close of the morning service, Amy was compelled to stop speaking, overwhelmed by the presence of God. It even became impossible to pray. One of the older children in the Boys' School tried to pray, but he broke down, and so did the other children. They cried bitterly and prayed for forgiveness. Their sorrow then spread to the women.

"It was so startling and so awful," Amy Carmichael wrote, "I can use no other word, that details escape me. Soon the whole upper half of the church was on its face on the floor crying to God, each boy and girl, man and woman, oblivious of all others. The sound was like the sound of waves or strong wind in the trees. No separate voice could be heard." She continued, "I had never heard of such a thing as this among Tamil people. Up in the north, of course, one knew that it had happened, but our Tamils are so stolid, so unemotional I had never imagined such a thing as this occurring."

Non-Christians rushed to the church to look through doors and windows. But nothing could stop the people from praying, and they continued to pray, with only one short break in over four hours. Amy said, "They passed like four minutes." For two weeks "life was apportioned for us much as it was for the apostles when they gave themselves continually to prayer and to the ministry of the Word. Everything else had to stand aside."

Months later Amy Carmichael reported that almost all of the children were truly converted "out and out," and that most of the workers were thoroughly revived. Backsliders were restored. There were notable conversions in the village, and Christians "were quickened to walk in newness of life." She added, "For all this we do praise God. . . . We have seen just enough to make us very hungry to see more."

From across Tamilnad came reports of increased prayer, continuing confession of sin, restitution and changed lives, followed by a deep soul burden for the salvation of friends and neighbors. From Dohnavur and other places in the far south were reports of crowded prayer meetings, sorrowful crying and confession of sin, and many conversions.

CONVERSIONS IN KERALA STATE

A Salvation Army captain led a Tamil convert into a new victorious Christian life. This new convert, V. D. David, became known as Tamil David. In 1892 he and a missionary, L. M. Wardsworth, were invited to hold meetings in central Kerala. God sent a great awakening with "usual accompaniments of confessions of sin, with great brokenness and weeping and public witnessing of faith in Christ."[9] Ten thousand people were converted in three months. In the largest meeting, twenty-five thousand gathered at Maramon in 1895, and at that time the Maramon Convention was founded.

In 1900 the Metropolitan Titus Mar Thoma of the Mar Thoma Church invited Rev. Thomas Walker of Tinnevelly to evangelize in Kerala. Walker's ministry brought great spiritual thirst and expectancy of revival. When news of the Welsh revival came to Trivandrum, profound interest was manifested and Christians became "obsessed" with prayer for an outpouring of the Spirit. On July 23, 1905, at Kottayan, a special day of intercession for worldwide revival was proclaimed and for four months daily prayer meetings for revival were held across India. At Kunnankulam a Malayali Anglican gave a report of the Welsh revival. From then on daily prayer meetings were held in the town with deepening intensity. In Cochin, Anglicans held daily prayer meetings. Many of all denominations, including Anglicans, Congregationalists, and Mar Thomists, became hungry and expectant for revival.

In fact, revival had already begun at Trivandrum with a three-day ministry of the Salvation Army. Three hundred people made inquiries during the three days, and God gave spiritual quickening to the local churches. Blessings spread to rural congregations. Hundreds were added to the churches.

The Church Missionary Society called the revival "a remarkable spiritual work."[10] It brought thousands into their membership in a couple of years. The Mar Thoma church doubled in ten years. Parish after parish among the Anglicans reported rising spiritual power. Punchamannil Mammen, a convert of the revival under Tamil David, was called by God. Mammen began holding meetings characterized by deep conviction of sin, weeping, repenting, and confessing. People flocked in from other towns, and the revival extended to Alleppey, Niranam, Kattunilam, and Venmoney.

The next year Mammen preached in many Kerala cities and to Malayalam-speaking churches in Madras. Genuine repentance was manifested in practical ways with open confession of sin, immediate restitution, unity, and love. Personal animosities ended. Quarrels were settled. Congregational disputes were reconciled. Former enemies united in prayer, formed preaching bands, and traveled to nearby villages. There was a new interest in witnessing, prayer, unity among the Christians, and church attendance.

Walker of Tinnevelly reported concerning 1906: "This closing year has been in a very special sense, a year of grace for India. . . . Congregation after congregation was bowed before the power of the Holy Spirit in deep conviction and confession of sin. At times the solemnity and power were almost painful, and we were often in church till midnight. The people of a 'revived' congregation would follow us to the adjacent villages to give their testimonies there, and their witness did far more than our preaching."[11]

The revival that began in Kerala in 1905 lasted until the end of the decade, and there were thrilling reports of revival and God-blessed evangelism throughout Kerala and Cochin.

KARNATAKA STATE COMES TO THE LORD

On January 1, 1905, the London Missionary Society held a special prayer meeting in Bellary. An account of the revival in Wales was given, and immediately deep and intense conviction of sin settled upon the people, resulting in confession, reconciliation, and restitution.

Revival spread to the Girls' Hostel, and night after night midnight prayer and praise were heard. In the middle of the night girls under deep conviction of sin called for the matron to pray with them.

Praying bands from Pandita Ramabai's Mukti center arrived in Belgaum. Revival soon started in the girls' orphanage and spread to the local churches. The Mukti women also went to Bangalore, where God gave the same revival phenomena of intense prayer, deep conviction of sin, and confession, followed by wonderful conversions. Revival was reported from the Kolar goldfields and from Tumkur. Congregational missionaries reported the casting out of demons as members of a prayer band prayed. As a result, villagers were impressed with the Christians' God who had such amazing power, and they "flocked in for instruction in the faith."[12] The whole attitude of the village was changed. It resulted in a movement of an entire caste group toward Christ.

From 1905 onward the American Methodists enjoyed the results of a People Movement among the lower-caste people. Four thousand in 1905 grew to forty thousand by 1925. There were People Movements at Sholapur and Rachur, and the German Lutherans in the Basel Mission around Bangalore reaped a harvest. Every part of Dravidian India (South India) shared the 1905 awakening—Telegus, Tamils, Malayalis, and Kanarese. The 1905 awakening was even stronger in southern India than in the north.

CHAPTER THIRTY-TWO

Revival in Andhra State

News of the revival in the Khasia hills in northeast India encouraged the Baptists in Andhra Pradesh on the southeast coast of India to pray even more earnestly for revival. In 1905, under the preaching of evangelist S. E. Morrow, three villages in Akidu District, Andhra, were visited with a foretaste of revival blessing. The Holy Spirit brought upon many people a deep conviction of sin and need for confession. Villagers were unable to sleep at night and had no peace until they received forgiveness from God. But it was ten months later until the full revival began.

On Sunday, August 11, 1906, God sent simultaneous revivals to Akidu and Yellamanchili. Meetings lasted five to ten hours and even longer. "There is no order of service, no leader, no sermon in any meeting, except the divine order of the Spirit as He leads. Be it noted that there has been absolutely no human instrument in this wonderful visitation. We missionaries have taken no part in it except to pray, not even that in public at first."[1] On the very day that revival began in these two centers, the secretary of the Canadian Baptist Foreign Mission Board and two Baptist missionaries were praying, deeply burdened and with tears, in an upper room in Toronto for awakening in that very part of the Telegu field.

THUNDER FROM HEAVEN

One evening, in Nellore, the Telegu church agreed to pray every evening until the blessing of revival came. For ten days they prayed. Then one evening in the church while someone was praying, "the Spirit came down with power." Dr. David Downie reported, "There was a rumbling noise like distant thunder, and a simultaneous, agonizing cry went up from the whole congregation. Some were sobbing, some crying out, and all were confessing their sins and beseeching God for mercy. The prevailing prayer continued far into the night."[2] Typical revival phenomena occurred. Some of the girls went into trances, were unconscious of anything around them, and spoke to some unseen person.

In the evening, thinking the girls needed rest, Dr. Downie tried to close the meeting by singing the Doxology and pronouncing the benediction. But no one moved. Then a girl got up and said, "Let us pray." It was ten o'clock but the meeting went on until long after midnight. Another night Dr. Boggs tried to close the meeting, with the same result.

Revival began thus in the Nellore church, in the boarding schools, and then spread to the village churches. The leadership of the Holy Spirit was particularly evident in prayer and praise meetings. Sunday schools also showed real revival. After the revival season passed, the head mistress reported that the Christian girls no longer had quarrels. Restitution had been made for wrongs done and things stolen, and valued little treasures such as jewelry were surrendered to God as a freewill offering for His work.

At Ramapatnam, where the seminary was located, no unusual revival phenomena were reported. Instead there was a quiet, substantial work of grace among the seminary students and the pupils of the boarding school.

REPORTS BRING REVIVAL

James A. Baker, forty years a missionary, reported from Ongole that some Telegu leaflets describing the great revival in Wales were distributed without comment to some of the preachers. They had never heard of such a revival and began to ask questions about it. There had been no united prayers and nothing unusual was expected. Suddenly, one Sunday evening at the high school students' weekly English service, everyone present felt that the Spirit of God was there.

Missionaries were in tears. Eleven high school boys arose and requested special prayer. That prompted a new movement of prayer for an outpouring of the Holy Spirit. The regular Wednesday evening prayer meeting became a "New Life" meeting. Each Wednesday the attendance grew larger and the meeting lasted longer, with more intense praying.

The April quarterly meetings at Ongole contained the customary lectures, papers, and discussion. On Monday morning while the Lord's Supper was being observed, "suddenly without warning the usual stoical mindedness of our Indian assembly was broken as by an earthquake. Everyone present was shaken. One of the most quiet and retiring of our workers arose and, striking his breast, cried in Telegu in a loud voice, "Perishudatma! Perishudatma! (Holy Spirit! Holy Spirit!). Many others followed. For the first time at Ongole, the Holy Spirit of God was glimpsed in the act of convicting His people of sin."[3]

Ordinarily the quarterly meetings lasted only four days, but the workers stayed on at their own expense two weeks longer, holding meetings day and night. Many confessions were made, old quarrels settled, and wrongs put right. Various schools in Ongole began to hold meetings late into the night. The chapel room was constantly in use by praying bands of students. Children in the boarding schools started saving rationed grain to share on Sunday with others in famine areas. When the workers reached their homes, they spread the report of revival throughout the villages.

Throughout the hot months of April and May, revivals were constantly in progress in many places. In July a large crowd attended two meetings on Sunday and were powerfully affected. That evening a Welsh missionary told the story of the revival in Wales in simple Telegu. When he sat down, all heads were bowed in intense stillness. Then "in a flash, the spirit of confession broke forth and swept through the assembly. A thousand Indian Christians were in the church. The noise was tremendous. Non-Christians from nearby places came running in to see what was the trouble, but no one heeded them."

The whole congregation was weeping and wailing. The Holy Spirit took over, and people personally opened their hearts and consciences before God. "It was impossible to talk to individuals, much less to the audience. A voice could not be heard three feet away—everyone seemed to be living in another world."[4] After an hour, a few people gathered around the organ and tried to sing but no one noticed. After two hours someone with a strong voice started a hymn and the congregation began to sing. From that time on there was perfect order in all the meetings.

The meetings went on for days, and each day more and more faces glowed with peace. From the time of giving out the tracts, the revival lasted a year and a half. Large numbers were baptized, lives were changed, and Christians felt a responsibility to serve. Even the quality of the congregational singing changed. From Eluru came the report of "an outpouring of God's Spirit such as I have never before witnessed in this land or in any other. The revival came as a cleansing fire and quickening spirit."[5]

LIFE-CHANGING POWER

In Kurnool District in the interior of India, typhoid, smallpox, and cholera raged and a famine swept over the villages. Right when conditions were at their worst, "suddenly and unexpectedly like the rushing of a mighty wind revival came. A common quarterly meeting was turned into a revival lasting two weeks. Without any leaders, it began in a great volume of prayer, rising higher and higher, all the people praying aloud and crying to God for mercy. All day and far into the night this continued—'burning, cleansing, quickening and transforming lives by divine power.' "[6] It was the mightiest movement of the Holy Spirit that Kurnool had ever known. In real revival lack of a human leader does not cause confusion. The Holy Spirit is in charge.

Six years later, in 1912, God sent a great awakening among the non-Christians, and more than a thousand received Christ and were baptized. The same thing happened in Secunderabad: first revival and the confession of hidden sins and then evangelism resulting in many conversions and a new zeal among the Christians.

The revivals in Nellore and Ongole created a tremendous stir in the American Baptist Churches. Soon revival came also to the Canadian Baptists, beginning in the Kakanada Girls' School on August 14. For days, lessons, housework, food, and rest were almost forgotten while God worked in the hearts of the students and teachers. Then began a series of meetings that lasted seven weeks for hours both day and night in church and school. The Holy Spirit visited the church in overwhelming power.

At Ramachandrapuram people were shocked to discover that teachers and even preachers had been living in sin right up to the moment revival began, while others had been living holy lives before God. At Samalkot, revival came to the seminary. They reported that words would fail to tell all the amazing things that God did. The fruit was abiding. The school teachers even reported that the pupils changed their habits of study, and their written examinations showed the difference.

One report said, "The Spirit came like a flood and we had three glorious weeks, which to experience is worth a lifetime."[7] A teacher was so convicted that he jumped up and ran from the church but fell upon his face a few yards from the door. He was brought into a full confession and cleansing and began to pray and witness.

The neighboring American Lutheran field at Guntur reported that in the revival decade the baptized membership rose from 18,964 to 40,198, and in the Godavery District baptized membership rose from 11,938 to 16,953 in the five years. During the time of revival caste people showed a new interest in Christ, and nearly five hundred were baptized in the Guntur locality alone. The village congregations increased about 25 percent in number, and in the Anglican area of Andhra revival took on the proportions of a mass movement. In the Dornakal District of Hyderabad, Bishop Azariah baptized three thousand people a year for thirty years. He followed the methods developed earlier in the Tinnevelly revival.

CHAPTER THIRTY-THREE

Mighty Waves of Revival in Northeast India

At the turn of the century many Welsh Presbyterian missionaries were ministering in the hills of Assam in northeast India. In early 1903 a Khasi (tribal area) church at Mawphlang in Central Assam began a Monday evening prayer meeting to seek the outpouring of the Holy Spirit in Khasia and all over the world. In 1904 these prayer meetings intensified in fervency.

Near the end of 1904, the Khasi Christians heard that revival had come to their mother churches in Wales. The reports week after week of God's work of revival in Wales brought joy and hunger for revival to come to Assam. Not only did the Khasi pray in chapel services for revival, but they held special prayer meetings for revival in homes. Young people took an active part, and even young girls stood up and prayed, often with deep emotion.

Revival actually came one or two months earlier to Assam than to Ramabai's Mukti, but it spread more slowly and did not touch as many other parts of India as did the Mukti revival.

At the beginning of 1905 the Khasi Christians decided to have prayer meetings every night until God sent revival.

Often it was difficult to close the meetings at 10:00 P.M. On the first Sunday in March 1906 the Bible lesson was on the baptism of the Spirit. There was an unusual sense of the Spirit's presence, with prayer, weeping, and praise.

At the presbytery meeting held in Pariong soon afterward, two were asked to lead in prayer but others also stood up and began to pray. A spirit of intercession came over the meeting, and the next Sunday there was simultaneous prayer, weeping, and praise across the congregation. At the third Sunday service in the evening two very powerful messages were delivered by Khasi preachers. When the minister was about to pronounce the benediction, someone stood up in the middle of the congregation and fervently prayed, "O God, pour down Thy Spirit upon us all now. Whilst Thou art blessing the people of Wales so much do not send us away empty!"[1] Men and women began to call out to God. Some cried aloud for mercy, and nearly all wept. Some men fainted, and many began to sing. At 7:00 P.M. they tried to close the service to eat, but prayer continued through the meal time. The chapel became packed as people prayed into the night. For eighteen months people gathered daily in the church to pray for revival.

In 1906 revival awakenings spread to the northeast through the Assam centers at Nowgong, Golaghat, Sibsagor, and north Lakhimpur areas. The Baptists also reported remarkable workings of the Spirit along the Brahmaputra valley. December 2, 1906, had been set apart as a day of prayer for India. At Nowgong the 2:00 P.M. young men's group was followed immediately by a women's meeting. All of the youth continued praying. There was bitter weeping, confession of sin, groans, crying, and earnest prayer until 8:00 P.M. The churches held a united concert of prayer for revival and salvation of the lost. For several months the Spirit's working extended from the valley below up into the hills.

REVIVAL AMONG THE TRIBES

In 1907 for nine months the awakening spread north of the Brahmaputra into the tribal areas. Almost every church was blessed and quickened. Then revival began to spread south of the river. A district conference was in session at Golaghat. On Saturday night the whole congregation began to weep. Many were in agony because of their sins, and young and old cried out to God for mercy. The Sunday meetings began at 6:00 A.M. and continued until almost midnight.

From there the revival movement spread south and southwest into the Naga hills. Three times as many baptisms were performed that year among the Nagas than had been the average for the previous five years. The Mizo tribe in the Lushai Hills far to the south heard of the revival among the Presbyterians in the north and the Baptists in the south. A party of ten—seven Presbyterians and three Baptists—set out to walk two weeks through mountain jungles to the Khasi assembly. They marveled at God's presence and the power that was evident during the assembly. Not one of them, however, could understand the Khasi language. At the close of the service, the Mizos started back home with great sadness.

Along the way they stopped near the place where the seven Presbyterians lived. The Baptists still had four more days of walking to reach home. As the ten were singing "God be with you till we meet again," in farewell to each other, the Holy Spirit was suddenly poured upon them. Others came from nearby houses and joined them. Revival spread in all directions.

A Presbyterian missionary, Rev. D. E. Jones, prophesied that revival would break out at a large village named Phullen. A teacher was sent to that village to start the movement. But after walking four days, the teacher arrived to find that the revival had begun four days before this, at the very time that Rev. Jones was prophesying. Persecution soon began in the Phullen area, and the Christians suffered greatly. Some were evicted from their homes at midnight and driven into the jungle.

Then in 1908 an antirevival movement surged across the area. People gathered to sing songs with heathen lyrics, and young people of both sexes danced in ecstasy and then joined together in large feasts. There were demonstrations in every village, and the antirevival movement spread like wildfire. Paganism ran rampant in the Lushai Hills until 1911–12.

At the time when the bamboo flowered, a horde of rats invaded the area. They appeared almost overnight and devoured the stores of food and grain that the people had in the fields. Suffering was terrible. People were forced to live on roots dug from the hills, and refugees poured down to the plains. Many died of starvation. Missionaries cared for the orphans. In Wales, offerings were collected and sent to Lushai. Christians shared their food without hesitation with their pagan neighbors. The distress of the people and the loving charity of the Christians brought an end to the pagan revival. Revival fire broke out again in 1913 at the presbytery meetings.

In 1919 an even greater revival broke out simultaneously in three separate places and spread to the easternmost border of India in the Manipur state, an area with a proliferation of headhunters. Four thousand were converted, more than the previous total of Christians. This region of former headhunters eventually became the most evangelical area in India. Within half a century the total number of Christians in the tribal areas of Assam was 567,049. Schools were established all across the area by the churches, and the vast majority of these new Christians were taught to read and write.

THE KHASI CHILDREN'S REVIVAL

In the Khasia revival movement, God particularly blessed, revived, and used children. When the revival broke out in the churches, the children felt they should hold special prayer meetings of their own every day. An adult reported that as he was returning from Cherra, he could hear the sound of crying and sobbing as he neared the chapel. He hurried in and found all of the children bathed in tears. Two young men were staying with them, and God worked mightily in each child. One child after another prayed simple prayers, showing real signs of sorrow for their sin.

One of the boys stood up and, with a terrified expression on his face, told how the night before he had seen hellfire and was so frightened that he fled to Jesus for refuge. He seemed very earnest, and obviously the experience was very real to him. Other children were deeply moved, and a wave of prayer overflowed them all.

Even when the meetings were over, some of the children did not want to return to their homes. Little ones would linger, go back to the chapel, and pray simple prayers all by themselves with only their teacher with them. In Shangpung the children did not seem able to leave the chapel. When some children went out, others came in, and the meetings went on for many hours, sometimes lasting all day long and late into the night. Some of the revived children went to the marketplace and witnessed to the people who had come to buy and sell. God used them so greatly that a large crowd of people ran to the Christians' chapel, and a powerful service was held.

A report from Jowai described daily prayer meetings that had been held with the children for more than a month. On Monday, May 8, the children's service began at 2:30 P.M. A man got up and with tears confessed his sins and asked God's forgiveness. Two of the boys then prayed for him.

The man stated that he had never realized what a child's prayer could be until then.

Another little boy got up and related that the day before God had showed him his sin. He began to describe Christ on the cross and how He had suffered for us. Some of the children began to sob, one after another, until the whole chapel was filled with the sound of children crying to God to forgive them, to have mercy on them, and to save them. Adults, hearing the cries, came running from their homes until the large chapel was nearly filled. The boy who was speaking seemed totally unaware of what was going on. A man poured out his soul to God. Several began to sing. Some of the children were still crying. Then the children began to sing and wave their hymnbooks. The meeting did not close until 7:00 P.M., when the people separated and returned to their individual homes, praising God for the manifestation of His presence.

YOUNG EVANGELISTS

Many of the children deeply desired to work for Jesus. They visited the homes of the pagans, held meetings in the marketplaces, and even walked to distant villages, some taking older relatives along just to get a chance to tell what God had done for them. The pagans treated them with respect.

During the revival movement in Khasia, a teacher felt the burden of prayer for a certain girl and kept praying for her day after day. One night the teacher lay awake for hours thinking about the girl and praying for her, and she fell asleep to dream of her. In the dream she was urging the little girl to give her heart to Jesus. Two days later the teacher spoke to the girl and told her of her dream. To her surprise, the girl told her that on that very night she had felt her conscience convicting her of her carelessness and thoughtlessness. She had given herself to Jesus and now she wanted to belong to Christ and to work for Him.

This girl lived with her mother nearby, but her father was a pastor stationed at a distant place. The girl traveled for two days to reach him and told him she had come to stay with him a week or two because there was going to be a revival in that village. The church there was rather cold, but the father began nightly meetings. After two weeks he told his daughter that she had better return to her mother after that service. She got up to sing by herself a Khasi hymn. While she was singing, the Holy Spirit came down in revival fire and a great work was done for God in that village.

At the presbytery in Laityra in February 1906, God's Spirit was unusually present. It was a great time of prayer and praise. Because of the great crowds the second meeting on Sunday had to be held in the open air. Rain fell and it was very cold, but no one seemed to notice because of the unusual sense of the presence of the Holy Spirit. After they sang for a long time, a young girl was led to the platform. She had recently been converted and greatly blessed in the revival.

The girl began to speak with a sweet and tender voice, saying that although she was weak and ignorant, she felt she must testify to what God had done for her. She did not want to crucify Jesus afresh by not speaking. She related that she had been a pagan, worshiping demons, and her parents had threatened to kill her if she ever became a follower of Jesus Christ. Her father was the leader of the pagan religion in her village.

She explained that Jesus had shown her hell and heaven and told her that He would use her to bring her parents and many others in her home village to Himself. He had fulfilled His word. Now her parents and over 140 others in her village had received Jesus Christ as their Savior. She said God would do the same thing for anyone who would obey Him. She pled with the people, and the crowd heard God's voice speaking through this young girl.

At the end of the service, they all sang "Crown Him Lord of All." The bond of love was wonderfully manifest throughout the presbytery. There were about two thousand of them standing in the open field, and the faces of the people as they sang and danced lit up with heavenly joy. Many of the people in the fields seemed to be in a trance and appeared as if they were looking into the face of Jesus.

The presbytery at Shillong in August 1905 was the first one to convene after the revival. On Sunday from ten o'clock until midnight there were three services held with two short intervals of about an hour, so that at least twelve hours were spent in services. Three sermons were preached and the rest of the time was given to singing and praying. "The fervor rose at times to boiling heat, and scores of men were almost beside themselves with spiritual ecstasy. We never witnessed such scenes, scores of people literally danced, while large numbers who did not dance waved their arms in the air, keeping time as they sang some of our magnificent Khasi hymns to equally magnificent Welsh and English tunes. Hundreds in the congregation were young people under thirty years of age."[2]

CROWN HIM LORD OF ALL

Jesus Christ was never so popular in northeast India as He had now become. To be a Christian meant something. Prominent themes in all the people's prayers were Jesus Christ crucified, the blood of the cross as God's means for the cleansing of sin, and similar subjects. All came to the meetings determined not to go away empty. Meetings began as soon as people arrived and, in fact, many little prayer meetings were held along the roads. From the first service on Friday morning at 8:00, the chapel was packed out, with hundreds watching and listening from the outside.

"All Hail the Pow'r of Jesus' Name" was sung over and over for at least an hour. Nearly everyone sang with eyes shut, and their bodies swayed back and forth in time with the music. Some were in trances and others danced for gladness and joy, seeking to crown Jesus Lord of all. As soon as the singing stopped, prayers instantly arose simultaneously from all parts of the building. On Sunday morning there were about eight thousand people assembled in the open air, and God's Spirit moved visibly over the whole congregation. They had never expected such numbers to be present.

One missionary in a far-away jungle village told of a big market deserted at the busiest hour of the day. All buying and selling had come to a standstill while people flocked to an open-air service nearby led by a simple village teacher. Women whose business was selling liquor returned to their stalls in the market to pour out their liquor on the ground. They went home and destroyed their distilleries and then returned at night to the schoolhouse to offer themselves and their families to the Lord. These people lived in an uncivilized jungle, scarcely seeing the light of the sun, steeped in drunkenness and immorality, and now they had obtained the righteousness which is in Jesus Christ.

For six years the teacher had worked in this village and had seen no spiritual results. Suddenly one Sunday morning at daybreak the teacher was awakened by the sound of singing in the schoolroom, and he found it filled with men, women, and children all singing heartily one of the hymns he had tried over and over to teach them for some months.

Now the Holy Spirit was working so mightily that they were singing with all their hearts. Prayers were called out to God, including cries for pardon and praise for sins forgiven. The meeting continued all day and all the following night, and the work of God continued. At a place where the ministry was hardest, the Gospel had gone the deepest. The Holy Spirit was working in mighty power.

A boy from this village came to a district school and was asked, "How many services do you have on Sunday?"

"Only one," the boy replied, "because that one lasts all day."[3]

REVIVAL MIRACLES

An old man, saved almost on the edge of eternity, wanted to spend the rest of his time on earth at the house of God. Whenever any reference was made to the death of Christ by word or song, the old man called out, "Oh, I do love Him. I do love Him." And then he would ask, "Did He suffer all that for me?" Another old drunkard, who was considered utterly hopeless, was wonderfully saved and delivered by the power of the Lord.

Some distance away was an area that missionaries had tried to open up for Christian work for years, but the chief official was very much opposed to Christianity, many of the people there were addicted to opium, and there seemed no hope. But when revival came, the whole area opened to the gospel, and the larger villages began to beg for teachers. The prayers of years were answered, and large numbers of people turned to Jesus.

Many miraculous healings took place. A poor woman who had suffered from a painful, loathsome skin disease for many years was on the verge of being driven away from her village. She came to revival meetings, heard of the one true God who loves, and trusted in Jesus. One day, in the midst of a crowded meeting, she stood up and cried out, "God has given me medicine. God has given me medicine. He will heal me with this medicine." And she rubbed her body with both hands. In a short time she stood up, saying, "I'm well. God has taken away my disease, He has heard my prayer." And it was absolutely true.

One deacon came in from a village noted for its drunkenness and, in deference to Christ, testified about the change that had come over his village since the revival. Only two men in his village were left who were not Christians. The deacon said he and his wife were going to pray together for those two men until they were saved. Later news came that both men had been saved and they were now very busy and active in the church. Neighboring churches caught the Spirit's fire, and everywhere men and women were added to the Lord. In one district more than six hundred in one year alone were added to the small village churches, and the next year they expected twice that many. Christians were living on a much higher spiritual level than they did two years before, and the non-Christians developed a tremendous respect for these believers.

WAVES OF REVIVAL IN KHASIA

Eighteen months after the revival in the Khasi district began, the Holy Spirit continued to work in power. The Gospel was spreading, and villages far and wide were turning to Christ in the Khasi Hills, the Lushia Hills, and in the plain. News of the revival traveled throughout India and lifted the hearts of Christian workers in the darkest areas. Revival blessing spread to many churches across the country as they heard the story of the Khasi revival. The revival in Khasia seemed to come in a succession of mighty waves, each one like the tide coming in from the ocean. Whenever the Christians felt that the power was subsiding, they would return to prayer again, humbling themselves before God, and God's presence and power would be renewed.

The result of the Assam revival was that believers were more united in love than ever before. Christians were careful not to get in debt, and those who had debts were quick to pay them. There was a great desire to extend the kingdom of Christ. Men, women, and children came, giving financial gifts as had never been seen before. One little girl of six went to one of her friends and asked if she would pay her something for washing her dog. "Do you like dogs?" the friend asked. "Oh, no. I'm afraid of them," replied the little child. "But I love Jesus, and I'll do it for Him."[4]

The Christians decided to raise a thank offering of ten thousand rupees to be used for home missions work. When people heard of the thank offering, they became excited and said, "It does not matter if we have only a little to eat for a few days. We'll do with less gladly. Only let us have something to give to our Lord." Village pastors in place after place were amazed to see even poor people bringing in thank offerings. The goal of ten thousand rupees was more than attained—twenty thousand were gathered in offerings.

CHAPTER THIRTY-FOUR

Korean
Presbyterian Pentecost

The Presbyterian Church in Korea looks back to January 6–7, 1907, as the beginning of a mighty outpouring of the Holy Spirit in revival. The churches of Korea had been known for their study of God's Word, joy and power in prayer, generosity in giving, and zeal in witnessing.

Dr. William Blair, Presbyterian missionary leader at that time, described the church in these words: "Many had come into the church sincerely believing in Jesus as their Savior and anxious to do His will, without great sorrow for sin because of its familiarity. We felt the whole Church, to become holy, needed a vision of God's holiness."[1]

Again and again revival has only come in power to God's people when Christians have realized how infinitely holy God is in His wonderful nature and how heinous sin is in His sight. When people humble themselves before God, and when repentance and confession are complete, then revival tides may begin to sweep over a church or area.

PREPARATION FOR REVIVAL

The Korean Presbyterians had long emphasized seasons of group Bible study. Each church at least one week a year laid aside secular work and all other activities to gather to study God's Word. Uninterrupted, prayerful Bible study has always refreshed, blessed, and revived the local churches. The whole Korean evangelical church to this day is a Bible-believing, Bible-loving church. Not only was there extended Bible study once a year, but many district or circuit Bible study classes were held also.

The city of Pyongyang, then capital of Korea, held a general Bible study conference for ten days to two weeks each year with eight hundred to a thousand in attendance. Many walked ten to a hundred miles to attend the conference at their own expense. For half an hour each morning they sang, and then for three hours more they heard God's Word expounded and taught. A new song was taught each year and then taken back and taught to all the local churches.

A visiting Presbyterian leader in the fall of 1906 reported that he had seen God's blessing and revival come to India following the great revival in Wales in 1904–1905. Many in Pyongyang hungered for God to work similarly in Korea. For weeks that winter, missionaries met every evening to pray for a revival in the churches. When the general class began on January 2, the missionaries' evening meeting had to stop, so they began noon prayer meetings for all who would come. When the general class began, all were hushed before God, and one right after another was eager to lead in prayer.

The meetings continued all week. On Saturday evening there was a message on the unity of the body of Christ. Sunday services, however, seemed so lifeless and spiritually bound that many were discouraged. On Monday at noon the missionaries wept and prayed, as the services seemed to be blocked.

Monday night, however, a new spirit of expectancy settled on the group, and God's presence was realized in a very precious way. When the Korean leader arose and called for prayer, so many began to pray that the leader said, "If you want to pray like that, all pray."

Instantly, the whole fifteen hundred in attendance began to pray audibly, not in excited shouting, but in deeply moving, harmonious sighs directed toward God. Then the prayers turned to weeping. One after another rose, confessed a sin or sins, broke down and wept, and then threw himself on the floor in an agony of deep conviction for sin. Sometimes after a confession, the whole fifteen hundred broke out again into audible prayer.

THE FRUITS OF REVIVAL

There had been bad feelings between two of the Korean church leaders, a Mr. Kang and a Mr. Kim. On Monday night, Mr. Kang confessed his hatred and bitterness toward Mr. Kim, but Mr. Kim did not respond. On Tuesday night, Mr. Kim suddenly came forward and began to confess the animosity he felt toward Mr. Kang and one of the missionaries.

That missionary arose and called out to God, "Father! Father!" Suddenly the heavens seemed to open. The missionary later recalled, "It seemed as if the roof was lifted from the building and the Spirit of God came down from heaven in a mighty avalanche of power upon us. I fell at Kim's side and wept and prayed as I had never prayed before.... Some threw themselves full length upon the floor; hundreds stood with arms outstretched toward heaven. Every man forgot every other. Each was face to face with God. I can hear yet that fearful sound of hundreds of men pleading with God for life, for mercy."[2]

The missionaries did not dare to interfere. Like Dr. Andrew Murray on a similar occasion in South Africa, they could only stand back and let God work. The Korean leader started a hymn and soon all quieted down as they sang. Then public confessions began as people saw themselves in the white light of God's judgment throne.

Dr. Blair, who recorded this mighty movement of the Spirit, added, "We may have our theories of the desirability or undesirability of public confession of sin. I have had mine; but I know now that when the Spirit of God falls upon guilty souls, there will be confession, and no power on earth can stop it."[3]

When the series of Bible classes closed on Tuesday night, the Christians returned to their homes and churches across the country, taking revival fire back with them. In almost every Presbyterian church across Korea revival flamed. In Pyongyang special meetings continued for a month, and even school classes were put aside for days as the children prayed, repented, and wept before God.

Hundreds of people made restitution for their wrongs as far as they could possibly do so. Throughout the city, men went from house to house asking forgiveness from those they had wronged and returning stolen money and property to both Christians and Buddhists.

Each person convicted by the Holy Spirit could get no rest until he or she had confessed and made restitution as far as possible. A few were deeply convicted but were so stubborn and ashamed that they refused to confess. In case after case, soon afterward the sin came to public attention and the person left the church disgraced, in some cases never to return.

The 1907 Korean Pentecost prepared thousands of Christians in one way or another for victorious living, for victorious Christian ministry, and even some for victorious martyrdom.

To this day the evangelical churches of Korea have much in common. They all pray, fast, and believe and read the Bible. In one of our own OMS-related churches in Korea in the 1970s, I saw a small-print, four-page insert in the Sunday church bulletin. When I asked for interpretation, I was told that the church was divided into twenty-four groups. Each group kept a weekly record of various statistics, including the total number of Bible chapters read by each member, the number of new believers won to the Lord by each member, the attendance at the various prayer meetings, and the offerings given.

A LASTING IMPACT

Eighty-seven years have gone by, but Korea still bears the imprint of the 1907 revival. Korean Christians are, on the whole, still deeply committed. In our own work, our church leaders have told me they have records of more than twenty thousand of their members who have spent forty days in fasting and prayer. Still today an average of about one-third of the church members attends the 5:00 A.M. prayer meeting every day.

Now the Korean church is beginning to send missionaries across the world. Our own related Korean church has joined with us to start a theological seminary in Moscow. We now have over fifty students. This church has also financed the building construction for several hundred of our poorer village churches in India. Every six months twelve more seminary graduate couples are given six months of special missionary orientation and then sent out to various parts of the world. Still today when the churches pray, regardless of denomination, they call on God with one voice.

Practically every evangelical church in all of Korea received blessing in the 1907 revival. Everywhere the phenomena were the same: hunger for God, conviction of sin, deep confession and restitution, and audible prayer by the entire group, a form of prayer that was then completely new in Korea. In five years there was a net growth of nearly eighty thousand believers in Korea—twice the number of

Protestants in China after the first eighty years of missionary work. Bishop C. M. Harris of the Methodist Church said that the general effects of the revival movement as a whole were completely good. He believed that the whole church was raised to a higher spiritual level, and there was little fanaticism because of previous careful instruction in the Bible.

Many people look back on the Korean revival of 1907 as the real spiritual birth of the Korean church. But we must remember that there had been touches of revival in 1895, in 1903, and in 1905. In one decade after the Korean revival, church membership quadrupled. Korea, today, is the most evangelized and most Christian part of the Orient.

CHAPTER THIRTY-FIVE

Goforth and the North China Revival

God sent a spirit of revival across Manchuria and north-eastern and central China in the early years of the twentieth century. The man God used perhaps most extensively in these times of revival harvest was Jonathan Goforth, a Canadian Presbyterian missionary. He went to China in 1887 and served there until 1934. During the approximately ten years of special revival, it seemed that almost everwhere Goforth went God sent revival to the church and a continuing harvest among the non-Christians. Conservative in his theology, intensely earnest in his evangelism, and a man who exemplified 2 Chronicles 7:14, Goforth dared to expect and experience revival.

A REVOLUTIONARY REVIVALIST

Goforth escaped the tragic Boxer Rebellion in China in 1900, in which 189 Protestant missionaries and their children and several thousands of Chinese Christians were martyred. But he returned to China in 1901 and soon became deeply dissatisfied with the spiritual harvest in his work. When he had first arrived in China, he felt that there had to be a period of seed sowing before harvest could come. But now Goforth began to study the Scripture. He was greatly

259

encouraged by the reports of the revival in Wales in 1904 and 1905.

In 1905 Goforth was given a pamphlet containing excerpts from Finney's autobiography and revival lectures. His heart was set ablaze. He read one of Finney's statements that just as a farmer would not expect to receive a harvest in his fields by merely praying and not obeying the laws of nature, so Christians should not expect spiritual harvest without obeying God's harvest laws. Goforth said to himself, "If Finney is right, then I am going to find out what those laws are and obey them, no matter what it costs." Early in 1906 someone loaned him a copy of the full autobiography of Finney. Goforth's life was spiritually revolutionized. A few days later Goforth preached a message in a rented hall, and the whole audience stood up and cried, "We want to follow this Jesus who died for us."[1]

In the autumn of 1906, Goforth sensed how cold and fruitless missionary work was in so many areas of China. He wanted to tour these areas and seek to revive the Christians. But God first reminded him of a tension between another missionary and himself. Goforth felt that he was in the right, but the Holy Spirit clearly led him to go and make things right. Goforth protested that the other missionary had already come to him in tears, confessing his fault and asking forgiveness, but God reminded him that love had not yet been restored between the two of them. Goforth felt God telling him that unless he made this right he could not expect God's blessing on the trip he was planning.

In the middle of one of his messages, Goforth promised the Lord that as soon as the meeting was over he would go to his missionary brother and make things right. Instantly the whole atmosphere of the meeting seemed to change, although no one knew what Goforth had promised God in his heart. At the close, person after person rose to pray, many of them weeping. In twenty years they had not seen such brokenness before God. At each place thereafter where Goforth stopped on that trip, the Holy Spirit convicted the people and wrongs were made right by restitution. In place after place people broke down and wept as they confessed their sins. Within the next year there was phenomenal growth at the centers where revival had come.

KOREA SETS THE EXAMPLE

A few months later, in early 1907, Goforth was invited to accompany the foreign missionary secretary of his denomination to Korea. They intended to visit the work there and see the revival area.

Goforth learned in Pyongyang that both Methodist and Presbyterian missionaries had heard of the great revivals in northeast India and Wales. Missionaries in Pyongyang determined to pray every day until revival blessing was poured out upon them. After five months of waiting on God, mighty revival came to Pyongyang.

Goforth was deeply moved as he visited Korea shortly after this mighty revival. Thousands of Korean men and women had been set ablaze by the fire of the Holy Spirit. Services were crowded, and people went everywhere testifying and trying to win people to Jesus. Even little boys would run up to people on the street and plead with them to accept Jesus as their Savior. Everyone carried a Bible.

The spirit of prevailing prayer that had preceded the outpouring of God's Spirit in Pyongyang amazed Goforth. He was more conscious of the presence of God in the Korean prayer meetings than he had ever been during his own life and ministry. He saw that thousands of lives had been transformed by the holy fire of God.

Goforth traveled back to his home in Honan province in China. Wherever he stopped in Manchuria and northern China, he shared the story of the Korean revival, and in every place the missionaries and Chinese were gripped with hunger for such a revival. They begged Goforth to return for special meetings.

At Kikungshan, as Goforth spoke on the Korean revival, God so gripped the people that following the benediction no one stirred for six minutes. Then gradually people began to weep. Missionaries went to one another, confessing their faults and asking forgiveness.

A missions conference was scheduled to begin the following week, but they decided to put aside the planned schedule and just seek God's face in prayer. Hunger for revival ached in every heart. As the missionaries parted to return to their own stations all over China, they vowed to stop whatever they were doing at four o'clock each afternoon and pray for revival.

REVIVAL ARRIVES IN MANCHURIA

In February 1908 Goforth made the long journey to Mukden, the capital of Manchuria. He had agreed to come on the condition that the people prepare for the meetings by united prayer. But Goforth discovered when he arrived that no prayer sessions had been held and the local missionary leader was not in sympathy with the meetings. Meanwhile, however, some three thousand of the revived Christians in Pyongyang, Korea, were in special prayer for the Mukden meeting. In spite of the disappointing situation there in Manchuria, God heard the prevailing prayer of the saints in Korea.

On the second day of Goforth's meetings the spirit of repentance and confession came upon the people. By the fourth day there was much mutual confession and forgiveness. At the final meeting, a burden came upon the Chinese pastor and people as they prayed for many who had sinned, backslidden, and drifted away during and after the Boxer Rebellion. The whole assembly stood together in pleading intercession like a mother begging for her rebellious son.

That year hundreds of backsliders came back to God. Many confessed that they did not believe they had ever been truly saved before this time.

Goforth then went to Liaoyang. This revival began a movement that spread throughout the whole surrounding country. Revived bands of believers went out from village to village. The non-Christians would often say, "The Christians' God has come. . . . If you don't want to go the same way, you better keep away from them."[2]

When Goforth began meetings in Kwangning, he was told not to expect oral prayer from the people. The men would only pray if they were called on by name, and the women would never pray aloud. At the close of his first message, Goforth said, "Please let's not have any of your ordinary kind of praying. If there are any prayers . . . which you have used for years, just lay them aside. We haven't any time for them. But if the Spirit of God so moves you that you feel you simply must give utterance to what is in your heart, then do not hesitate. We have time for that kind of praying."[3] Immediately eight men and women got up one right after another and prayed. Later that day in another service, twenty followed one right after another in prayer.

By the next day even the schoolboys and schoolgirls were leading in prayer. People remarked they had never heard such praying as that before. They could not wait to bring their confessions and petitions before God. For the first three days, none of the church pastors, evangelists, or leaders were praying. But by the fourth day God took over with tremendous power.

As Presbyterians, the people in Kwangning had always stood to pray. But now more than half of the congregation fell on their knees and began to call on God. Before long all were kneeling. Then one elder asked forgiveness from another. Soon a pastor was on his feet, confessing to God the sins of adultery and accepting a bribe. He was wearing a fur garment that had been given him as a bribe, and he tore it off and threw it away from him. As the pastor continued to pray, a heavenly fire fell upon the audience. Even little children began to cry to God for mercy, and the meeting went on for six hours.

Non-Christians heard about the strange doings, and many of them came into the meeting. The Holy Spirit fell in convicting power on these non-Christians, and they fell on their knees and began to repent and pray to Jesus for forgiveness.

A prominent local church lay leader was unable to be in the service that evening, but the Holy Spirit convicted him in his own home. Such pain came on the man that he thought he was going to die, and all of his sins loomed before him. He dictated a confession of how he had stolen building materials from the church when the church was being built. He instructed his son to read his confession before the whole church the next day, but by the next morning he was so much better that he went to the church himself and confessed before everyone.

NO SIN TOO LARGE

Bands of revived Christians began to tour the surrounding area, and wherever they went with their testimonies, God sent revival blessing. In Goforth's meetings at Chinchow, a pastor from another place was deeply ashamed of his violent temper. He and his wife did not dare live in the same room anymore. The pastor confessed and made things right, and soon revival broke out in his church, where the scandal of the quarreling pastor and his wife had hindered the church.

The meetings at Chinchow had been going on for a week when a missionary named Dr. Phillips arrived. This man was deeply prejudiced against revival and displays of emotion. As soon as Dr. Phillips entered the church building, he was gripped by the reverence and presence of the Lord. There was vibrant singing, silent prayer, and then one after another began to pray. Soon the whole church was united in intercession with such weeping that the whole floor was wet with the tears. "The very air seemed electric," Phillips reported.

One sobbing man after another made agonizing confession, not of shocking sins, but of the sinful state of their hearts. "Never have I experienced anything more heart-breaking," Phillips related,[4] as those souls were stripped naked before their fellows. Hour after hour the praying continued. A strong farmer, a timid woman, and a schoolboy prayed, each in deep sincerity and repentance. After each confession, the whole group united in prayer for the person who had confessed.

REVIVAL BRINGS FORGIVENESS

The Christians of Shinminfu had seen fifty-four of their members martyred seven years earlier before the Boxer revolt of 1900. The Christians had prepared a list of 250 people who had taken part in the massacre, and they hoped some day to take revenge. When the Goforth meetings began, many of the Christians could not sleep for several days. When Goforth tried to dismiss one session, the people pled for him to continue the service.

An evangelist came forward and confessed sins, apparently very sincerely. Goforth told him to go in peace, and that God, according to 1 John 1:9, forgave him. The man cried out, "But I have not confessed the worst sin of all." His heart was still unwilling to forgive the man who had murdered his father seven years before. Instantly Goforth replied, "Then God can't forgive you."[5] The evangelist wept, but he could not forgive.

Then a schoolboy got up and told how he had been planning to grow up and take vengeance on the one who had killed his father. He told how he, too, had been unable to sleep or eat the past few days. The boy begged for prayer. Another boy related that the Boxers had killed his father, mother, and older brother. One after another, nine boys got up, telling such stories and asking for prayer that they might have grace to forgive. The meeting continued for hours. The next day the list of those who had killed the Christians was brought in. Everyone on it was publicly forgiven in absentia, and the list was torn to fragments.

Newchwang was said by all to be the most spiritually hopeless church in the district. One of the missionaries went there a few days early to hold special prayer meetings before Goforth arrived. When Goforth reached Newchwang, he heard about a Christian who had denied Christ in 1900 to escape martyrdom but had now been tremendously convicted by the Spirit and was restored. A Christian contractor had confessed to cheating a firm out of two hundred dollars and said he would pay it that very day.

The next morning Goforth began his first service. When he entered the pulpit, he bowed in silent prayer. When he opened his eyes, everyone in the building, even the children, was tremendously convicted by the Spirit, and many began to weep. One by one people began to confess their sins. God sent a mighty revival before the message was given, a hymn was sung, or an audible prayer was said. The prayers of the revived brethren in the other churches had released great power on Newchwang.

In the fall of 1908, Goforth went to the Taiyuan church in Shansi. Shansi is called "the martyr province" of China because in 1900 a hundred missionaries and many, many Chinese believers and even children were killed. In one afternoon sixty missionaries and Chinese were beheaded. A pagan Chinese scholar said everyone, even the women and children, died with smiles on their faces.

For some years the professing Christians of Shansi had so backslidden that they were known for quarreling, beating their wives, dishonoring parents, and cheating neighbors. When revival came, lives were so transformed that the people publicly confessed their sins and went from house to house to ask forgiveness and make restitution. Husbands publicly asked their wives' forgiveness. The non-Christians were frequently heard to say that "a new Jesus" had come to Taiyuan.[6]

GOD'S OWN TIMING

Goforth had only one day to spend in Hsichow, where the church had split and Christians were setting a poor example. A prominent teacher in the mission school, known for her violent temper, had become instantly blind during a fit of rage. The leader of the church division was known for drunkenness and anger. In one day of revival power, both of these backsliders were converted, saved, and delivered. Many other lives were changed as well. Mr. Kuo, the church leader, said that when conviction fell on him he had an awful burning within him, and he felt that he would burn up if he did not confess.

When Goforth arrived at Chuwuhsien, he spent four days with leaders from twenty-one stations in three provinces. He began by describing the revival God sent to Manchuria. Immediately people began to weep, and the entire four-day period was marked by continuing broken-ness and confession. At every moment, even late into the night, people prayed in their rooms or in small groups.

At Chuwu, revival came much more slowly. After Goforth held his services, the principal of the boys' high school began to get up long before dawn to pray. At day-break many of the boys joined him. After twenty days, the Holy Spirit was finally poured out on them. Quarrels ceased, and confession and restitution proved how deeply

God had worked. The girls' high school was not in session, but when the girls returned and heard of the news, they insisted on a day of fasting and prayer. Suddenly the Holy Spirit came upon the whole group, and the girls stayed for hours on their knees asking God for forgiveness.

CHAPTER THIRTY-SIX

The Great Chinese Harvest

It was in the spring of 1908 that revival came to Goforth's own station of Chengteh. Christians gathered from the surrounding area. The boys' and girls' schools closed so all could attend, and as many as possible of the hospital staff were also allowed to attend. God began working suddenly and intensely. When the principal of the girls' school arose and confessed her sins, God's Spirit moved in power among the girls. On the fifth day, the principal of the boys' school was deeply humbled and broken before God. By nightfall the revival fire swept through his school as well.

Some people were so blessed that they went quickly to their villages and brought back relatives and friends. Others hired messengers to go and bring their people. So many were praying and confessing that meetings went on for hours. On seven occasions the people were so broken before God that Dr. Goforth was unable to bring his message. New bands of Christians were constantly arriving from distant places, eager to share in God's blessing.

The meetings were planned for eight days, but by then the Spirit was working so powerfully that the meetings went longer. A few people tried to run away from God, but the

Spirit's pressure on their souls became so unbearable that they returned and repented.

Great waves of prayer often swept over the congregation when someone would ask prayer for a particular church or for an unsaved loved one. Instantly scores of people would burst out with fervent intercession. Outsiders were irresistibly drawn to the services, convicted, and then rejoiced in Christ, their newfound Savior. The missionaries and Chinese leaders of Chengteh formed revival bands and carried the blessing far and wide.

FACING OPPOSITION

On occasion Goforth was severely tested when the services brought no response and the speaking became difficult. But he held on to God's promise in Jeremiah 23:29: " 'Is not my word like fire,' declares the LORD, 'and like a hammer that breaks a rock in pieces?' " Suddenly the Holy Spirit would move upon the people, and so many would want to pray and confess that the meeting would go on for hours. Non-Christian Chinese began flocking to the services. One Christian was walking home when ninety non-Christians surrounded him and asked him to explain "this Jesus and His way of salvation." Noted witches and their whole families were converted. Hopeless opium addicts were saved and became powerful witnesses for Christ.

In the adjoining province of Honan, in the city of Kaifeng, meetings seemed to stagnate until key people yielded to God and confessed their sins. In Kwangchow the meetings were hindered by two demon-possessed people: the wife of a prominent evangelist and a pagan. The demons were cast out in the name of Jesus, and then God's blessing came to the crowd. There was great blessing in the eight days of meetings, and within four years the Christians in Kwangchow had increased from two thousand to eight thousand.

Twelve days of meetings were held in Sinyangchou. From the sixth day on the Spirit worked intensely among the schoolgirls. But the boys, most of whom were from non-Christian families, resented the meetings and determined not to be moved. Several of them planned to attack Goforth and kill him. On the tenth afternoon, the boys had returned to their dormitory when suddenly the Holy Spirit gripped them with irresistible power. Both students and teachers were in spiritual agony over their sins, pleading for someone to pray for them. By the eleventh morning boys gave numerous testimonies of victory and clung to Goforth as if he were their father.

In Chihli some of the key missionaries and Chinese teachers began to confess their anger, lack of love, selfishness, and unworthiness. Deep conviction fell on all the people. Although they had always stood when they prayed, now one after another fell on their knees humbled before God. Within minutes, hundreds had fallen to their knees. Suddenly, "like a wind sweeping over a field of grain . . . every last man, woman, and child was down on the floor of the church crying for mercy."[1] The key to the Chihli revival seemed to be a renowned medical doctor, a brilliant man known far and wide for his piety. But he had on occasion showed impatience. When this doctor humbled himself in public confession, the Chihli revival came in full force.

Goforth responded to invitations from the Methodists in Peking and the American Presbyterians in Hopeh province. In Peking many of the university students were determined not to disgrace themselves by confession and self-humbling. Because of their reluctance, the Methodist mission station experienced only small blessings.

This was Goforth's experience in place after place. In almost every Christian center there were some who had tensions, quarrels, or divisions, and these problems hindered the revival. When those involved refused to submit to the

Lord and confess their sins, revival was delayed. But when sinners humbled themselves before God and repented, revival spread quickly through the community and often even out among the pagans surrounding them.

REVIVAL SWEEPS THE SCHOOLS

When Goforth had to leave for England, he requested Dr. Pike, a Methodist missionary who had previously been greatly used in revival, to continue the meetings. On the twelfth day of Pike's meetings, the preachers and evangelists became broken before the Lord and began to confess. Suddenly the Spirit of God swept like an avalanche through the university students. For days it was impossible to hold regular classes. Impromptu prayer meetings followed in one student room after another. Meetings began at 5:00 A.M. and often lasted until 10:00 P.M. When the holidays came, 150 of the university students toured the whole surrounding area two by two, evangelizing and holding services.

At Chowtsun the missionaries had been facing rebellious attitudes among the male students. All the furniture in the school had been smashed, and the missionary headmaster had been burned in effigy. When Goforth spoke, the boys all sat in a choir loft behind him and were undisciplined and disrespectful. For four days not a boy opened his mouth to sing, and their faces showed their obstinacy. Goforth simply trusted God to deal with them.

As Goforth entered the service on the morning of the fifth day, every boy was in tears. The moment the service began, all sang wholeheartedly. Goforth opened the time of prayer, and boy after boy came running to the front to confess sins, including drinking, gambling, and visiting brothels. Some fell to the floor in intense spiritual agony as they prayed. Every prayer, confession, and testimony revealed the working of the Holy Spirit.

In the next town in which Goforth preached, five hundred to six hundred students attended in addition to the regular church members. The very first day the Spirit powerfully convicted many of the church members, and a deep work began and then spread among the schoolgirls. The young men, especially those in teacher training, remained unmoved and read their books while Goforth preached.

On the seventh day a student came up to the platform carrying a pile of books, which he threw on the floor with disgust. He said, "These are devil books." The students had bought them in the city, and while Goforth preached, they were reading these immoral books. The boy confessed how he had already been led into sexual impurity through them. One after another of the boys came forward and confessed. Confession and prayer went on for five and a half hours until the missionaries insisted Goforth take a rest. The whole morning of the eighth day was such a stream of confession that Goforth could not preach.

At Chefoo the Chinese church leaders had warned people in advance not to confess sins publicly. On the fourth day of the meetings, when several women began to be convicted by the Holy Spirit, two deacons went to them and reminded them: "Remember what we agreed." On the fifth morning as Goforth began to speak, an elder came forward and said he could not stand the burden any longer; he just had to confess. He then confessed to lying, stealing, and adultery. Goforth tried to speak again, but once more he was interrupted by confession, and he had to stop altogether. For several days the Spirit moved in revival fire and power. The large tent specially prepared for the services could not hold all the people.

Many of Goforth's revival meetings were characterized not only by confession but also by healing. In the province of Shantung, at the first service on the sixth day, the Holy

Spirit's fire swept so powerfully through the audience that many people were healed of bodily illnesses. No mention whatever had been made of healing, yet many had the same wonderful experience. The same unexpected work of healing also occurred in a meeting in another province.

MORE OBSTACLES OVERCOME

As Goforth neared the next place where he was scheduled to hold special services, he was met by a delegation of missionary and church leaders. These leaders tried to discourage him. "Don't expect the Holy Spirit to use you here as He did in Manchuria," they said. Goforth replied, "The Holy Spirit is always ready. It depends on you to be ready." The second day an evangelist was preparing twenty-seven people for baptism and found he could not continue. He felt he was not worthy since he himself was not filled with the Spirit.

On the afternoon of the sixth day there was a tremendous spirit of prayer, and then this prayer died away. A holy silence fell upon the people, and for some time no one said a word. Suddenly an evangelist called out, "O Lord, You've come." Instantly others began to call out the same words. For one hour everyone prayed, confessed, or sang at the same time. Yet Goforth said it seemed like the most perfect order. He tried to pronounce the benediction and dismiss the service, but no one paid any attention.

For an hour and a half longer the Spirit moved more mightily than Goforth had ever known. Even little boys wept as they prayed for unsaved parents. High school boys were gripped most powerfully. No one knew that these boys had formed a secret infidel club and were already infidels. But spiritual fire burned among them, and one after another came forward and agonized in prayer for forgiveness. The meeting went on, and at 3:00 A.M. the next morning men, women, and children again filled the church and prayed and sang praises until sunrise. It was mid-winter, and there was no heat in the building, yet no one seemed to notice. What light and joy showed on their faces! As the final service began at 10:00 A.M., not a single man, woman, or child remained unconverted.

In some areas, it seemed the devil threw up every possible obstacle to defeat the meetings. The headmaster of a large school was an elder of one of the churches. Several years earlier he had denied Christ in order to save his own life. When the church tried to discipline him, he changed denominations and remained unrepentant. He tried to keep the schoolboys from responding to God. Another man, pastor of the local Chinese Baptist church, called a special meeting and attacked Goforth for his Presbyterian views on doctrine. One of his own Baptist missionaries retorted that the hindrance was not Goforth's views on baptism but their own unconfessed sin. Missionaries and pastors opposed each other, and the Chinese members took sides.

Goforth spoke on "Have Faith in God." The headmaster of the boys' school came to the platform and tried to stir up antiforeign sentiment. The high school boys sided with him. By the close of the seventh day, the meetings seemed a failure, and a missionary came to Goforth weeping. Goforth said, "Why are you talking like that?" He told the missionary to have faith in God. God would not allow His name to be disgraced.

That night many of the high school boys could not sleep. On the eighth morning God's Spirit broke upon them, and the students came as a body and confessed their wrong. Then the headmaster came weeping and confessed his sin. Within three years over three thousand new believers were added to the Lord in this community.

For a special cooperative campaign in Nanking in the early spring of 1909, a large pavilion to seat fourteen hundred was built, since no church there could seat more than six hundred. The pavilion was made of mats which leaked badly when it rained. Rain poured until the day the campaign began, and it rained constantly for two days after the meetings ended. But not a drop fell on the pavilion during the nine-day campaign.

On the third day of the Nanking campaign, revival came upon the Adventist Mission schoolgirls. On the fourth day the Friends schoolgirls received the Spirit, and on the fifth day revival came to the Presbyterian schoolgirls. Then the Holy Spirit began to work on the strongly resistant boys at Union High School. By the seventh day of the campaign, the boys began yielding to God. On the eighth evening the Methodist girls' school experienced mighty conviction. And on the final day the service continued for six hours. Leaders and missionaries of many denominations made humble confessions.

At the close of his autobiographical account of revival in China, *By My Spirit*, Jonathan Goforth asserted, "We wish to state most emphatically as our conviction that God's revival may be had when we will and where we will. . . . Our reading of the Word of God makes it inconceivable to us that the Holy Spirit should be willing, even for a day, to delay His work. We may be sure that, where there is a lack of the fullness of God, it is ever due to man's lack of faith and obedience. If God the Holy Spirit is not glorifying Jesus Christ in the world today, as at Pentecost, it is we who are to blame."[2]

Goforth then asks, "Are we ready to pay the price of Holy Ghost revival?" He outlines what he considers to be the indispensable factors in preparing God's way in revival: (1) prayer, (2) a "back-to-the Bible" movement, and (3) exalting Jesus Christ as King of Kings and Lord of Lords.

The old Presbyterian missionary and prayer warrior, the man of unshakable faith in the Word of God, concluded his book with these words: "Brethren, the Spirit of God is with us still. Pentecost is yet within our grasp. If revival is being withheld from us it is because some idol remains still enthroned; because we still insist in placing our reliance in human schemes; because we still refuse to face the unchangeable truth that 'it is not by might, but by my Spirit.' "[3]

CHAPTER THIRTY-SEVEN

Revival Fires in Africa

During the decade of revival in the early twentieth century, numerous areas of Africa experienced revival blessings. Many places were influenced by reports of the revival in Wales. A Methodist evangelist held mission campaigns among several Bantu tribes and in major cities in South Africa. Many restorations and conversions from paganism occurred. In the Transkei, God sent powerful conviction of sin. Many confessions were made—even of murder—and restitutions were accomplished.

By God's providence, Rees Howells and his wife, who had experienced the revival in Wales, were called to go to South Africa under the South Africa General Mission. They sailed in 1915, and upon arrival Howells began to speak about revival. Within six weeks the Holy Spirit began to move upon the Christians. Twelve missionaries were praying together. They sang, "Lord, send a revival, and let it begin with me."[1] God assured Howells that revival was on the way. Three days later revival began.

In the Sunday evening services a young African girl who had fasted and prayed for three days began to pray and weep in the service. Within five minutes the whole congregation knelt, weeping and praying. The Holy Spirit fell upon them. That night the sound of prayer could be heard in every village. For six days the Spirit convicted people, and in the prayer services people continually stood to confess their sins. Everyone who came near would seem to be gripped by the Holy Spirit. For fifteen months there were two revival meetings each day. Hundreds came to Christ.

The Howells received an invitation to visit the station of another missionary organization forty miles away. In the very first meeting at 9:00 A.M. the building was crowded. Some visitors who had come from Rusitu testified that God had just given them revival. In a few minutes the crowds began to cry for mercy and confess their sins. The meeting went on until 1:00 P.M. and then reconvened at 2:00 P.M. Teachers, evangelists, students, and church members continued praying, singing, and confessing until sunset. One even confessed to brutal murder. When God assured him of His forgiveness, he began calling out over and over, "Thank You, Lord Jesus." About one hundred received deliverance and victory that day. Scores more found forgiveness and salvation the next day. By Sunday over two hundred had been gloriously saved. God's power was so mightily present that black and white people prayed, wept, confessed, and testified together without any awareness of racial differences.

REES HOWELLS BECOMES A REVIVALIST

After fifteen months, the head of the mission in Capetown asked every missionary to pray each morning from 7:00 to 7:30 for revival. One morning as Rees Howells was claiming God's promise in Malachi 3:10, God gave him a vision of the Holy Spirit coming down on all the mission stations. For a whole day Howells was so full of the Spirit that he walked for miles on the mountainside shouting the praises of God.

A month later the mission head convened a conference of all the missionaries. He wrote Mr. and Mrs. Howells to bring enough clothes for six months. Forty-three missionaries were present. Howells felt that because he was so new on the field, he should not play a leading role in the conference. But the mission head insisted, and Howells was asked to speak the first day. After that the mission head asked him to speak every day. For three weeks the conference ran like a revival. Some nights the services went on until the early morning hours. The missionaries were so full of joy that they were even singing in the streetcars. At the close, the missionaries unanimously asked the Howells to visit every one of the mission stations. Then they all went back to their own stations to pray and prepare the way of the Lord. For two years the Howells journeyed from station to station in Swaziland, Pondoland, Bomuanaland, Tmbuland, and Zululand, traveling some eleven thousand miles.

At the first station, on the third day of meetings, the Holy Spirit came down and "swept the place." Two African deacons objected to the confession of sins. Howells urged them to pray. After Jephthah, one of these stubborn deacons, had prayed for three days, the Spirit broke through in the early hours of the morning. Jephthah, like Saul of Tarsus, was immediately blinded but filled with joy. His mother went from house to house, calling the people for a service. At three A.M. they filled the church. Jephthah was led into the church. He confessed the sins he had committed, and scores were converted. After three days God restored Jephthah's sight.

For three months afterward, the Howells took Jephthah with them in the meetings wherever they went. Whenever Jephthah gave his testimony, "It was like shots from a gun all the time as one after another would go down under the Spirit's conviction."[2] In each place many were saved.

Next the Howells went to Bethany, the home of the queen of Swaziland. The first day the Howells were in the chapel for thirteen hours, meeting all the time with seeking souls. On the third day the power of the Lord came upon them. The queen of Swaziland sent for Howells and asked him why her people were going after his God. Howells told her it was because they had met the living God and had received forgiveness of sins and the gift of eternal life. He preached to her, and she was much affected when she realized that the Howells had left their only son in Britain to come to minister to them in Africa. She permitted Howells to have a private meeting with her chieftains, explaining that he must not look at her, but speak as if he were only talking to them. God powerfully anointed Howells in the meeting, and when Howells called for a response, fifty stood up, including the daughter-in-law of the reigning queen. Before three days were over, 105 had accepted Jesus.

At one of the stations in Pondoland, Howells preached on Good Friday concerning the Crucifixion. When he came to the words, "Away with him, crucify him!" people were instantly convicted by the Holy Spirit. The whole congregation rushed forward and fell on their knees to get right with God.

At a place in Zululand, an evangelist was concerned about his lack of power to win souls. He went out into the bush and cried all night to God. The next day he was filled with the Holy Spirit, and God's anointing came upon him with such power that before long his small out-station had become larger than the main station.

In every one of the twenty-five stations, God fulfilled His promise and sent revival. He had promised Rees Howells ten thousand souls, and He gave them.

In Johannesburg, for twenty-one days Howells conducted great revival meetings in one of the largest churches, and it was packed every night. He spoke through three interpreters so that different tribes could understand. Every night hundreds came forward to receive Christ as Savior.

INWOOD IN MALAWI

Rev. Charles Inwood, a leader in the Keswick movement, visited Malawi. For months the missionaries had been urging the Christians to pray, and about one hundred prayer meetings were being held regularly. When Rev. Inwood began his ministry in Malawi, there was little response at first. Then on a Saturday morning a man began to weep profusely. After a period of silent prayer, one after another of the elders began to pray and confess their sins before all. Sometimes two or three prayed together in a quiet voice. Suddenly the spirit of intercession came upon them like the wind. Twenty-five hundred people were praying audibly at the same time. No one seemed to be conscious of anyone else. To control the meeting, a missionary started a hymn, but with little effect. Finally the praying dissipated, a song of confession was sung, and the congregation dispersed in total silence to pray.

At the next session the women met separately and the men met in the large church. In both gatherings there were torrents of prayer, and the whole audience engaged in prayer simultaneously. On Sunday seven thousand were present. Thousands of pagans heard the account of the revival and came to see what was happening.

Inwood went from convention to convention with the same mighty results. Debts were paid, feuds were healed, quarreling was replaced by brotherly kindness, prayer became a joy, candidates volunteered to serve the Lord, and many pagans were brought into Christian faith. All were convinced that there is no power in the world so irresistible as the power of the Holy Spirit.

REVIVAL SPREADS ACROSS AFRICA

Evidence of the Spirit's working in Zambia soon became apparent. In the eastern provinces revivals among the Dutch Reformed brought hundreds to Christ. In Congo, revival came to the Luebo station in May 1902, with hundreds coming to Christ. By 1906 there were nine thousand members and two thousand others preparing for membership, and 2,180 were added to the church that year. In Kifwa, 648 were baptized in 1906, and 1,800 more were being prepared for baptism. On Saturday evenings crowded prayer meetings prepared for fruitful Sunday services.

From 1906 on, revival began to transform southern Cameroon. By 1909, Cameroon reported continuous revival and several thousand inquirers. In Uganda, the Anglican church services had thousands in attendance. There were many conversions, and the impact was felt all over East Africa. In Nigeria a spiritual awakening in the Niger delta brought agonizing conviction of sin among a people who had hardly known what sin was. Within a decade, membership rose from one thousand to nearly twenty-one thousand.

In the Ivory Coast and Gold Coast, William Wade Harris, a Liberian, won thousands to Christ, and the Methodists gained more than 100,000 attending their services. Awakenings continued there for at least ten years.

In Upper Egypt revival came to Nachaileh, a town of twenty thousand. Thieves, robbers, and drunkards were converted, and at least one person in every household turned to Jesus. In Algeria, crowds of two thousand thronged services night after night to hear a French evangelist. The decade of 1901 to 1910 was recognized as the period of the greatest progress of the Gospel Africa had ever known.

MADAGASCAR REBORN

On the western island of Madagascar, the family of a nominal Christian who had been a witch doctor became ill. The man, whose name was Rainisoalambo, heard a voice one day saying, "Pray for them and they will be healed." He did pray, and his entire family was healed. Rainisoalambo gave up alcohol, became loyal once more to his wife, began to study the Scriptures and to attend church services. In 1894, as a result of this vision, he became a witnessing Christian. He had only limited activities until 1899. Slowly the story of Rainisoalambo's conversion drew other people to his house and many were converted. Rainisoalambo became their teacher. He won another witch doctor to the Lord after his prayers brought healing to that man. The two of them began to go from village to village evangelizing. They recognized the role of evil spirits and cast out demons in the name of the Lord.

Rainisoalambo's converts became known as Disciples of the Lord. They visited people in their homes and visited every home in a village. They preached in churches or wherever they could in each district. The Bible was their only authority. They always worked as teams, and they received no financial support from anyone. They preached on sin, hell, healing, the cross, and brotherly love. Their ministry involved healing by the laying on of hands and casting out demons. An indigenous awakening began to spread. These Disciples of the Lord reached all parts of the island of Madagascar. When Rainisoalambo died, the progress of the Disciples of the Lord began to decline. But by then the Welsh revival had begun. The Disciples of the Lord maintained a strong impact upon the Christians in Madagascar.

In 1905 a second Madagascar revival began in a small village. Christians there heard of the Welsh revival and also of revival in the Norwegian settlements where Welsh missionaries had first evangelized eighty years before. As the people in the village began to pray, quarrels were healed, mutual forgiveness offered, and hindrances were removed. Several weeks were spent in intercession and reconciliation. Then came a profound sense of God's presence in the prayer meeting. The following week eighty-three people in this village publicly professed their faith in Christ. The movement began to spread all over Madagascar. Heart searching, confession of sin, open repentance, and conversions resulted in transformed lives. An unusual number of witch doctors and sorcerers hardened by paganism threw away their charms and paraphernalia and publicly professed faith in Jesus.

God greatly used two women in this second revival movement: a Welsh woman named Mrs. Rowlands and a Malagasy woman named Ravelonjnahary. Both women had a great love for people and a burning desire to help people in need. God especially used Ravelonjnahary to heal many of the sick. She would carefully register each visitor and pray and counsel each one personally. Some people had to wait fifteen days to see her. While they waited, each day they would attend the services in the village church. Frequently people were healed during the church services. Ravelonjnahary exhorted the people to total faith in God, and great blessing was poured out on the services. A general awakening took place; many of the converts were used in exhorting and prophesying. Missionaries preached with renewed zeal and dedication.

Thirty intercessors gathered in a village church at 1:00 P.M. and prayed until 4:00 A.M. the next morning for the salvation of a witch doctor who had been a bitter enemy. At 4:00 A.M. they felt God had heard their prayers. They went to the witch doctor's house and preached Jesus to him. He listened quietly, removed his charms and fetishes, and received Jesus as his Savior. Then the former witch doctor became severely ill, and he and the other Christians believed it was from Satan. But they prayed, and soon he was delivered.

The Malagasy Awakening continued to advance into 1908, characterized by much prayer, consecration meetings, spiritual agony, and deeply moving confessions of sin. The spontaneous open confession seemed prompted by the fact that many people received visions of the sufferings of Christ. Converts quickly made restitution to those they had harmed by their sins. Women were particularly used by God in speaking, praying, visiting the lost, and soul winning. Madagascar experienced results similar to those in Wales.

Enemies from other tribes came and requested that someone come and evangelize them. Crowds attended the services, and many asked for baptism. The village chief and the new believers burned their wooden altars, fetishes and idols in village after village. In 1898 there had been 41,134 Protestant church members and 86,406 adherents. By 1908, as a result of the revival, there were 66,264 church members and 218,188 adherents. The Madagascar awakening was indeed a movement of the people.

CHAPTER THIRTY-EIGHT

The Shantung Revival

In 1932 God sent one of the greatest revivals of the twentieth century to the Shantung province of northern China. It began in the North China Mission of the Southern Baptists through the ministry of Miss Marie Monsen, a Norwegian Evangelical Lutheran missionary who was a refugee in Chefoo. The revival spread specifically throughout the Southern Baptist work, but it also spread to a number of other missionary societies and to other provinces of northern China.

The Shantung revival was born in prayer groups, some of which began as far back as 1925. Miss Monsen wrote: "Visiting the different stations of this mission was a wonderful experience. In each place one felt everything had been prepared in definite, believing, unceasing prayer. It was marvelously open everywhere, and there was a unity between the missionaries in the work."[1]

In Honan, Southern Baptist missionaries had been praying many years for revival in their province. Beginning in 1929 there were two daily prayer meetings for revival, one for missionaries and one for Chinese. Then for five months these two groups united in prayer twice daily, and finally God sent revival.

The Shantung revival has been reported in some detail by Dr. C. L. Culpepper, respected missionary leader of the Southern Baptist board. The revival was characterized by conviction of sin, confession, clear experiences of the new birth, and emphasis upon a definite experience of the fullness of the Spirit. Like all revivals, prayer abounded, even all-night prayer meetings, as people hungered for the mighty workings of God and the experience of the fullness of His Spirit. It was in no sense a Pentecostal movement, for it did not emphasize a particular gift of the Spirit.

Miss Monsen's methods were simple. She gave personal testimony and she posed two simple personal questions to everyone: "Have you been born again?" and "Are you filled with the Spirit?" Many of the Southern Baptist missionaries had attended a conference in Peitaiho in 1929, where Canadian Presbyterian missionary Dr. Jonathan Goforth spoke. Goforth had been mightily used of God in the North China revivals of 1908–1909. The spiritual hunger of the Chinese people deepened.

When Miss Monsen met Dr. Culpepper, her first words to him were, "Dr. Culpepper, have you been filled with the Holy Spirit?" When he stammered an indefinite reply, she told him how "fifteen years earlier she had prayed for and received the promise of the Holy Spirit as recorded in Galatians 3:14."[2]

The next day some twenty missionaries and friends gathered to pray for the serious eye condition of Mrs. Culpepper. After two hours of earnest prayer, Dr. Culpepper anointed his wife and prayed for her eyes. Suddenly, "it was as though God had walked into the room. Everyone prayed aloud. We felt that heaven had come down." As they prayed, two Chinese cooks known for their mutual hatred walked into the room. They were gripped by the convicting power of the Spirit, confessed their hatred of each other, sought forgiveness, and were gloriously saved. Suddenly someone said to Mrs. Culpepper, "What about your eyes?" She had been completely healed.[3] This was the prelude to the Shantung revival.

The awakening began in 1927 with a series of preparatory meetings. Miss Monsen went from church to church and mission station to mission station asking everyone—pastors, evangelists, laymen, Chinese and missionaries—the same personal question: "Have you been born again?" She spoke on the seriousness of sin, the need for the new birth, reconciliation and restitution, the deeper spiritual life, and prayer for revival in China. She always gave her testimony and afterward asked everyone the same question: "Have you been born again?"

There was no sensationalism in Marie Monsen's meetings. She spoke in a quiet voice. Some were insulted or angered, but they could not escape her question. Many, even missionaries, realized they had never been born again or that they had never been filled with the Spirit. Some lied to her but became so convicted that they humbled themselves before God and were clearly converted.

One young Christian worker insisted he was saved, but he could not deceive the Holy Spirit. One night in his courtyard the Holy Spirit struck him down, and he was carried in stiff, blue, and cold. People knelt around him, praying. A missionary urged him to confess his sins. As soon as the young man could open his mouth, he confessed and was instantly joyous and completely well again.

A MISSIONARY REVIVED

In 1932 real revival came. The mission reports were thrilling. Every member of the faculty of the North China Baptist Theological Seminary had been filled with the Holy Spirit. Many of the hospital staff at Hwanghsien had been saved and others filled with the Spirit. At Tsinan more people had been saved than in any previous year. Nearly every one of the preachers, teachers, Bible women, and missionaries there "had an experience of the deeper life, and each one began to have genuine victory and power in his life."[4] Another report said, "The sheer joy and rapture of this new marvelous, intimate fellowship into which we were brought with the glorified Redeemer Himself is beyond the power of human expression."[5] Revival had indeed come.

The revival spread. From Pingtu a missionary wrote, "We estimate that 3000 have been saved this year. There have been about 900 baptisms, with others waiting. 'The Acts of the Holy Spirit' are being reenacted in a remarkable way right here in our midst."[6] Revival began to spread all over Shantung.

Dr. Culpepper went to Pingtu to see for himself the place where God had worked so mightily. He saw the transformed living of revived people, the many new converts, and how God was working. He returned to Hwanghsien, a large Baptist center, and reported. Those at the center arranged for special meetings with an outside evangelist.

On Monday morning they began special prayer meetings to prepare for the revival services. They met at 5:00 A.M., 10:00 A.M., 2:00 P.M., and in the evening. The Holy Spirit applied Romans 2:17–24, and Dr. Culpepper became deeply convicted. He spent much of the night in prayer. In the morning he confessed to about forty missionary and Chinese coworkers his unworthiness, spiritual impotence, and heart need. Soon the others began to fall on their knees. A missionary and a Chinese leader confessed to each other that they had hated each other.

Confessions and prayer continued all that day and night, all the next day, and many even prayed through the second night. Others arrived, some gripped by the Spirit, and they began confessing their sin. The prayer meeting continued unbroken from Monday morning through Thursday. By that time two hundred were in attendance. By Friday night nearly all two hundred were revived, and they sang and praised God for hours.

Culpepper and two Chinese preachers had agreed to meet Saturday night to pray to be filled with the Spirit. Culpepper had been hesitant and fearful to make a full surrender, but God applied Luke 11:9–13 to his heart. He was able to trust God's promise as he surrendered all. The Holy Spirit flooded his soul, and for half an hour he was "completely enraptured" in Jesus. "Human words and man's mind cannot understand nor explain what I heard and saw. The experience is as if it happened yesterday. The Lord became more real to me than any human being had ever been. He took complete control of my soul—removing all hypocrisy, sham, and unrighteousness—and filled me with His divine love, purity, compassion, and power."[7] It seemed to Culpepper that his heart burst with love and compassion for others: for his wife, children, coworkers, and the unsaved. For the first time he experienced the Holy Spirit powerfully interceding through him (Rom. 8:26–27).

TEN-DAY REVIVAL

Sunday was a glorious day. Culpepper had never before experienced such prayer and fellowship in the morning service. That night fifteen people came to the Culpepper home for further prayer, and all fifteen were filled with the Spirit.

On Monday students came back from their homes. Revival broke out in the girls' high school, boys' high school, seminary, and the hospital. They began services in the large chapel, which seated fifteen hundred, and the two schools filled it in special services twice a day. In every service dozens came forward to pray. They filled the front and the aisles, kneeling, praying, confessing their sins, and weeping before God.

The revival services lasted ten days. All six hundred girl students professed salvation, and nine hundred of the

thousand boy students. A number of students had formed a
secret communist society, but when their leader stood up to
challenge Dr. Culpepper, the Holy Spirit knocked him to
the floor and under a bench. The student confessed, but he
refused to repent and left the school. Within a week he was
dead. Other members of the communist society confessed
their hatred of God and the missionaries, but only about half
were saved. All of the others left school.

The revival spread to every Baptist church and chapel
in the county. About twenty to thirty people were baptized
every month. Then the revival spread into adjoining counties. Five revival centers developed, and revival fire spread
across Shantung province and then to Honan, Manchuria,
and Anhoei provinces. Eventually it spread into other
denominations.

Repeatedly the revival spread or received new outpourings as people became filled with the Holy Spirit. Perhaps the most outstanding result of the Shantung revival was
that witnessing became spontaneous and empowered by the
Spirit.

FROM THE INSIDE OUT

As key evangelistic teams moved from city to city
across the province, they first helped Christians seek right
relationships and the infilling of the Spirit. The Spirit-filled
were then led by the Holy Spirit to seek the lost. In the
words of a team member, "It's easy to win the lost when
Christ's Spirit has free, clear channels through which to
work."[8]

Many examples from this period reveal God's working. In a mission school in which nearly all of the students
had come from pagan homes, two teachers were filled with
the Spirit. Soon every student was saved, and the teachers
traveled from house to house evangelizing. They saw many
converted.

Revival reached all three Baptist hospitals. Several nurses were saved and filled with the Spirit. The sick were saved daily. Two women were filled with the Spirit and walked ten miles to their home village. They testified to their home church, and soon people were "confessing their sins" and then "searching for the fullness of the Holy Spirit. After receiving it, they, in turn, began telling the story; and revival spread like fire throughout the countryside."[9]

Spirit-filled students and lecturers used Saturdays and Sundays to witness everywhere. Reports were given in the daily evening prayer meetings. "One of the outstanding features of the revival is personal testimony. People went everywhere witnessing."[10] Another outstanding result of the revival was a new interest in Bible study. Shops kept selling out of Bibles. Short-term Bible classes were held, many meeting every night. Before the revival, seminary enrollment had decreased to four. Now it increased to 150.

Within a few months church attendance multiplied enormously. Many churches began to discipline their members when Bible standards were not upheld, something that had not been done before.

REVIVAL BRINGS CHANGE

Another outstanding result of the revival was a new spirit of prayer. People loved to pray. Often prayer meetings lasted two to three hours. "The prayers were not long and monotonous, but fervent, sometimes tearful, always as if those praying were simply talking to the Father with the confidence that He was listening. It was beautiful to hear them pray for each other. . . . There was no cheap advertising of prayer for the sick; but in simple, childlike faith these people prayed for the sick, and many were healed."[11]

Repentance and confession of sin, not healing, were the main emphases of church teaching. But God gave unusual healings. A man who crawled like a worm because his legs were grown together was instantly healed and became a gospel preacher. An old man dying of tuberculosis, with his coffin and grave clothes already prepared, suddenly leaped up and said, "I am well." He sold the coffin and started a church building fund. Through the healings, God opened new doors for the Gospel.

In another village a dying woman was already dressed in her grave clothes when a new convert came and prayed for her. The woman was instantly healed. The new convert witnessed to her and then sent for a missionary. Her whole family and a large number of other villagers were saved. About twenty in the village were filled with the Spirit.

In Pingtu a graduate of a renowned missionary hospital had joined an anti-Christian political party and had taken a public oath to reject the foreign religion. He remarked that if two of his paralyzed patients were healed he would believe in Christ. Two of his patients, one who had been paralyzed eighteen years and the other twenty-eight years, were instantly healed. The doctor began to tremble from fear and Holy Spirit conviction. He repented and was saved. He immediately began to do personal evangelism among the members of the anti-Christian political party.

Another result of the revival was constant singing. Many put Scripture verses to music. Old illiterate people memorized the songs and sang with tears of joy flowing down their faces. Dr. Culpepper said many old women who could not carry a tune were filled with the Spirit and began singing almost like angels.

A wonderful spirit of worship settled on the services. At times entire congregations would bow in silent worship. Then suddenly people would pray aloud and praise God for up to an hour. Without even a sermon, when an invitation was given to come forward and accept Christ, many were saved. Even baptismal services were so marked by God's presence that they led to conversions.

During the revival many were called into the ministry. One skeptic and scoffer was wonderfully saved. In the closing service of the series of meetings he was filled with the Spirit. Within a few days he had read the whole Bible through. God gave the former skeptic great compassion for the lost. Wherever he went the power of God was upon him, and he led many to Christ.

Dr. Culpepper journeyed throughout the entire province of Shantung, visiting hamlets and farms, and wherever he went he found evidence of the revival. Churches were crowded and at times had to be enlarged to accommodate crowds of up to a thousand. Old habits and pagan customs were changed, and people testified to cleansing from sin. Christians had new soul-winning zeal.

In previous years it had been difficult to get the interest and attention of the non-Christians. Now the Holy Spirit was convicting and working so powerfully that unbelievers came at their own initiative seeking salvation. God gave new unity, and Christians confessed openly and prayed for one another. Even missionaries confessed their hidden sins. Personal and racial problems between missionaries and Chinese were dissolved. Thousands of people gave up their idols. The Christians found new joy in giving, and many paid up their tithes that were in arrears. The revival spread into university circles, and many college students were saved.

The Shantung revival is a wonderful example of how God sends a harvest among the non-Christians after the Christians are revived. The Shantung revival lasted for about five years. Hundreds of churches were revived and thousands of people were saved.

CHAPTER THIRTY-NINE

The East Africa Revival

Beginning in 1930, a fifty-year revival characterized by church planting and harvest occurred in East Africa, primarily in the east-central African countries of Rwanda, Burundi, and Uganda. The revival stemmed from the work of the Church Missionary Society, one of more than thirty Anglican missionary societies. CMS was conservative in its theology, especially during this revival period, and was strongly influenced by the Keswick movement's emphasis on experiencing new birth, being filled with the Holy Spirit, and living a life of spiritual victory.

REVIVAL HUNGER IN RWANDA

The Rwanda Mission of the Church Missionary Society was founded in 1920. The missionaries and members soon sensed the need for revival. They were greatly helped and blessed by the book *How to Live the Victorious Life* by An Unknown Christian. After five years, there were already 150 village churches and a large central church seating two thousand. But soon the church began to suffer when members became involved in drinking, sexual vice, witchcraft, and other sins. In 1927 a week of prayer and humiliation before God was held on the field and in the homelands by supporters. They sought "a wonderful outpouring of God the Holy Ghost . . . that in its flood will reach the uttermost parts of Rwanda in the days to come."[1] The immediate result was an increase in attendance to sometimes a thousand people at a service. People had to sit outside because the church buildings were too small.

In 1929 Dr. Joe Church, one of the missionary leaders, felt depressed, weary, and at the end of his rope. For months he had struggled to deal with the seeming endless deaths from famine and the inability to meet all the needs. He longed for a companion who also hungered for the fullness of the Holy Spirit and the victorious life. God gave him a key young African, Simeon Nsibambi, a government employee who agreed with Church heart and soul. As the two prayed together, God gave Church his "share in the power of Pentecost."[2] From August 1931 there began a series of revival events that prepared the way of the Lord and deepened the revival work of the Spirit. God prepared godly local African leaders at Gahini, both among the manual workers and the staff. Opposition, problems, and persecution increased. Satan realized that God was at work.

Even before the new large church at Gahini was complete, the members met there for their first confirmation meeting. On Tuesday they began having meetings twice a day for Bible study and prayer, especially on the subjects of consecration and the Holy Spirit. At least a thousand people attended. Morning prayer meetings sometimes began even before 4:00 A.M. In November great enthusiasm came when the first New Testaments in their language arrived. At Christmas, over two thousand people packed the new church and overflowed to the outside.

THE ABAKA

From 1931 on the Holy Spirit revived men and women everywhere in Rwanda and set them aflame. Many became deeply convicted of their sin, humbled themselves in real repentance, confessed their sins, asked forgiveness from people they had wronged, and made restitution. They sought and received forgiveness and cleansing and lived victoriously over the sins of their past. Those born again began to be called the "Abaka" (those on fire). "They were marked men, joy shone in their faces, and everywhere they went they had a testimony."[3]

Little teams of revived believers began to go from place to place witnessing. One old villager and a friend journeyed five hundred miles witnessing and learning the needs of the various places they visited so they could pray for them better.

The leader of the evangelists' training school was burdened by the unresponsiveness of his students. He took a week's leave of absence to pray, fast, and study the Word, pleading for a new endowment of the Holy Spirit. Soon he became radiant with the presence of the Lord.

God also raised up William Nagenda, who became a mighty leader of revival among Africans and Europeans throughout the churches in Rwanda, Uganda, Kenya, and the Sudan.

In October 1933 a two-man Keswick delegation arrived from Britain and held the first Keswick convention on the field at Kabale. During that convention the Spirit worked deeply among the missionaries, and they realized that they were not really a praying mission. They began quarterly meetings for prayer and fellowship. God led them to deal with tensions arising between the clergy and the lay people.

At a second revival convention that year, God broke through during the final prayer session, and deep conviction of sin and a spirit of confession prevailed for two and a half hours. Some of the wives of the coworkers were also mightily changed by the revival. Roman Catholic opposition increased, backed up by some Belgium representatives.

From 1933 on, Bible teaching conferences were held each year. Soon senior Christians organized themselves into evangelistic teams. Several of the saved hospital staff built small, thatched prayer huts or separate rooms on their houses so they could spend more time alone with God. When a missionary suggested an early morning prayer meeting for the hospital staff at 5:00 A.M. each day, they smiled and said they already prayed earlier than that each day. The next morning the hospital workers were on his veranda at 4:00 A.M., and they prayed for two hours. One day after Christmas, during an "ordinary" prayer meeting, God suddenly broke in with real conviction of sin. For two and a half hours there was brokenness, confession of sin, and earnest prayer.

God convicted the missionaries about their British reserve and lack of intimacy with one another, with the Africans, and even with their families. Many also, both Africans and missionaries, felt a new freedom in personal and group evangelism and a new burden for the lost.

In 1935 the Protestant Alliance of Rwanda-Burundi was formed by the Anglican, Danish Baptist, American Friends, Free Methodist, and Nazarene missionaries.

FROM RWANDA TO UGANDA

The African bishop of the Uganda church desired revival in his theological college at Muono. He asked two missionaries from Rwanda, Joe Church and Lawrence Barham, to bring a team from Rwanda. Joe Church sent out a call for prayer in the form of a pamphlet. God used his message to raise up a great volume of prayer for the first time in the history of the mission. As prayer ascended, the whole revival movement surged forward. Prayer intensified for several months. In June 1936, a convention was held, and the Holy Spirit worked mightily.

Simultaneously revival broke out at Gahini in Rwanda on June 24, 1936. It seemed as though the Holy Spirit with His unseen hand gathered together the hospital staff, men from the nearby village, and others in a room in the hospital. They prayed and sang, and some were smitten down under a tremendous conviction of sin. Revival swept into the girls' school, and similar manifestations came from five different centers across the mission. Everywhere the mysterious power of the Holy Spirit was at work. Fifty students at the theological college were revived. Revival song and prayer prevailed in each place as confessions and reconciliations were made.

In the holidays that followed, the seventy evangelists in training were so on fire that they traveled in revival teams of two or three at their own expense. During the next three years, revival teams went out from Rwanda to Uganda, Kenya, Tanganyika, the Sudan, and Congo.

The East African revival continually emphasized the cross and the power of the blood of Jesus. The revived Africans were afraid of the nominalism in the church among the unrevived. They boldly denounced sin and hypocrisy among both Africans and missionaries. Often those who were rebuked broke down and confessed, though there were some who were strongly opposed to humbling themselves in public.

By 1942 the African Rwanda Mission numbered 20,000 converts, with other adherents bringing the total to 50,000. The seven hundred village congregations had 2,210 baptisms the previous year, and there were 1,400 trained workers, five of whom were ordained.

CONVENTIONS IMPACT THE CHURCH

During the war God used interdenominational conventions year after year to bring refreshment and revival. The largest convention, held in 1945, had fifteen to twenty thousand in attendance. The theme of the conference was "Jesus Satisfies." God intervened in a striking way. One mission after another was filled with the Spirit, and with tears of joy they celebrated in their deeper unity.

These thousands were not the fruit of some mass movement but were drawn to Christ by the victorious living of spiritually hungry and radiant believers. The fourfold emphasis of the conference was: (1) victory over sin; (2) confession and repentance; (3) fellowship with believers; (4) and the lordship of Jesus Christ.

The main work of the Spirit at this time, however, was in maintaining and deepening the life of the churches. A serious famine provided opportunity for the Christians to show love in practical ways. Even during the famine enthusiastic services of praise and song went on night after night to the amazement of the non-Christians. Misery and despair were all around, but the Christians were full of joy. There was a steady stream of conversions, many of them quite notable. High standards of honesty and morality were enforced everywhere, home and family life was transformed, and practical holiness was demonstrated everywhere. There was a constant emphasis upon the cross of Christ and on the Holy Spirit.

In 1952 great conventions were held in East Africa at Kako in Uganda, where one hundred Europeans and eight hundred Africans were present. Never before had so many tribes been present in such a convention. God gave revival-type blessings. In the meantime, God was using the East Africa message.

Spiritual warfare could be expected, and there were those who were critical as the revival movement continued year after year. Some thought the revival singing and dancing, which often lasted late into the night, went to an extreme. But this is the African way to express joy. Some objected to the constant emphasis on sin and repentance. In

Rwanda Mission there was a God-given hunger for more holiness and Christlikeness. The Christians there saw revival as repentance and daily coming to Jesus with a broken and contrite heart.

Some criticized the revived people for acting superior and exclusive. But revival is a kind of revolt against low spirituality. The revived people did not want to compromise God's standards for His church. The reluctance to cooperate with Christians who did not cooperate in the revival may have gone too far at times, but the desire to maintain the spirituality of the church fellowship is commendable and understandable.

These tendencies did not cause nearly as much criticism and questioning in the young church in Rwanda as it did in the older church of Uganda, which had had its church structure and leadership for years before the revival began. Some Church of England friends felt someone should be sent to "control" the revived people, but this could easily have led to grieving and stopping the work of the Holy Spirit. Leadership from within the revival needed to be raised up and guided. Someone from the outside could not as fully understand or as wisely lead.

FIRE, FELLOWSHIP, AND THE CROSS

Looking back on the work of the Spirit over the first twenty-five years of the Church Missionary Society in Uganda, Dr. Stanley Smith, an integral part of the revival movement, summarized it with three words: fire, fellowship, and the cross.

God's promise is, "He will baptize you with the Holy Spirit and with fire" (Matt. 3:11). The revival demonstrated that the church's one vital need is the fire of the Spirit. The revived people over the years were known as the Abaka ("those aflame"). Praise God, the revival fire continued to burn in their hearts year after year.

Unity in fellowship is essential if God is to give revival. Continuing holy fellowship was the secret to the continuance of the East African revival. The revival was characterized by: (1) regular fellowship meetings for the revived; (2) transparent sincerity—there was freedom but no compulsion to confess faults and failures in the fellowship meeting; and (3) honesty—Christians took the iniative in reproof and reconciliation.

The East Africa revival began within the Church of England and spread most greatly within that church. Separation from the Anglican church was not encouraged; instead the African Christians sought an even stronger relationship with all evangelicals. The twenty-five years of revival helped produce within the Anglican church 25,105 baptized members, 7,362 communicant members, and 1,089 village churches.

Taking up Christ's cross meant, for some in east Africa, persecution and martyrdom. As the story of the Rwanda revival spread and both missionary and African leaders from Rwanda told the revival story in surrounding African countries, the work of revival spread wider and wider. Revival conventions were held at times in Uganda and Kenya. The goal of the revived people was to continue walking with Jesus (1) in holy obedience, (2) in daily submission to the cross, (3) in daily transparency, and (4) in daily victory. It was the men and women of the revival fellowship who saved the church during the persecution and martyrdom of the Mau Mau uprising in Kenya in 1953.

In the 1960s others died heroically in Rwanda and Burundi because they hid or rescued members of an opposing tribe. In the 1970s when Muslim ruler Idi Amin killed hundreds of thousands of Christians, again it was the revival Christians who stood the test. Their slogan was, "We live today and are gone tomorrow." Bishop Bates states, "During this period Archbishop Luwum of Kampala, Uganda, was murdered. Four thousand people walked unintimidated past Idi Amin's guards to the Luwum funeral on February 20, 1977, where they sang the Martyr's Song, sung first by the Ugandan martyrs in 1885. Luwum and thousands of those who attended his funeral were products of the East Africa Revival and members of his fellowship were part of a deeper spiritual movement within the framework of the Anglican church in which they were often holders of high offices."[4]

A WIDENING IMPACT

Bishop Gerald E. Bates of the Free Methodist Church, who spent twenty-seven years in East Africa, states that the revival movement "revolutionized the spiritual orientation of whole missions and denominations, brought salvation to hundreds of thousands, and left an indelible stamp on the character of mid-African Christianity."[5]

In 1988 Bishop Bates reported that in some areas the revival had virtually disappeared, but that in others there was still "a beloved stratum of authenticity which springs to the surface at times of spiritual renewal or in times of great stress."[6]

In the meantime, God used the East Africa revival message to bring hunger and open doors for revival challenge in centers in Switzerland (1947), Britain (1949), France (1949), Moldavia (1951), Angola (1952), and India (1952). In East Africa itself the pattern from 1952 to 1972 became smaller missions and widespread weekend gatherings. Team members visited the United States in 1952, and France, Germany, and Switzerland in 1953. Other team members took the revival message to Ethiopia, Pakistan, Australia, the Far East, and Brazil.

The movement of the Spirit in the East Africa Revival differs in some aspects from other revival movements recorded in earlier chapters. In earlier revivals, a mighty outpouring of the Spirit came to an area over a limited period of time, and during that short period brought many to Christ through deep awareness of the presence of God, overwhelming conviction of sin, and instantly transformed lives. Often the impact upon the community and area brought profound moral blessing and change. These revivals for the most part took place among people in a nominally Christian civilization who had had long previous acquaintance with Christianity.

In East Africa, the revival movement came first to Christian groups: churches and educational and medical institutions founded by Christian missions. Then God used the revived Christians to bring new people to Christ and His church. The Spirit moved from "islands" of at least nominal Christians out into hitherto unevangelized areas.

The East Africa revival went on for many years, with outstanding occurrences here and there of spiritual blessing at conventions, ordination services, or other church or mission conferences. There were from time to time fresh outpourings of the Spirit. Often these occasions were interspersed with longer periods during which Christians sought to live and serve in a revived manner, to pursue godly living and transparent relationships, and to be constantly ready to ask forgiveness, confess sin or failure, and endeavor to preserve the unity of the Spirit.

The holy influence of these revival emphases and teachings has impacted widening areas of Anglican missionary work and the life and ministry of many other church groups, particularly those in Africa. For a period of time in the 1950s, a missionary leader and a key African leader of the revival shared the reports and blessings of revival in East Africa in selected churches, conventions, and gatherings in Europe, Asia, and America. Undoubtedly God used the East Africa revival to contribute to harvest and church growth as is found in Africa today.

CHAPTER FORTY

The Revival
in the Hebrides

The island of Lewis and Harris, the largest island of the outer Hebrides, lies off the northwest coast of Scotland. Lewis is the northern part of the island. From time to time since 1828, God in mercy has visited Lewis with revival. Three Presbyterian denominations had churches on the island.

A number of Christians prayed that God would again send revival. In one village a minister felt God confirmed His promise that there would be a harvest in his congregation. His wife in a dream saw the church filled with anxious people and an unknown minister in the pulpit.

PREPARE YE THE WAY

In 1949 in the village of Barvas, Rev. James Murray MacKay was the parish minister. For months he and his church leaders prayed for an outpouring of the Spirit. In a small cottage lived two elderly sisters: Peggy Smith, aged eighty-four and blind, and her sister Christine Smith, eighty-two and almost bent double with arthritis. They were unable to attend worship, but for months they prayed in their cottage for God to send revival to Barvas.

The sisters prayed by name for the people in each cottage along the village streets. They loved their church and respected their minister, but longed for a new visitation of God. God gave them the promise, "I will pour water on the thirsty land, and streams on the dry ground" (Isa. 44:3). The Smith sisters prayed this promise day and night.

On the other side of Barvas, knowing nothing about the prayer burden of the Smith sisters, seven young men met three nights a week in a barn to pray for revival. They entered into a covenant with God in accordance with Isaiah 62:6–7 that they would give God no rest until He sent revival. "I have posted watchmen on your walls, O Jerusalem; they will never be silent day or night. You who call on the LORD, give yourselves no rest, and give him no rest till he establishes Jerusalem and makes her the praise of the earth" (Isa. 62:6–7). Month after month they prevailed.

One night one young deacon took his Bible and read to the other young men on their knees from Psalm 24:3–5, "Who may ascend the hill of the LORD? Who may stand in his holy place? He who has clean hands and a pure heart. . . . He will receive blessing from the LORD." The deacon said to the others, "Brethren, is it not so much humbug to be waiting thus night after night if we ourselves are not right with God?" Lifting his hands toward heaven, he cried, "Oh, God! Are my hands clean? Is my heart pure?" Instantly he fell prostrated on the floor. An awesome awareness of God filled the barn. God released "a stream of supernatural power in their lives."[1] The blood of Jesus Christ poured in and cleansed their souls (1 John 1:7). That night they found themselves searched by the holiness of God and saw things in their lives they had never suspected.

That same morning God gave one of the Smith sisters a vision. Peggy Smith saw the churches crowded with people, including many young people, and hundreds being swept into the kingdom. She saw the Lamb in the midst of the throne with the keys of heaven in his hand (Rev. 5:6; Matt. 16:18). Peggy Smith sent word to Rev. MacKay that God had shown her He was going to send a mighty revival. She asked him to call together the elders and deacons of the church for special times of waiting on God for revival.

The pastor and church leaders prayed repeatedly for several months. Rev. MacKay felt led to plan a parish mission in the winter. The question was, who should he call? In September he went to the Strathpeffer Convention and asked the speaker, Dr. Tom Fitch, to recommend someone to come to the Hebrides for a revival series. Dr. Fitch told him there was a Gaelic-speaking minister in Edinburgh, Rev. Duncan Campbell, who was free to hold missions.

When Campbell arrived, Rev. MacKay and two of his elders met him at the pier. Campbell looked so pale after the choppy voyage that one of the elders wondered if he was fit to preach. One elder asked him, "Mr. Campbell, are you walking with God?" Duncan Campbell realized that these men were living on a high spiritual plane. As he walked along the village road the next day, he sensed that God was hovering near and was already at work.

GRIPPED BY THE SPIRIT

That night Campbell preached on "The Wise Virgins" and the following night on "The Foolish Virgins." The second service closed with intense silence. God was speaking to hearts. At the close, Campbell dismissed the crowd and the building emptied. But suddenly the church door opened again and an elder motioned for Campbell to come to the door. The entire congregation was standing outside, so gripped by the Holy Spirit they did not want to leave. Other people who had not attended were drawn from their homes by the irresistible power of the Holy Spirit. Many faces showed deep distress.

Campbell called everyone back inside the church. The awesome presence of God was so profound that unsaved people began to groan with distress and pray in repentance. Even Christians felt the weight of their sinfulness. Suddenly a cry pierced the air. One of the prayer warriors of the young men's prayer group was burdened to the point of agony as he poured out his soul for revival. He fell prostrate on the floor in a trance. Strong men cried for mercy, and as person after person received assurance of salvation, some praised God and even shouted for joy. A mother stood with her arms around her son, thanking God, as tears of joy streamed down her face. Prayers of years were answered.

Rev. MacKay went the next day to the Smith sisters to tell them what had happened. They told him they had prevailed in prayer the previous night. "We struggled through the hours of the night, refusing to take a denial. . . . Our God is a covenant-keeping God and He must be true to His covenant engagements. Did He fail us? Never! Before the morning light broke we saw the enemy retreating, and our wonderful Lamb taking the field."[2]

News of the revival spread immediately across the island. The next night buses arrived from various places filled with men and women anxious to hear and see what God was doing. In a few days, work throughout the area was largely set aside as people prayed for themselves, friends, and neighbors. People prayed and found God in homes, barns, loom-sheds, by the roadside, and by peat stacks. Revival fire spread to other villages and calls came from other churches.

SATURATED WITH GOD

The whole region seemed saturated with God. Wherever people were—in their homes, fields, on the road—they were awesomely aware of God's presence. Visitors to the island noticed it and remarked on it. An unsaved man came to the minister's home one day for prayer. Rev. MacKay told him he had not seen him in the services. The man responded, "I haven't been to church, but this revival is in the air. I can't get away from the Spirit."[3]

A man from another village had been running from God for years. When his sister told him what was happening in Barvas, he was frightened and even prayed to God to keep this man Campbell away from his village. When Duncan Campbell came for several nights the man refused to attend. Eventually he gave in and came. In his message, Campbell described people who made vows to serve God when they were in danger at sea but had not fulfilled them. The man, who had experienced something similar, became tremendously angry. He thought that his sister had told Campbell about his experience on a torpedoed boat during the war. He determined to get even with his sister. God gripped him with deep conviction, and the next day Campbell visited his home and prayed with him there.

That night the man became burdened with such unbearable conviction of the Holy Spirit that at the close of the service he scrambled over people to get to the place of prayer. He called out, "I am lost, really lost! There is nothing but hell for me!" Duncan Campbell said he had better pray for himself and ask God for mercy. The man fell on his knees and began to pray. Almost instantly he received the assurance of the forgiveness of sins. He seemed to see on the floor "the locks and chains of sin which had bound him." Christ set him free. "Later as he met an elder by the roadside, a circle of light seemed to envelop them, and looking up to locate the source he found himself gazing into the face of his Savior."[4]

"Have you done business with God today?" was a frequent way people greeted each other on the roadside. Christians seemed led by the Spirit to homes where people were praying. A woman milking a cow was led to go immediately and plead with a neighbor. A bus driver became so burdened he stopped the bus and pled with the passengers to repent, feeling sure that someone was hearing God's last call to salvation and would not be returning home with them. The warning went unheeded, and before the return journey a young man who had been on the bus was killed in tragic circumstances.

WATER UPON THE DRY GROUND

Campbell was beginning meetings in another church in another part of the island. The minister was out in the field when suddenly Campbell came running from the pastor's study, calling out, "It's coming! It's coming! We've got through at last! We are over the top!" That very night revival broke and God's presence was everywhere. People were drawn to the church. Even people who never came near it were convicted.

Campbell went to the village of Arnol, but many people there remained aloof. He called for a night of prayer in the home of an elder. Around midnight Campbell turned to a blacksmith and said, "John, I feel the time has come for you to pray." With his cap in his hand, John rose to pray, and in the middle of the prayer he paused, raised his right hand to heaven, and said, "O God, You made a promise to pour water upon him that is thirsty and floods upon the dry ground, and Lord, it's not happening." He paused again and then continued, "Lord, if I know anything about my own heart I stand before Thee as an empty vessel thirsting for Thee and for a manifestation of Thy power." He halted again, and after a moment of tense silence, cried, "O God, Your honor is at stake, and I now challenge You to fulfill Your covenant engagement and do what You have promised to do."[5]

At that very moment the house shook, dishes rattled in the sideboard, and wave after wave of God's power swept through the building. Some thought there had been an earth-quake, but Duncan Campbell remembered Acts 4:31. When Campbell pronounced the benediction and they went out-side, the people felt as if the whole community was alive with an awareness of God. A stream of blessing was released which brought salvation to many homes during the suc-ceeding nights.

One night the service did not end until between one and two o'clock in the morning. People were just beginning to disperse when a messenger arrived saying that revival had broken out in another church several miles away. Rev. Campbell, the minister, and about two hundred people started across the fields, taking a shortcut to the other church. Suddenly the sky was filled with the sound of angelic voices singing. Everyone heard it, and they fell on their knees in the field. Some were saved as they knelt there. Then they went on to the other service.

A fifteen-year-old boy named Donald was wonder-fully converted and became an outstanding helper in the revival. One day Campbell called at Donald's home and found him on his knees in the barn with an open Bible before him. Donald quietly said, "Excuse me a little, Mister Campbell, I am having an audience with the King." In a ser-vice one night this youth stood up, clasped his hands together and uttered the one word, "Father."[6] Everyone was immediately melted to tears by the presence of God invad-ing the house. And this extraordinary young man went on to play an important role in the Berneray revival.

BERNERAY REVIVAL

A second wave of revival came in April 1952, this time to the small island of Berneray. On Easter Monday 1952, Duncan Campbell had just given an address at The Faith Mission Convention being held in the Hamilton Road Pres-byterian Church in Bangor, Northern Ireland. Campbell sensed God calling him to Berneray, and so he went immediately.

Campbell told me, "Now mind you, I had never met anyone from Berneray, I had never had any letter from Berneray, and I did not know anyone on Berneray." When they reached the island's shore, the boatmen lifted out Campbell's suitcases and started back toward Harris. Campbell had to climb a steep bluff, and when he got to the top, he found he was in a field. He saw a young man plowing in the field.

Campbell lugged his two suitcases over to where the young man was and asked him to take him to the home of their pastor. The boy responded that they had not had a pastor on the island for some years. Campbell asked him, "Do you have elders?" "Oh, yes," he said. Duncan Campbell said, "Go to the nearest elder and tell him that Duncan Campbell has arrived. If he asks which Campbell, tell him the minister who was in Lewis." Duncan was exhausted and sat down on the heavy suitcases.

After some time he saw the young man hustling across the field toward him. The young man said, "Here, let me carry your suitcases. The elder said to tell you that the service will be at nine o'clock tonight." When Duncan met the elder, he asked him, "How did you know I was coming?" The elder told him that three days before he was in his barn and had spent most of the day praying. As he prayed he felt impressed that God would send Duncan Campbell. "Lord, I don't know where he is," the elder prayed, "but You know, and with You all things are possible. You send him to the island." The farmer was so certain that God would bring Campbell in three days' time that he sent announcements all around the island announcing a service at nine o'clock Thursday evening.[7]

In the first services there seemed to be no response. Campbell was tired, but the elder insisted God was going to send revival. At the close of the service one night, Duncan Campbell dismissed the congregation and then stayed behind after all had left the church. Suddenly the elder came back and called him to the door. He said, "Mr. Campbell, see what's happening! He has come! He has come!"[8] The Holy Spirit had so gripped the people as they went down the lane toward the main road that they had stopped. No one could move any further. People began to sigh and groan from the burden of sin. Campbell called them back into the church, and a mighty movement of the Spirit began.

When Campbell encountered spiritual resistance, he sent for some people to come from Barvas and help with prayer. Fifteen-year-old Donald was among them, and he carried a deep burden for souls. One night, sensing difficulty in preaching, Campbell stopped and asked Donald to lead in prayer. The young lad rose to his feet, made reference to the fourth chapter of Revelation, which he had read that morning, and then prayed, "O God, I seem to be gazing through the open door. I see the Lamb in the midst of the throne, with the keys of death and of hell at his girdle." He began to sob.

Then lifting his eyes upward, Donald cried, "O God, there is power there, let it loose!" Instantly it was as if a hurricane swept through the building. "The floodgates of heaven opened. The church resembled a battlefield. On one side many were prostrated over the seats weeping and sobbing; on the other side some were affected by throwing their arms in the air in a rigid posture. God had come."[9] Throughout the island there was immediately a new liberty and a new sense of God's presence at work.

Meetings continued day and night. During one twenty-four-hour period, Campbell preached eight times: in crowded churches five times, twice in an open field to crowds, and once by the seashore. At times when Campbell left one church to go to another, he left behind hundreds of people who were crying to God for mercy. As he left another church, elders sent a young man to call him to a field where he found three to five hundred people waiting. Some were prostrate on the ground asking God for mercy. Four teenage girls gathered around a deeply convicted sinner, and as they prayed with him they told him the God who had saved them the night before could save him now.

Duncan Campbell preached to the newly converted to make a full surrender of their lives and receive the fullness of the Spirit. He said, "I believe it was because the people of Lewis grasped that truth we can say today we know practically nothing of backsliding from that gracious movement of years ago. It is because they entered into the fullness. Because of that, a stream of men and women went into full-time service."[10]

In December 1957 the third wave of revival came to the Hebrides, this time on the island of North Uist. Uist had never known revival. God began to work sovereignly in the village of Lochmaddy. As the news spread of what was happening in Lochmaddy, revival spread to a neighboring parish. The meetings were crowded, and night after night souls were seeking God. People walked miles over roads and fields to where services were being held.

GOD'S GRACE AT BIBLE COLLEGE

In place after place where Campbell visited, God's presence accompanied him in an unusual way. God seemed to give him an extra dose of the supernatural, demonstrated not so much in powerful and amazing works, but in people becoming aware of the presence of Jesus, the glory of the Lord, and the nearness of the heavenly world. But like Charles G. Finney, Duncan Campbell did not give his whole life to revival ministries. He also became involved in Bible college work.

After recurring health problems required Rev. Campbell to slow down in his itinerant ministry, he was invited in 1958 to become the principal of Faith Mission Bible College in Edinburgh. Friday mornings were devoted to prayer and waiting on the Lord by the college family. Campbell continued to deliver burning messages, and the students sat trembling as he taught them God's Word. "There was something sacred about the way he used God's name, and often the atmosphere of heaven filled the room when, with reverence and tenderness, he simply said, 'Jesus.' We felt we were standing on holy ground."[11]

In March 1960, during one of these Friday morning prayer sessions, God visited the college in special revival grace. One student said, "It seemed that if I lifted my head I would look upon God."[12] Wave after wave of the power of the Spirit swept over the group. Many experienced inner cleansing and were empowered for more effective Christian service.

Twice before during Campbell's ministry, God in His amazing grace had caused the people to hear heavenly music. Once during the Lewis revival in the early morning hours, as a group was walking through a glen, "the heavens seemed to be filled with angelic praise, until another minister present cried for joy: 'This is heaven! This is heaven!' "[13]

Campbell did not seek such manifestations, but he appreciated when God drew so amazingly near. He sometimes checked excessive emotions. He was to have retired in 1963 but agreed to remain on for three more years until a successor was appointed.

BEYOND SCOTLAND

At a 1964 convention in Lisburn in Northern Ireland, the convention chairman, sitting alone in a room, suddenly felt the room filled with the brightness of the Lord's presence. He was so overawed with a sense of unworthiness that he went outside. There seemed to be a holy brightness on the plants and flowers. The chairman, overcome with emotion, stepped back into the house. Just then Duncan Campbell stepped up, his face all aglow; he had been praying. Throughout the day God's presence hovered near, and that evening Campbell preached his final message. When the benediction was given, God took over the service. The organist attempted to play, but her hands were powerless to touch the keyboard. The congregation was gripped by holy awe and silence, and no one moved for half an hour. Then people began to pray and weep. Several heard sounds from heaven.

In Aberdare, Wales, after the second service, prayer continued all day and until three o'clock in the morning. People took time off from their employment to pray. On that particular night, after Duncan Campbell had spoken for an hour, six young men sitting side by side suddenly saw the glory of God come down upon Campbell. They fell on the floor weeping. The congregation was gripped by prayer, and one after another people began to repent, confess their sins, and make things right with one another and with God.

God sent to Duncan Campbell a prayer burden for Canada. In June 1969 he preached in a small Baptist church in Saskatoon, Saskatchewan. The pastor for three years had prayed that God would send Duncan Campbell. One night as Campbell preached, he prophesied that God would send revival to Canada and that it would begin in that church. Two years later it happened. Just before the revival broke, Campbell was in his home in Edinburgh and one day was tremendously moved to intercede for two hours in special prayer for a Canadian revival. He felt that God assured him that He was working.

Though weak in body, Duncan did not want to retire. His last words in his last message were, "Keep on fighting, but see that you are fighting in the love of Jesus."[14] Moved by this, the students gathered for a special prayer meeting and asked him to join them. He prayed with them for a little while but felt exhausted and went to bed. At 2:00 A.M. he had a heart attack. On March 28, 1972, the revivalist entered heaven.

CHAPTER FORTY-ONE

Revival Fire on Campuses

Over the past two hundred years God has from time to time sent Holy Spirit revival to the campuses of Bible schools, Christian colleges, and theological seminaries in various parts of the world, but especially in the United States. Among the better known of these have been Asbury College in Wilmore, Kentucky, and Wheaton College in Wheaton, Illinois. However, dozens of other institutions, large and small, have been visited by revival movements of the Spirit.

Just as revival fire has leaped from church to church and nation to nation in a worldwide movement of the Holy Spirit, so campus revival fires have at times leaped from school to school in a holy blaze of revival blessing.

AN AMERICAN PHENOMENON?

Why were revivals more frequent and conspicuous on American campuses than elsewhere in the world? First, the earliest colleges in the United States were not part of large universities but collegiate institutions founded primarily for theological training. This was true of Harvard, William and Mary, Yale, Princeton, Columbia University, Rutgers, Dartmouth, Brown University, and others. In Britain, revival movements have begun more in voluntary societies, such as Wesley's Holy Club at Oxford.

Second, revivals have tended to come to schools where all students were required to attend chapel services. In many schools the students took the initiative in the intercession that prepared the way of the Lord to send revival.

At the time of the American Revolution a tide of skepticism from France and Europe destroyed the Christian emphasis, and a high percentage of college students became atheists. Colleges became centers of profanity, gambling, intemperance, rowdiness, and licentiousness. One year only two students at Princeton professed religion. Colleges were called "seed-beds of infidelity."[1]

The first of the American college revivals occurred in Virginia at Hampden Sydney College in 1787. Praying students formed a small society, and nearly half of the student body was saved in the ensuing revival. Similar groups in other colleges were used by God to prepare the way for spiritual awakenings. Little prayer groups of two or three began to meet privately for prayer. In 1802 one-third of the Yale students professed to receive Christ, and at various colleges twenty, twenty-five, and even as many as fifty students professed to receive salvation.

By the mid-1800s, however, spiritual life was in decline both in society in general and in the colleges. Many actively Christian students became involved in the antislavery movement. Compulsory chapel attendance in many colleges ceased, and the main spiritual awakenings after that in the secular universities occurred in the small student-led Christian groups.

1858–59 CAMPUS REVIVALS

The mighty movement of the Holy Spirit in the revival of the United Prayer Meetings that swept across the United States in 1858–59 saw from one to two million new people

receive Christ and join the churches. Nearly all denominational colleges were touched by this movement of the Spirit.
Collegiate prayer meetings led to repentance, confession,
and restitution. In 1857 God sent revival to Oberlin College
in Ohio, led by Charles G. Finney. Twenty or more college
campuses experienced revival in 1858. Many state universities were impacted by the revival, with many student conversions. Dr. J. Edwin Orr estimates that some five thousand
students made commitments to Christ that year.

In 1858 God sent revival to Williams College, and at
Amherst College nearly all the students were saved. The
most powerful revival since 1821 came to Yale. Almost half
of the students testified to receiving Christ as Savior. There
were effects of the revival experienced in Dartmouth College, Columbia University, and the College of the City of
New York.

In Georgia the 1858–59 revival came to Emory University, Mercer College, and the University of Georgia.
Every student in Oglethorpe University was under deep
conviction of sin, and many were saved.

Student revivals occurred at the University of North
Carolina and at Wake Forest College. At the University of
Virginia there were prayer meetings, conviction of sin, and
conversions. The YMCA was organized at Virginia, and the
revived students went out evangelizing among the black
people and those in the nearby mountains.

The 1858–59 revival swept across the north and
brought new spiritual life to the University of Michigan.
Dennison College in Ohio saw many student conversions,
and the president of the college baptized them in a cold
creek. There were great results at Miami University in
Oxford, Ohio, and a record number entered the ministry.
Wilberforce University in Ohio, for black students, saw
many come to Christ. All these campus revivals were

"solemn and serious, not one charge of fanaticism being found in any record."[2]

A student campus group at Princeton prevailed in prayer for the Moody campaign of 1875 in which about one-third of the student body was converted. In 1872 the intercollegiate Young Men's Christian Association was set up, and by 1890 there were 250 student associations with twelve thousand members focusing on evangelism and prayer.

The 1859 revival profoundly moved the British universities of Oxford and Cambridge, and Prayer Unions were formed. Moody had later campaigns at Oxford and Cambridge. God was beginning a worldwide interdenominational student movement. Among the results was the founding of the Student Volunteer Movement, from which in the next fifty years some twenty thousand students were sent to the mission fields. Indirectly, as a result of this revival, the China Inland Mission was founded as the first of the faith missionary societies, and the InterVarsity Christian Union was established on British campuses.

1905–1908 CAMPUS REVIVALS

In the first decade of the 1900s, God began a mighty revival movement in Wales through young Evan Roberts, who for thirteen years had been pleading with God to send revival. We have described how the Spirit's fire kindled revival as the holy flame leaped from Wales to India to Korea to north China to the United States and other parts of the world. That holy fire also kindled new spiritual life on college campuses. Revival came to Cornell University in 1907–1908. At Princeton at that time more than a thousand of the 1,384 students attended weekly evangelistic meetings.

In the first decade of the century, unusual spiritual interest and responsiveness were found both in cities and on campuses. Atlantic City, New Jersey, claimed that not more than fifty unconverted people were left in the city of sixty thousand. Town after town in New Jersey reported revival. At Rutgers University in 1905, half of the students were in voluntary Bible classes. Newark reported that Pentecost was being repeated, and at Princeton University an average of more than 70 percent of the students attended weekly evangelistic meetings.

Across New England, without any special campaigns, revival and "an intense sensation of the presence of God in the congregations, as in the Welsh revival," was reported in Maine, New Hampshire, Vermont, Massachusetts, Rhode Island, and Connecticut. During the campaigns by evangelist J. Wilbur Chapman in Atlanta and Louisville, stores, factories, and offices almost unanimously closed at noon for prayer. In many educational institutions in 1905, both smaller colleges and large universities, students and faculty led evangelistic meetings without any special campaign or speaker. It was reported that "the Spirit of God is being graciously poured out."[3]

At Trinity College, Durham, North Carolina, one-third of the student body was saved during the revival, and only twenty-five students did not claim to be born again. Similar reports came from South Carolina, Florida, Georgia, Alabama, Louisiana, and Texas. "An extraordinary upheaval shook the Baylor University campus at Waco, Texas. It began in meetings for prayer, continued in confession of sin, resulted in many conversions, and enrolled the majority of the students in classes for missionary preparation."[4]

Space does not permit the recounting of the many thrilling revival events in 1905–1906 at the University of California in Berkeley, Stanford University, Northwestern University, Iowa State College, and McGill University in Montreal. The same evidences of the Holy Spirit's working in Canada occurred as in the United States: prayer for revival, concern for the unsaved, ardent evangelism, and instant response in churches, in the communities, and on the campuses.

At Seattle Pacific College, now a university, revival came on December 19, 1905. "At times the Spirit was so out-poured as to make it impossible to describe the scenes. Wave after wave of blessing, billow after billow of divine glory rolled over the entire congregation. . . . So great was the power of God that the unsaved were unable to resist and a number of them broke down and commenced to seek the Lord. The meeting continued in power and interest until long after midnight, and a number were saved."[5]

At Taylor University in Upland, Indiana, President Winchester preached on "The Baptism of the Holy Spirit" on January 6, 1905. God put such prayer burdens on the active Christian students and such conviction on the unsaved students that academic and social matters were sus-pended for a week and God gave the greatest revival ever known on the campus.

The 1905–1906 collegiate revivals demonstrated that organized campaigns were less fruitful on campuses at that time than spontaneous movements of revival. Out of the revivals came thousands of volunteers for missionary ser-vice, and new interdenominational faith missions were founded. In 1896 some two thousand college students were enrolled in missionary study classes, but in 1906 there were eleven thousand.

WHEATON REVIVALS

Several of the American colleges have maintained their evangelical doctrinal commitment and spiritual fervor throughout this century and have seen revival fire kindled again and again on their campuses. Out of these have come also a large number of foreign missionaries, evangelists, pas-tors, and Christian leaders. Two of these are Wheaton College in the Chicago area and Asbury College in Wilmore, Kentucky.

Wheaton College has long been a bulwark of evangelical life and faith influencing the evangelical movement far and wide since its founding in 1860, right after the 1859 revival. It is not surprising that God has visited Wheaton a number of times with spiritual revival.

In the fall of 1935, a Wheaton student gospel team met Dr. J. Edwin Orr in Toronto and became hungry for revival to come to Wheaton. Don Hillis, Adrian Heaton, Robert Evans, and Jack Murray began to pray. After several months of prayer, Hillis met Orr and asked him when they should expect revival to come to the Wheaton campus. Orr replied, "Whenever Christians get right with God about their sins."[6]

Dr. J. Edwin Orr, who for several decades was much used by God in revival evangelism in various parts of the world and who became the greatest historian of revival, spoke of the Wheaton revival that began in the Wheaton chapel on January 13, 1936. Orr pled before a thousand faculty and students for another campus awakening. Student prayer meetings went on until midnight.

Several weeks later a week of special services was held on the campus. At the close of one message the Dean of Men rose and said he could not understand what was hindering the work of the Spirit. Perhaps there was unconfessed sin. Don Hillis, a student body leader, rose and lamented that Wheaton students so feared emotion that they often hindered the Spirit's power. He then began to confess sin in his own life.

One student after another began to confess. Classes were canceled, lunch was skipped, and after a brief pause at the dinner hour, the service went on with confessions and testimonies till the early morning hours. Profound changes came to the campus. There were many apologies, and restitutions were made day after day. Hardness of heart was replaced by a tender humility. Even faculty members made apologies.

Wheaton was again visited with the Spirit's work in revival during 1943. In February during the midwinter evangelistic services, while a comparatively unknown pastor was speaking, a prominent student athlete came running down the aisle and on to the platform, and in deep repentance confessed sins committed while at Wheaton. People began to stand all over the auditorium, weeping and waiting to confess their own sins and to ask forgiveness.

Throughout the day confessions, testimonies, and prayer continued. After the evening service, the confessions, testimonies, and prayer continued until midnight, when President Edman sent the students to their rooms. Friday morning the speaker turned and wondered if there were no needs among the faculty. Then one after another professor arose, wept, confessed, and testified. Again the service went on until midnight. Sunday afternoon closed with a blessed praise service. Dr. Edman said he believed every person on the campus—student, faculty, and staff—was moved by the Holy Spirit during that revival. Many of the students eventually became evangelical leaders around the world in succeeding decades. Over 30 percent of the graduating class went into full-time Christian service.

In 1948 the Holy Spirit sent another revival breakthrough. It started in Wheaton Bible Church as a young British evangelist, Stephen Olford, was conducting special services. He had spent the entire previous night in prayer under a sense of heavy spiritual burden.

The convicting power of the Holy Spirit came upon the meeting. At the conclusion, every head bowed in prayer. Several prayed and broke down. Then Peter Joshua came forward. He was the brother of Seth Joshua, the man so vitally used by God before and during the Welsh revival of 1904. Joshua had preached the gospel many years, but God convicted him of hypocrisy. "I have been told by God to confess my sin," he said. The Spirit of God moved upon the meeting.

Then the pastor, Rev. Joseph Macaulay, stood and confessed the sin of professionalism. "I have not shed tears for souls. I have tailored my prayers and preaching to impress the university and professors."[7] Then the pastor's wife stood and confessed that she had encouraged him in this. The service went on until 2:00 A.M.

The next day the revival fire leaped from the Wheaton Bible Church to the Wheaton College chapel hour. For two weeks classes were canceled, and the Spirit worked deeply in revival that swept the entire campus. Wheaton acting President Dr. Roger K. Voskuyl said everyone on the campus was touched in one way or another by the revival. A number were born again for the first time. Many others were challenged to a deeper consecration than they had ever known before. The Holy Spirit probed hearts deeply, and many things were made right with the Lord.

Among the many students who responded to God's challenge were all five of the men who later became known as "the Ecuador martyrs." Jim Elliot, perhaps the most famous of these, at Olford's suggestion began keeping a journal of his quiet times, a journal that has challenged thousands. Many other students also responded to God's call to the mission fields.

In 1950, after months of earnest prayer by a number of students, winter evangelistic services were scheduled to begin at Wheaton February 4. Classes met together to implore God for revival. On the evening of the fourth day the Holy Spirit took charge during a planned ten-minute time for testimony. Testimonies and confessions continued without a break. Fifty to one hundred students stood for hours waiting their turn to speak.

In dormitory rooms and houses spontaneous prayer and praise meetings began. The confessions always tended to be specific in the naming of sins, but the sensational was avoided. Most testimonies and confessions were comparatively brief.

At first revival spread mainly among professing Christians, but after twelve hours of the long chapel, unconverted and backslidden young men and young women were gripped by the Holy Spirit. Students immediately began to make restitution at the college and even back in their home communities.

That same night the debate team was in Florida. The Spirit convicted them, and confession and prayer led to precious victory there in Florida. Elsewhere in the South, the chapel choir on tour was gripped by God and brought into revival at the same time. By this time the revival made the headlines in American and overseas newspapers.

When the students who had gone to their rooms late Wednesday night reached the chapel on Thursday morning, they found about a hundred who had spent the whole night in the chapel and were still waiting their turn to speak. The chapel service continued unbroken all Thursday and Thursday night and until 9:00 A.M. Friday morning when President Edman stopped them. Outside people and the press were arriving, and President Edman did not want the revival to be sensationalized.

The Friday night praise meeting was filled with heavenly congregational singing. The revival services continued with blessing for a total of nine days. Hundreds of lives were transformed by the grace of God. Revival fire leaped across Chicago to Northern Baptist Theological Seminary, where God gave twelve hours of revival.

In 1970 a fifth touch of revival fire came to Wheaton College and followed a pattern similar to earlier times of revival.

LATER REVIVALS ON OTHER CAMPUSES

By the end of February 1936, God had not only sent revival to Wheaton but also to Eastern Nazarene College and Gordon College, both in Massachusetts. Eastern Nazarene had also experienced thrilling revival in 1930.

In May and June 1949, God sent revival stirrings to the Minneapolis area that affected six college campuses. There was prayer, heart-searching confession and restitution, and lasting spiritual results in perhaps more than two thousand students' lives.

In August 1949 a College Briefing Conference was held at Forest Home Conference grounds near San Bernardino, California. The conference had been arranged by Miss Henrietta Mears. A thousand students from a dozen western universities were moved by the Holy Spirit, as Billy Graham and Edwin Orr spoke. God gave people grace to seek Him with all their heart. There was repentance, private and public confession of spiritual need and sin, restoration of backsliders, and deep revival.

It was at this conference, long after midnight one night, that Billy Graham testified he received a deeper transforming spiritual experience out in the woods when he was alone with God. Within weeks his historic Los Angeles campaign began, which gave birth to his new and greatly expanded worldwide ministry.

By November of 1949, God had sent revival with ardent prayer, confession, and testimonies to Northern Baptist Theological Seminary and North Park College, both in the Chicago area. Within ten months' time new revival poured out on dozens of campuses, including Wheaton College, Asbury College, Seattle Pacific College, and Baylor University in Texas.

In the next month of March 1950, a mighty revival came to Seattle Pacific College. The Holy Spirit gave unusual prayer burdens to many students and faculty. There was much personal counseling, confession, and testimony. Dr. J. Edwin Orr ministered twice a day. As many as 150 went forward for prayer in a single service. A similar awakening came to Simpson Bible College, then located also in Seattle.

Houghton College, near Buffalo, New York, experienced revival in October 1951 while evangelist Dr. Dwight H. Ferguson was speaking. Prayer went on all night, morning classes were canceled for several days, and students traveled to nearby towns and cities to witness and conduct services.

CHAPTER FORTY-TWO

The Spirit Comes to Asbury

Perhaps no major campus in America has experienced revival more frequently than Asbury College. Revival fire has leaped from this small college to innumerable campuses across the nation. Asbury College, an interdenominational institution founded in 1890 in the small town of Wilmore, Kentucky, by a godly Methodist minister, is deeply committed to the holiness movement and its emphasis upon the Holy Spirit. Some have suggested that those colleges that emphasize the fullness of the Spirit tend to expect and experience revival more frequently than do other evangelical institutions.

THE 1905 REVIVAL

During a winter blizzard early in 1905, God sent the first of several revivals to Asbury College. Dr. E. Stanley Jones, much used by God in India, told the story. Four of the young male students were having a prayer meeting in a private room. To their surprise, at about 10:00 P.M. the Holy Spirit seemed to enter the room, and suddenly they were all swept off their feet. Other students heard them and came running. For four hours they continued in the Lord's presence, and none of them slept the rest of that night.

In the morning they went to the college chapel service. The Holy Spirit took charge by His mighty revival workings. There were confessions of sin, spontaneous intercession, and new deep commitments to the Lord. People were on their knees throughout the chapel seeking God. Many were melted to tears. Some were prostrate before God. Revival spread throughout the college and town, and people began to flock in from the surrounding area. The moment they came on the campus they would fall on their knees and be converted even before they got to the auditorium.

This in a small scale reminds one of the "zone of holy influence" that seemed at times to extend off the eastern shore of the United States during the 1858 revival. For three days there were no classes. Every classroom was a prayer meeting. "At the end of three days I think every student was converted and many people from the outside," said Stanley Jones.[1]

For several days while many of the students were rejoicing in their newfound victories, Jones sat quietly. Many felt that his mighty prevailing prayers were part of the preparation for the Lord to bring this Pentecost to pass. But Jones merely sat in the front row and listened. Suddenly Sunday morning the church door opened and Jones came running down the aisle, shouting praises to God. He leaped into the pulpit and began like an Old Testament prophet to pour out the truth in the name of the Lord.

Jones was asked to address a student missionary meeting. He felt inadequate but prayed until he knew in his heart that at least one person would feel God's call when he spoke. He told this to the students as he began to speak and, to his amazement, at the conclusion of his first appeal, God told him "You are the one." For several weeks few classes were held because so much time was given to intercession and revival services.

Stanley Jones said this revival was the most formative experience of his time at Asbury. "I could only walk the floor praising Him and praising Him."[2] At this same time, God sent revival to colleges and seminaries in Louisville, Kentucky, and Kansas City, Missouri. Asbury-like revival fire was also reported at Wheaton College, Taylor University, Seattle Pacific College, Bethel College in Minnesota, and Baylor University.

Early in 1907 God sent another outpouring of the Spirit in real revival to Asbury College. It was described in particular as a revival of praise.

REVIVALS OF PREVAILING PRAYER

On February 18, 1908, revival came to Asbury for the third time in four years. While someone was praying during a chapel service, the spirit of intercession suddenly fell upon the whole student body, and it seemed the very heavens would be rent by the agonizing importunate cries of young men and women. That service lasted until midnight, with only slight intermissions for meals. Throughout the whole time sinners were seeking God. For two weeks the spirit of revival continued. Almost the entire school wrestled in agonizing prayer. Repeatedly the joy of the Lord was displayed, but primarily this was a revival of prevailing prayer.

There was no appointed leader. The students prayed from dawn until chapel time. A spirit of mighty intercession seemed to come upon all of them throughout each chapel service. This spirit of prayer was almost irresistible in its fervor.

One day a supper intermission was announced, but revival fire fell at the dinner table and few ate anything. Students led the evening services, which were characterized by many public and private confessions. Letters were sent asking forgiveness, and restitution was made. A spirit of revival continued throughout the rest of the school year. Many testified that they had learned the secret of prevailing prayer.

There was a tremendous missions emphasis, and in one service thirty-three testified to being called to the mission field.

During the 1915–16 school year, God used the Student Ministerial Association to spark great revival at Asbury. In a weekly session a student preached with unusual urgency. He felt someone needed to find God. Ding Bing Chen, a Chinese student, came forward and confessed that he had never been born again. He sought God's face in definite prayer and was wonderfully converted. This brought a widespread spirit of prayer to the student body. The college began holding nightly meetings led by the student preachers. The meetings grew in intensity and power from night to night. Special services continued for three weeks and had tremendous effect upon the spiritual life of the campus.

In February 1921 the annual mid-winter special revival meetings were planned. The college prepared for this by convening days of prayer during the fall and early winter months. Dr. C. W. Butler was the speaker and preached on great doctrinal truths. In the first days of January, God's Spirit was graciously present as the college family and the community prepared the way of the Lord in prayer. Dr. Butler's preaching was plain and unemotional, dealing specifically with the topics of justification and sanctification. Deep conviction fell upon the students and faculty. At each invitation to come forward for prayer, people were ready. Singing and urging were unnecessary; people wanted nothing more than to seek God.

At the very first service there were scenes beyond all description. People seemed to touch God for victory the moment they reached the altar and knelt there. Revived students surrounded some who did not come forward, and prayed and pled with God until they came into victory. A powerful sense of God's presence was felt throughout. In the first evening service some trusted God for victory while walking down the aisle toward the altar and began praising God for newfound blessing.

By the end of the week the students were totally absorbed in planning and praying for the revival. In the final Sunday services many from the community sought God, and it was announced that almost everyone in the college had found new victory in Christ. On the last night of the services, prayer around the altar continued all night until six o'clock in the morning. It was then decided that one of the faculty members would carry on services three days longer.

Throughout the entire meeting people sought God almost continuously. Everyone seemed eager to obey God. Prayer was obviously the main factor; drama and supernatural phenomena played no part. Hunger for holiness was universal, and great blessing was received by all.

THE 1950 REVIVAL

During early 1950 Asbury College experienced another in the series of revivals God has sent there since 1905. It continued unbroken for 118 hours. A small group of male students had been praying and fasting for revival every night for many weeks. Often they prayed all night long in the gymnasium and in their rooms. The group kept growing in numbers. Groups of students assembled for fasting and prayer in dormitory rooms, in various chapels, in the gymnasium, and in other places. They claimed God's covenant revival promise in 2 Chronicles 7:14.

During chapel on February 23, a student arose and testified, and one after another followed. Since an outside speaker was scheduled to speak in the chapel, the chairman interrupted and asked for the message. The evangelist was so overcome by the presence of God that he spoke only briefly. The Holy Spirit came upon the entire college.

The presence of God seemed to move across the people. Young people began to stand all over the auditorium.

My friend and former teacher, Dr. W. W. Holland, reported, "So mighty was the presence of the Holy Spirit in that chapel service that the students could not refrain from testimony. Testimonies were followed by confessions, confessions by crowded altars, crowded altars gave place to glorious spiritual victories. . . . Thus it ran for several days. Wave after wave of glory swept the vast audiences. Triumph after triumph took place at the altar." A tremendous sense of sacredness rested upon the whole audience as students made bare their hearts in humble confession and asked forgiveness. Students pled with other students who did not immediately yield to the Lord.

An overwhelming sense of God's presence prevailed. It seemed as if a great magnet drew people to the large Hughes Auditorium. Students made phone calls to home churches, parents and loved ones, testifying, asking forgiveness, and reporting on what God was doing. Asbury Theological Seminary, across the street, dismissed classes for a time. Delegations from churches in other places arrived to be present and experience the Lord's blessing.

The service had begun at 9:00 A.M. on Thursday. It continued uninterrupted throughout the day and night. Few left the chapel. Hundreds prayed all night. Other crowds returned after 6:00 A.M., and thus it continued all Friday, Saturday, and Sunday, when many went to the local Wilmore churches. After midnight Sunday the dean requested the young ladies to retire to their dormitories, where group meetings went on. The young men prayed on in the chapel. It was not until 7:00 A.M. on Tuesday, March 1, that the chapel service concluded, after 118 hours. All the rest of the week capacity crowds filled the auditorium. Hundreds of people sought a spiritual experience from God.

Typical of the impact was the high school basketball coach at Paris, Kentucky. He came to investigate and was overwhelmed by the supernatural presence of God when he entered the building. Compelled by the Holy Spirit, he announced his name and position and his conversion; the next September he enrolled in Asbury Theological Seminary and is today a minister of the Gospel.

NATIONWIDE INFLUENCE

From the very first night, two newsmen were present getting reports and taking pictures. The Louisville and Lexington daily papers spread the report across the nation. By Sunday night, February 26, eight reporters representing the United Press, the Associated Press, and the National Broadcasting Company came to the campus and remained for eight hours. Revival had become the second largest news item in the United States, second only to the national coal strike. A nearby radio station asked permission to broadcast the services over their station. All this was unsolicited, and the reporting was sympathetic throughout. There were phone calls from many cities asking for news.

Students from nearby colleges attended services, were blessed, went back to their colleges, and then brought other students. Many of the townspeople were deeply moved. More than twenty of the Wilmore High School students were converted, including a number from the basketball team. Calls came from churches across the country asking prayer that God would send them revival.

At the end of the first week, more than 2,300 professed faith in these outside meetings where students or faculty gave testimonies. By the following week it was over four thousand. Five hundred churches from across the country called asking for student and faculty members to come and hold weekend meetings in their churches.

After five days of continuous services, classes were resumed, but each night crowds of a thousand to fifteen hundred continued to fill the auditorium. Night after night the long ninety-foot altar at the front of the auditorium was filled with people seeking salvation. Revival fires broke out in many sections of the United States when someone from Asbury visited. The college did not seek publicity, but God used the publicity greatly for His glory, as He often does in revivals.

One call came from Jackson, Mississippi, and when the delegation from the college arrived, revival broke out in Methodist and Baptist churches and continued for about a week. Another similar outbreak of revival came to Hattiesburg, Mississippi. From eighteen hundred to two thousand people found Christ in one week in Hattiesburg. Services were requested in colleges and high schools. In one school, when the invitation was given, 250 students moved forward to seek the Lord. Messages were usually only a few minutes long. No extremes of emotion or fanaticism were displayed. Denominational differences did not seem to arise.

At the Asbury revival, prayer was given first place. People prayed in relays twenty-four hours a day. Day and night people visited the prayer rooms. Preachers drove for miles to come and receive personal refreshing. It was not a time of religious excitement but a time of great peace and of praise. During the meeting fifty-one people were called to the mission field or to other full-time service. W. W. Holland told me, "It was a beautiful sight when Dean Kenyon asked how many in the audience had consecrated themselves to, and were preparing for full-time Christian service, to see more than six hundred young people rise to their feet, with uplifted hands, sing 'I'll go where you want me to go, dear Lord.' "

On the second Friday of the revival, an unusual outpouring of the Spirit came upon the seminary chapel across the street and lasted all morning. Asbury College president Z. T. Johnson said, "There was no feeling of elation or boastfulness on the part of any of us. Asbury College feels honored to have had such a gracious outpouring of the Holy

Spirit."[3] Dr. Bob Shuler, Jr., wrote, "It seemed to be as near to Pentecost as this modern day can come. . . . The revival was real. It was genuine. The actual power was present. . . . It was a genuine Holy Ghost revival and nothing less."[4] Dr. T. M. Anderson has estimated that the total network of revival blessing radiating out from the 1950 revival saw some fifty thousand people find a new experience in Christ.[5]

THE 1958 REVIVAL

On Saturday, March 1, 1958, God sent another mighty revival to Asbury. Students met at noon for prayer and fasting. The student body president, who was leading, asked the question, "What would you like to see take place at Asbury?" Many people, both students and faculty, expressed that they longed to see a sweeping revival. On Friday in the faculty prayer meeting, the day before the revival, faculty members expressed the same deep yearning. Groups of young people met in several rooms waiting before God in prayer.

In the Saturday chapel one of the faculty spoke on 2 Corinthians 13:5: "Examine yourselves to see whether you are in the faith; test yourselves." It quickly became evident that the Holy Spirit was in charge and was speaking deeply. A great awareness of the presence of God filled the room. As the speaker was about to close the service, a student body leader came to the platform and asked to say a word. He began to confess his own personal need and asked the students to forgive him for setting a poor example of Christian living. He started for the altar and invited campus leaders and others who had slipped away from the Lord to join him.

About seventy-five students responded immediately. As soon as they prayed through to assurance, they stepped forward to the platform and testified of what God had done for them. Before long forty or more students were waiting in line at the pulpit to testify. The long altar and front seats were filled with people seeking new victory from the Lord. Students prayed and sang choruses. Many confessed humbly to being lax and having a critical spirit. Classes were dismissed and did not resume until Tuesday.

There was no need for a preacher. The whole atmosphere was electrified with the presence of God already. Yet it was not a time of great emotion but a deep refining, quiet work of the Holy Spirit searching hearts, bringing deep conviction, breaking down stubbornness of will, and melting hearts. A wind from heaven blew through the school, clearing out impurities and bringing all sinfulness to light.

Intercession, repentance, and testimony continued unbroken except for choruses and prayers from 8:00 A.M. on Saturday until 11:00 P.M. on Monday. Most important were the testimonies that spoke of love for God and for one another. Many people, their hearts filled with love, confessed to pride, selfishness, and other sins.

Local people came to the auditorium to attend some of the services. High school students wept openly as they came before the audience to witness to God's saving grace. On Sunday night after the service was closed at the local Methodist church, some five hundred persons gathered without previous announcement in the college auditorium, where some of the students had continued constantly in prayer. This became the crowning service of the revival.

Ministerial students of the college and seminary who had been out in their pastorates on Sunday came back reporting gracious outpourings of the Holy Spirit. At the Wilmore Methodist Church that Sunday night the Holy Spirit came upon the service, which did not cease until 2:45 A.M. on Tuesday. Revival fire burned simultaneously in the church and in the college auditorium. Blessings spread to Asbury Theological Seminary, to the town of Wilmore, and to many other towns and communities in Kentucky,

Mississippi, Tennessee, Michigan, Wisconsin, Illinois, South Carolina, Ohio, and Indiana.

In Jackson, Mississippi, a television program entitled "Revival of Prayer" received countless letters requesting prayer. Within three weeks approximately a thousand people had been to a church somewhere seeking God.

After the 1958 revival, there was a continuous and most wonderful spirit of power and love and faith pervading Asbury. It flooded hearts and souls, and was voiced in holy songs, prayers, and testimonies. There remained a divine spirit of tenderness, sweetness, and love binding the whole student body in a beautiful unity.

CHAPTER FORTY-THREE

The 1970 Asbury Revival

For months a small group of students at Asbury College had been getting up a half hour earlier each morning for prayer, Bible study, and planning their day with God. Other groups, large and small, had been meeting for prayer at different times asking God to bring spiritual awakening.

During the last week of January 1970, Dr. Eugene Erny, my predecessor in the presidency of OMS, and I were in a committee session in Wilmore, Kentucky. Dr. Dennis Kinlaw, new president of Asbury College, heard that we were in town and sent word asking us to come to his office after we finished our committee business. Asbury then had about a thousand students, and the seminary across the street had about four hundred.

When we arrived, Dr. Kinlaw called in his dean. Both of these men opened their hearts to us, sharing their deep burden for the youth of America, the declining moral standards, the drug problem among youth, and the repercussions of these problems among the less spiritual elements of their student body. They had a great burden for what should be done. We spent two hours together in discussion and prayer.

Just one week later to the day, on February 3, 1970, the Asbury dean opened a chapel testimony service by sharing his own experience, then inviting others to do the same. Fervent, direct, and anointed testimonies followed. At the close of that allotted chapel hour one of the professors stepped to the platform and said that any students who wanted to pray should feel free to come forward. Instantly, from all over the auditorium students moved forward as the congregation began singing, "Just As I Am." When the class bell sounded, few heeded it. As they came forward to pray, other students who had been waiting to testify and had not been able to do so went to the platform and one by one began to speak.

Those who had come forward and knelt at the long Asbury altar joined those on the platform to make humble and tearful confessions of their needs. Some went to individuals in the congregation, asked forgiveness, and became reconciled. A long line of students began to form, each waiting to tell what God had done. As confessions were made, other students came forward and filled the long altar and the front seats. Intense divine manifestation continued into the noon hour.

Occasionally students or faculty members came to the microphone and sang their testimony. Members of the Women's Glee Club stood in their places around the auditorium and began to sing unitedly, "When I Survey the Wondrous Cross."

Classes were suspended for the rest of the day. At the supper hour some left, but others came and joined the group in the auditorium. At times every seat in the 1,550-capacity auditorium was occupied. Some were standing around the walls, others looking in from doorways. The whole front of the auditorium was crowded with people on their knees: some praying, some counseling, some just rejoicing in the Lord. In the meantime, the testimonies and confessions went on without pause. Some went to nearby classrooms in the basement to meet with God alone or in small groups. Often students sat or knelt together two by two with their open

Bibles, discussing the things of God. A beautiful spirit of unity prevailed as the revival services continued unbroken for 144 hours.

REVIVAL CROSSES THE STREET

The story of God's work at the college spread across the street to Asbury Theological Seminary. Seminarians met for an all-night prayer meeting. Many there had been feeling an intense burden for revival for many months. The next morning the seminary chapel service became a revival time also. Students moved forward to the altar to pray and meet God. Students and faculty made humble confessions from the pulpit. Jealousies, resentments, worldly attitudes, and lustful desires were confessed. Many confessed their indifference to spiritual things.

Some of the seminary classes met, but many students remained in the chapel where God's Spirit was so strongly felt. The next day and the rest of the week all classes were officially canceled.

Many of the married students brought their wives into the chapel. Often couples knelt together or sat together holding hands, talking and praying. They would rise with tears in their eyes and embrace each other and praise God.

On the weekend the seminary and college revivals merged together, and the revival went on around the clock. Even at 2:30 in the morning as many as three hundred people gathered to pray in the chapel. Before sunrise the number dwindled down to less than a hundred. Then as the new day began, the building began to fill again. Day after day the campus communities were absorbed in only one thing: getting right with God and seeking God's will. Many students stayed in the chapel the better part of a whole week. There were always a few faculty members on hand to counsel, pray with the students, and be available in any way God might use them, but they were not manipulating the services.

REVIVAL FLOWS

Telegrams, letters, and phone calls arrived with urgent appeals for prayer from all over the United States and Canada. As news of some new victory was shared, people would break forth into praise, and again and again the congregation, accompanied by the chapel organ, joined in singing "To God Be the Glory." Visitors came from as far away as California, Florida, and Canada. Many of these became revived and went to the platform to testify to what God had done in their lives.

Townspeople joined in the revival. Teenagers who had had no interest in religion were converted and began to win friends to Christ. On Sunday several of the local churches dismissed their regular services and encouraged everyone to go to the revival. One of the leading local pastors went into the pulpit and poured out the confession of his shortcomings. Then his wife followed with a very humble confession.

More than one hundred adults, faculty members, staff members, and town and community people moved forward and began to seek God. The whole front of the auditorium and front aisles were again filled with people weeping, praying, and becoming reconciled with one another. A beautiful spiritual and social healing took place on Sunday morning. No event in years had solved so many problems as did that Sunday in the auditorium.

The services continued in the auditorium for 185 hours without interruption. There was no pressure, no scheduled meetings, no offering, no prelude or postlude, and no benediction.

Appeals began coming from other campuses across the United States and from churches throughout the land asking for student delegations to come and share the news of the revival. By the end of May 1970, at least 130 colleges, seminaries, and Bible schools had received some revival blessings through the witness of the Asbury students. Some two thousand witness teams had gone out from Asbury College and seminary. To this must be added the hundreds of teams that went out from colleges and churches that were touched by revival when the Asbury witness teams arrived.

Two seminary couples went to Colombia, South America, to the Medellin seminary of OMS International. They spoke twenty-five times, seeing God work in various places in Colombia as He had at Asbury. Other witnesses during the summer visited five continents of the world.

Hundreds of articles appeared in Christian periodicals and secular newspapers. The book *One Divine Moment*, recounting the thrilling story of the Asbury revivals, had a widespread ministry.

CAMPUS RENEWAL

The president of Azusa Pacific University near Los Angeles asked for a student witness from Asbury to come to their campus. The Azusa faculty spent the entire night in prayer. The student arrived and did not preach but simply told what God had been doing at Asbury College and how his own life was affected. At the conclusion, 150 students moved en masse to the front and made altars out of the chairs. Testimonies began. Afternoon classes for the day were canceled. Students continued giving testimonies. Others met in dormitory rooms and classrooms for prayer.

Some left the campus to go to nearby colleges and share their testimonies. Students began telephoning their parents and pastors across the country to share their testimonies. The Friday chapel lasted for seven hours. The next Sunday the students scattered, testifying in many churches throughout the area. Often the pastor did not preach his sermon because people began to seek the Lord, and revival broke out in many churches. On Monday the students returned from their weekend witnessing and began to share in chapel.

Afternoon classes were again canceled, and for hours there were testimonies, singing, and prayer.

The next day the Azusa chaplain and ten students went to Pasadena College and shared the testimony of God's revival visitation to their campus. The college basketball coach came to the microphone and confessed his failure to be the witness God wanted him to be. The campus was electrified, and revival started all over again.

When the revival began at Asbury seminary, an alumnus of Greenville College, a Free Methodist institution, stood and shared his burden for his alma mater, telling of tensions and needs. Just then the local pastor stood and said a phone call had just come from Greenville asking for a witness team. Immediately graduates from Greenville who were enrolled at the seminary gathered around the altar to pray. They selected a team, and within half an hour the team was on its way. Driving through sleet and snow, the ten members reached Greenville. They shared the revival and immediately individuals were humbled before God, public confessions of wrong attitudes began, and revival continued through early Saturday morning hours.

Numerous teams went out from Greenville College to most of the churches of three Free Methodist conferences, and the spiritual tone of those churches was transformed.

For two years some students and faculty at Southwestern Baptist Theological Seminary in Fort Worth, Texas, had been praying for a movement of God on their campus. When the news of the Asbury awakening reached them, one professor told his class about it. The entire group fell on their knees before God, confessing, boldly interceding, and pleading for God's mercy. The same thing happened in another class. The next morning was Founder's Day, and after the observance it was announced that any wishing to hear more about the revival should stay in the chapel. Only about a dozen left, and twelve hundred stayed to hear the witnesses. Many were profoundly moved by the Spirit.

Olivet Nazarene University in Kankakee, Illinois, was mightily impacted by the 1970 revival. The president said he had never seen anything to compare with it in his twenty-one years as president. Classes were canceled and the Holy Spirit prevailed. Then hundreds of Olivet students fanned out across the country to their home churches to share the news of revival. One student went to the Nazarene Theological Seminary in Kansas City, Missouri. The Holy Spirit descended on the campus family with multitudes of blessings.

At Georgetown College near Lexington, Kentucky, six Asbury students gave their testimony, and the college administration and faculty and some seven hundred students joined in the "marathon revival." At least thirty-three other colleges and universities in the United States and Canada were touched with revival as the witnesses fanned out from coast to coast.

At the University of Tennessee, Ed Martin, a prominent faculty member, asked four students to share their testimony. Two hundred of the students sought the Lord, and until the end of the school year dozens of Tennessee students met every night in the dormitories for prayer. The Baptist Student Movement told the Asbury Seminary story at Texas A&M, the University of Texas at Arlington, and five of the largest state universities in Oklahoma. Hundreds of students were impacted, and some of the times of prayer, confession, and testimony lasted four or five hours.

THE ASBURY IMPACT ON CHURCHES

Hundreds of pastors across the country began requesting student teams to come to their churches. For months every Saturday a large procession of cars departed from the Asbury area to share in the witnessing. Many students traveled by air. Almost everywhere they went, pastors and congregations responded. Sermons and the order of service were forgotten. Church altars which for years had been little more than pieces of furniture now became hallowed places where men and women were reconciled with one another and with God. People forgot the clock and their dinners and sat for hours in the church sanctuaries meeting with God.

At the South Meridian Church of God in Anderson, Indiana, the Asbury team arrived on Saturday afternoon, February 21. They went straight to the Anderson College campus and began mingling with the students, inviting all to the Sunday morning service at this particular church. Sunday morning they gave their witness to about five hundred people, and while they were still speaking people began to move forward to the church altar to pray for their own spiritual needs. The service lasted three hours, and God was unusually present. The evening service was even more largely attended and went on for hours.

Monday evening about a thousand people crowded into the South Meridian Church sanctuary, which normally holds only 750. Many had to stand along the walls as the Asbury team shared their last witness in Anderson. God moved upon the entire congregation. Small groups began to pray throughout the building. High school and college students crowded around the altar, and time and again the pastor had to ask them to return to their seats and make room for others who wanted to come and kneel and pray. A large advertisement was put in the local paper, and Tuesday evening the sanctuary and gym were filled with about fourteen hundred people. Among the outstanding conversions were an alcoholic, a prominent athlete, and a Roman Catholic. Noon meetings began in the City Hall with up to two hundred in attendance. Visitors from out of the state began arriving from Kentucky, West Virginia, Illinois, Nebraska, Kansas, Canada, and as far west as California.

A special rally was held in the Anderson high school gymnasium on Sunday afternoon, March 8, with two thousand people and more attending. The next Sunday afternoon a city-wide rally was held with some 2,600 in attendance. Pastors in many states asked for witness teams to come from the Anderson church to their churches. By the first week of May, these teams from Anderson had visited scores of churches in thirty-one states and Canada. Wherever they went the power of the Holy Spirit was manifest, and hundreds of young people and adults made commitments to Christ. One Sunday in Roanoke, Virginia, over 250 people sought the Lord. In Huntington, West Virginia, revival spontaneously broke out, with services lasting for two weeks.

Meanwhile, at the South Meridian Church of God in Anderson, the services continued for fifty nights without a break, with an average attendance of about a thousand. Members of many denominations, black and white, young and old, came to the foot of the cross. Typical services lasted two and three hours and consisted primarily of singing, confession, prayer, and testimony. A front-page article in the *Chicago Tribune* called it Anderson's "Revival of Love."[1]

Testimonies abounded of alcoholics delivered, fractured homes healed, and churches visited with such Spirit-filled revival that congregations completely outgrew their sanctuaries and moved to nearby larger churches. People of many denominations came to be part of the movement of the Spirit. Often services lasted for hours. In one small community, five hundred out of seven hundred students in the local high school made commitments to Christ, and a pastor remarked, "Our town is a new town since the revival. Tough kids have been converted; broken homes reunited; alcoholics rehabilitated in society; and our churches revitalized. This is God's work!"[2]

A small Pennsylvania town asked for an Asbury speaker. The only one available was a girl from the college whose home was nearby, and she was home for the spring holidays. With trepidation, she went to the church and gave her testimony. The power of God fell upon the people, and revival began and continued for eight nights to standing-room-only crowds. In one service the girl's own father, who had been afflicted with curvature of the spine since childhood, was instantly healed. The whole community was shaken.

Within three months, some two thousand witness teams went out from Asbury College and Seminary, and hundreds of other teams went out from other colleges and local churches that were impacted by the revival. The little town of Wilmore, Kentucky, became the center of a network of revival that touched and brought new spiritual life and blessing to thousands of individuals in several thousand towns and villages in the United States and in other countries.

The 1970 revival at Asbury was a time of deep working of the Holy Spirit. It resulted in a multiplication of prayer, thrilling personal testimonies, and Spirit-filled singing. Thousands of lives were transformed. There were no awe-inspiring sounds, no mysterious winds, and no visible flames of fire. But perhaps it was the nearest thing to Pentecost America has experienced in this century.

The only complete record of the 1970 Asbury revival is recorded in heaven. What has happened at Asbury over and over throughout this century can happen again. God is the God of revival. He is no respecter of persons, places, institutions, or churches. No two revival accounts are exactly the same. But wherever God's people fulfill the covenant of revival God gave in 2 Chronicles 7:14, wherever God's people are willing to pray, God's Holy Spirit can be poured out again. The price of self-humbling, of seeking God's face, may seem great, but it will be eternally worthwhile. God is ready to send revival today. Are we preparing the way of the Lord for him?

CHAPTER FORTY-FOUR

Revival Is Coming

God at His own initiative voluntarily gave us, His people, the covenant of revival in 2 Chronicles 7:14. He must be true to His covenant word, and He waits for us to fulfill our part of this revival covenant. Thousands of times God has fulfilled the revival covenant for a family, a local church, a community, a region, or a nation. The more deep, widespread, and total the prayer and obedience of His children, the more widespread God's outpoured revival through the power of the Spirit can become.

We cannot produce revival, earn revival, or arrange God's timetable of revival visitation. We can only meet God's conditions and seek His face. What can we learn about the secrets of God's kingdom by studying the revivals of the past?

1. Savonarola proved that one person can turn the tide. God can work through anyone who is totally committed to Him, hungering for revival, and willing to pay the price in his or her obedience to the revival covenant. The same thrilling truth is seen in the revivals under Asa and Jehoshaphat.

2. No one is too young to be used by God. Whitefield at twenty-two showed that a young man ablaze for God can be a mighty instrument. Evan Roberts' spiritual hunger at

the age of thirteen led him into a dynamic ministry at twenty-six. And John Wesley's consuming passion for a holy life at twenty-six allowed God to fill him and begin a powerful ministry through him when Wesley was thirty-five.

3. Whitefield, Wesley, and Finney from the time they were filled with the Spirit seemed to be chosen specifically for revival. From the moment the Holy Spirit baptized them with His holy fire until their deaths, they carried revival fire wherever they went. Jonathan Goforth, Jonathan Edwards, David Brainerd, Miss Louisa Vaughan, Miss Aletta Jacobsz, and Duncan Campbell are examples of Christians who have been used in lighting revival fires in this way during a special period of their lives.

4. Witnessing and evangelism are God-ordained and are constantly used by God. They have their appointed roles, even during times of revival. But revival is about God's sovereignty, characterized particularly by the speed and the magnitude of the results and by the dynamic transformations of church and community. Evangelism without revival lacks the full manifestation of God's glorious presence and power.

5. Most revival movements have been characterized by deep conviction of sin and much public confession. God has used these confessions to convict others, both Christians and non-Christians, of their own sins. The Korea, North China, and U.S. campus revivals demonstrated the profound effect confession can have on listeners, especially when confession is accompanied by restitution and reconciliation.

6. Great joy in people who have found spiritual liberty is another common revival trait. Singing has been prominent, and those revived have sung and rejoiced for hours, drawing others to Christ. This was particularly true in the Welsh revival and in some revival periods in Africa.

7. Revival fires can be spread by oral and written testimonies, newspapers, on radio and TV, through letters, and over the telephone. In Wales, Northern Ireland, India, the

1858 revival in the United States, Korea, North China, and campus revivals, the Holy Spirit made great use of voices, books, and the media in spreading revival flames.

8. The Holy Spirit is the leader in all God-sent revival. He knows of God's longing to send revival to His people. He Himself intercedes with groanings deeper than words as He joins with Christ. The Spirit gives prayer concerns and prayer burdens for revival on many of God's children so that they may join in the same prevailing intercession.

9. Finally, revival history shows us that God can and will send revival again and again to the same place or to new places if there are people there who meet God's revival covenant conditions. It may seem that throughout history, revivals have tended to occur in the same places over and over: Wales, Northern Ireland, parts of Scotland, the Cape area of South Africa, and some American Christian college campuses such as Wheaton College and Asbury College.

Is this by arbitrary sovereign choice? Probably not. They seem to be places where over the years groups of people have demonstrated clear-cut evangelical faith, a reverent fear of God, and faithful prayer. They are places where the Holy Spirit has been honored, where His presence has been hungered for and sought, and where people have not only had the assurance of sins forgiven but have believed in and sought the infilling of the Holy Spirit.

God's covenant of revival was given at God's initiative. No human being begged God until He promised to revive. Because He is the God of revival, He voluntarily gave us His covenant as His invitation to us to seek revival. God is more hungry to give us revival than we are hungry to be revived.

God stated His covenant of revival in various forms throughout the Bible, especially in these Old Testament passages: Isaiah 41:18; 44:3; 62:1, 6–7; and 64:1–2, 4–5. But probably the most well-known and often-quoted promise is 2 Chronicles 7:14: "If my people, who are called by my name, will humble themselves and pray and seek my face and turn from their wicked ways, then will I hear from heaven and will forgive their sin and will heal their land."

God wants us to remember and reflect on how He has worked in the past. He wants this remembrance to make us hungry to see Him work again in all His historic power. If God's people hunger deeply enough, God will hear and send revival. That is why in this book I have given selected details of so many of God's revival workings over the past centuries and in our own day. Let us fulfill our part of His revival covenant. Let us accept His holy challenge in 2 Chronicles 7:14.

1. "If my people will humble themselves." How many of God's people do you know who take God's covenant seriously? How many are truly humbling themselves? Humble yourself in private prayer. Humble yourself in prayer meetings and solemn assemblies before God. Humble yourself with fasting like David did (Ps. 35:13).

2. "And pray and seek my face." Every time in the history of the church revival has come, it has followed extensive prayer and seeking of God's face by some of His children. When we study the history of God's work on earth, we will always find faithful praying saints, often hidden, holding on before Him in prayer, pleading for God to revive His people. Always there were people—often many—who in the privacy of their hearts cried out to God over and over.

God requires more than casual prayers for revival. He wants His people to hunger and thirst for His mighty working. To seek God's face is far more than occasionally mentioning revival in our prayer. It involves repeated and prolonged prayer. It requires holy determination in prayer, examining ourselves to see if anything in our lives is hindering God. A revival seeker is prepared to take any step that can help to bring answers. A revival seeker is eager to obey God in everything. Seeking God's face often requires asking forgiveness from others (Matt. 5:23–24; 6:14–15; Mark 11:25; Luke 6:37; Col. 3:13). It often requires resolving friction that has hindered prayer from being answered (1 Peter 3:7). Are you seeking God's face?

3. "And turn from their wicked ways." Anything that grieves God—whether things we did or things we failed to do—will hinder our efforts to respond to God's revival covenant. We need to be sensitive to the Holy Spirit and to His efforts to point out areas in our lives that hinder His working and rob us of God's full blessing. The Holy Spirit may at times with His strong voice correct us with deep conviction of our failure. At other times, His is a gentle touch to direct us more fully into God's will.

Instant obedience to anything the Holy Spirit shows us, instant repentance for anything that has grieved God—this is what prepares the way for revival. No one is as quick to sense the Spirit's reproof, no one is more sensitive and responsive to God than a Spirit-filled person. So it follows that no one should be as quick to repent over any failure than a Spirit-filled person! That is why God needs Spirit-filled people to play key roles in His revival strategy.

The above are the three essential steps in preparing the way of the Lord for revival. These are God's covenantal conditions if we would see His mighty working. But as sure as God is in heaven, when we fulfill His clear conditions, God will do two things: forgive us for any way we have grieved Him and give gracious healing to our land.

The whole world is wounded by Satan and sin. Every nation today is desperately in need of healing. Many churches, groups, and families need healing. Revival always brings healing to homes, churches, communities, and nations. "Oh God, heal our land" should be the heart-cry of every Christian.

Will another great revival come? It is never too late for God. If we will fulfill God's covenantal conditions, we will see God's covenantal promises fulfilled. So the question is not so much, "Will revival come?" but rather "Will we meet God's covenantal conditions for revival?"

Is it God's time? Just as it is always God's time to save, it is always God's time to give revival. Just as surely as "now is the day of salvation," so surely now is the day of revival, for now is the day of grace. It may take time for us to meet God's conditions, to prepare the way of the Lord, and to pray until we win the battles in prayer warfare. But God does not delay revival because He is arbitrary. He does not need to be begged.

Over the past several centuries God has given many revivals, large and small. The Finney revivals were perhaps more extensive than the Wesley-Whitefield revivals. The 1858–59 revivals were far more extensive than the Finney revivals and may even be considered God's follow-up to the Finney revivals. Certainly the 1858–59 revival was the first truly international one.

The 1905–1909 revival was probably preceded by prayer and hunger on a more international scale than any previous revival. God's blessing was poured out in more nations than in any previous revival movement. But never in Christian history has there been such a longing for renewal in so many parts of the world and by people from so many denominational backgrounds as there is today.

Surely this hunger is the result of the Holy Spirit calling God's people to prayer. There have been more books written on prayer than ever before. More organizations and more denominations have called for a year of prayer or a year for revival than ever previously known. Undoubtedly the Holy Spirit is calling God's people to their knees. Undoubtedly He is guiding His people to join Christ our great High Priest in His great longing and holy determina-

tion to see another great revival. Undoubtedly the Holy
Spirit Himself is groaning in prayer today for revival in the
church (Rom. 8:26).

The Holy Spirit does not play games with us or with
our prayer lives. When He gives us hunger and prayer burden for revival, He Himself and our beloved interceding
High Priest are one with us in that holy desire. Ours is but
a faint echo of the deep yearnings and desires and interces-
sions on their parts. Will their intercession be in vain? God's
prayer call in our hearts proves the Triune God is longing
to send revival. It is God's time.

Why should we not expect God to give one more great
outpouring of the Holy Spirit before our Lord's second
advent? Why should this not be the most widespread
revival the church has ever known? Of course the millennium will be the greatest revival of all. God has used the
media in the past to help spread hunger and expectancy and
news of revival. Why should God not do this in even
greater dimensions in this age of radio, television, and international communication?

But we are still too careless and ineffective in our
prayer lives. We need to recruit many more of God's children for serious prevailing intercession for revival. It will
probably be the regret of millions of Christians throughout
eternity that they failed so tragically in their prayer lives.
How ashamed they will be when they stand before Christ's
judgment throne. But, oh, the joy of those who wake up
now and invest quality time and an adequate quantity of
time in earnest intercession, particularly for revival.

Praise God for His revivals over the centuries. Praise
God that He is still the same today. Praise God that He has
promised to send revival if we meet His stated conditions.
We cannot earn revival; it is given through grace. But we can
share in preparing the way of the Lord, if we choose to do it.

Make a new prayer commitment to God. Join God the Son and God the Spirit in revival intercession. Set apart time regularly for prayer. Fall on your knees now and pray.

Give Us a Greater Hunger

Give us a greater hunger, Lord, than we have ever known.
Help us to wait in one accord until Your pow'r is shown.
Keep us Your children on our knees, beseeching You with mighty pleas
Till floods of blessing like the seas sweep over all Your own.

Give us a sense of urgency that will not be denied.
Give such desire Your work to see, till ease we cast aside.
Give us soul-hunger and soul-thirst, till hearts with longing almost burst,
Till we could wish ourselves accursed if souls but reach Your side!

Lord, now begin Your mighty work; make bare Your holy arm.
O God, forbid that we should shirk, or to this age conform!
Reveal Your Spirit's mighty pow'r; oh, come upon Your church this hour!
By Your own working, Lord, empow'r, till Satan's forts we storm.

Help each of us to do our part; O Lord, may we not fail.
Give clearest guidance to each heart, till highest mounts we scale.
Use us however You may choose; we would no burden, Lord, refuse;
But get us, Lord, where You can use and mightily prevail.

Oh, send the promised Holy Ghost upon us as we kneel.
We need His holy working most, till men conviction feel.
Lord, this is still the day of grace; have mercy on our dying race.
Revival send to every place; Your miracle reveal.

—Wesley L. Duewel

(Written at the Faith Mission Bible College, Edinburgh, after talking with Rev. Duncan Campbell, October 20, 1958.)

APPENDIX A

QUESTIONS FOR REFLECTION AND DISCUSSION

1. What is meant when a very spiritual person is said to be "on fire for God"? Do you know anyone like that?
2. What does fire teach us about the character and work of God?
3. Should all Christian leaders be "on fire for God" today? Should all believers?
4. Have you known times when God's presence was unusually real in your own life? Describe those times.
5. Have you had a special spiritual experience during worship in your church, an experience in which you were unusually aware of God's love and presence? At what point in the service did it occur?
6. Do you know people or churches for whom God once did great things, but for some reason they are not so effective now?
7. What steps should we as Christians take for moral reformation and revival in our own land?
8. John Wesley's hunger for God was so infectious that others gathered with him to seek to be more holy. Are you and your friends hungry enough for revival that you would adopt a spiritual lifestyle of prayer and fasting?
9. The ministries of George Whitefield and the Wesleys repeatedly stirred up tremendous opposition. Why is there such little opposition to our Christian leaders today?

10. What kind of spiritual background prepares people to receive the Holy Spirit into their lives?

11. Charles Finney became an instant soul-winner when he was filled with the Spirit. Can anyone who is filled with the Spirit expect immediate differences in his or her life and ministry?

12. Do you know any people today who could be called "prayer warriors"? What distinguishes a prayer warrior?

13. If revival came today, what impact would our media have on revival's effectiveness and growth? Why are spiritual matters so seldom covered in the secular media today?

14. What areas of our society most need revival today?

15. Is it possible for Christians today to unite in prayer for revival regardless of denominational differences?

16. Why do some Christians—Wesley, Whitefield, Finney, and others—light revival fire wherever they go, while others minister for years and are never used in revival? Does this mean God is not using them?

17. The great American revival of 1904–1905 is scarcely remembered today. Why do you think the effects of this revival have not lasted?

18. Praying Hyde and his companions spent months before conventions fasting and praying for revival. Would extended prayer today yield results? What keeps us from devoting this kind of time to prayer?

19. What do you think of extraordinary physical manifestations of the Holy Spirit? What purpose did they serve in past revivals? Would they be effective today?

20. Can Christian moral standards be maintained in churches and individual Christians without occasional revival? Do you think your moral standards are as high today as they were shortly after you became a Christian?

21. Why do we not hear of revivals on college campuses, even Christian ones, today?
22. Asbury College experienced revival in part because so many people had been praying for so long for revival. How might other Christian colleges today build up and maintain prayer support?
23. Most revival movements did not seek publicity, but revival spread through publicity anyway. Would spreading reports of prayer and hunger for revival help prepare the way of the Lord for revival now?
24. In what ways can your church have a prophetic role in your community? in your nation?
25. In many revivals, God used children's prayers. What can you do to help your children and those in your church develop more active prayer lives?
26. God frequently used elderly people in preparing the way for revival. Do you know any elderly people who have outstanding prayer lives? How can you learn from them?
27. If God sent revival to your church, what steps could you personally take to bring others to share in God's blessing?

A small booklet of questions for prayerful meditation, for most chapters, is available from the author at the following address: P.O. Box A, Greenwood, IN 46142-6599

APPENDIX B

ADDITIONAL REVIVAL MOVEMENTS

It is not possible to include in one book accounts of all the revival movements, especially of the past three centuries. Some readers may question why some outstanding movements of the Spirit in certain regions have not been recorded in greater detail or have not been referred to at all. The attempt has been to give some indication in the accounts included in this volume of the flow of the Holy Spirit in different parts of the world.

Among the revival movements, larger or smaller, that have not been included are the following:

The revival under Francis of Assisi (1209–25).

The Moravian revival in Germany (1722).

The Jonathan Edwards revival in New England (1734–35, 1740–41).

The Cambuslang revival in Scotland (1742).

The David Brainerd revival among the American Indians (1745–46).

The Kilsyth and Dundee revivals in Scotland (1839).

The William Taylor revivals around the world (1856–1900).

The Pentecostal Azusa revival (1906).

The Louisa Vaughan revival in Shantung among the Presbyterians and others (1896–1912).

The Shanghai revival (1925).

The Aletta Jacobsz revival among Presbyterian, Methodist, and OMS in Korea and North China (1938–40).

The Canadian Revival Movement (1970–   ).

NOTES

Introduction

1. Jonathan Goforth, *By My Spirit* (Minneapolis: Bethany Fellowship, Inc., 1964), 9.

Chapter 2: When Fire Really Fell

1. Helen S. Dyer, *Pandita Ramabai, A Great Life in Indian Missions* (London: Pickering & Inglis, n.d.), 100–101.

Chapter 6: A Monk's Revival

1. James Gilchrist Lawson, *Deeper Experiences of Famous Christians* (Anderson, Ind.: The Warner Press, 1911), 79.

Chapter 7: The Great Awakening Dawns

1. Albert D. Belden, *George Whitefield—The Awakener* (London: Sampson Low, Marston & Co., Ltd., n.d.), 54–56.

2. James Burns and Andrew W. Blackwood, Sr., *Revivals, Their Laws and Leaders* (Grand Rapids, Mich.: Baker, reprinted 1960), 288–89.

3. J. D. Douglas, general editor, *The New International Dictionary of the Christian Church* (revised edition) (Grand Rapids, Mich.: Zondervan, 1974), 476.

4. John Telford, *The Life of John Wesley* (New York: Hunt & Eaton, n.d.), 117.

5. Lawson, *Deeper Experiences of Famous Christians,* 178.

Chapter 8: George Whitefield: Ablaze for God

1. Belden, *George Whitefield—The Awakener,* 65.

Chapter 9: Whitefield's Continued Ministry

1. Belden, *George Whitefield—The Awakener.*

2. Ibid.

3. Ibid.

4. Ibid.

5. Ibid., 217–18.

6. Ibid., 219.

7. Ibid., 221.

8. Ibid., 222.

Chapter 10: Wesley the Revivalist

1. Telford, *The Life of John Wesley,* 8.

2. Ibid., 59.

3. Ibid., 92.

4. Ibid., 101.

5. Ibid., 122.

6. Ibid., 164.

7. Ibid., 312.

8. Burns and Blackwood, *Revivals, Their Laws and Leaders*, 326.

Chapter 11: The Revivals of Methodism

1. Telford, *The Life of John Wesley*, 199.

2. Ibid., 201.

3. Ibid., 263.

4. Ibid., 318.

5. Ibid., 320.

6. Ibid., 356.

7. Ibid., 345.

8. Ibid., 345.

9. Ibid., 349–52.

Chapter 12: Revival Fires Follow Finney

1. Lawson, *Deeper Experiences of Famous Christians*, 243.

2. Charles G. Finney, *The Memoirs of Charles G. Finney*, Garth M. Rosell and Richard A. G. Dupuis, ed. (Grand Rapids, Mich.: Zondervan, 1989), xxxi–xxxii.

3. Ibid., 13.

4. Ibid., 23.

5. Ibid., 75.

6. Ibid., 78.

7. Ibid., 80.

8. Ibid., 102.

Chapter 13: Revival Fire Spreads to Central New York

1. Finney, *The Memoirs of Charles G. Finney*, 147.

2. Ibid., 164.

3. Ibid., 168.

4. Ibid., 172.

5. Ibid., 195.

6. Ibid., 212.

7. Ibid., 239.

Chapter 14: Cities Ablaze

1. Finney, *The Memoirs of Charles G. Finney*, 325.

2. Ibid., 326.

3. Ibid., 331–35.

4. Ibid., 362.

5. Ibid., 378.

6. Ibid., 377–78.

Chapter 15: Oberlin and Beyond

1. Finney, *The Memoirs of Charles G. Finney*, 405–6.

2. Ibid., 451.

3. Ibid., 513–14.

4. Ibid., 622–23.

Chapter 17: God's Glory Over Land and Sea

1. J. Edwin Orr, *The Fervent Prayer* (Chicago: Moody, 1974), 18.

Chapter 18: Across the Sea to Ulster

1. William Gibson, *The Year of Grace* (Belfast: Ambassador Productions Ltd., 1989), 24–25.

2. Ian R. K. Paisley, *The "Fifty-Nine" Revival* (Belfast: The Free Presbyterian Church of Ulster, 1958), 39.

3. Ibid., 48.

4. Ibid., 50.

Chapter 19: The Belfast Connection

1. John Weir, *Heaven Came Down* (Belfast: Ambassador Productions Ltd., 1987), 48–49.

2. Ibid., 43.

3. Ibid., 109.

Chapter 20: The Irish Year of Grace

1. John Weir, *Heaven Came Down*, 126.

2. Paisley, *The "Fifty-Nine" Revival*, 90.

3. Ibid., 134.

4. Ibid., 141.

5. Ibid., 158–59.

6. Weir, *Heaven Came Down*, 172.

7. Ibid., 173.

8. Paisley, *The "Fifty Nine" Revival*, 101–2.

9. Ibid., 102.

10. Ibid., 102.

11. Ibid., 112–13.

12. Ibid., 41.

13. Weir, *Heaven Came Down*, 176.

14. Gibson, *The Year of Grace*, 85.

Chapter 21: The 1859 Prayer Revival in Wales

1. Thomas Phillips, *The Welsh Revival* (Edinburgh: The Banner of Truth Trust, 1989), 9–10.

2. Ibid., 31.

3. Ibid., 33.

4. Ibid.

5. Ibid., 37.

6. Ibid., 42.

7. Ibid., 54–55.

8. Ibid., 56.

9. Ibid., 75–77, 122.

10. Ibid., 64.

11. Ibid., 78–79.

12. Ibid., 60.

Chapter 22: Revival Fires in South Africa

1. Orr, *Evangelical Awakenings in Africa* (Minneapolis: Bethany Fellowship, Inc., 1975), 58.

2. Ibid.

3. Ibid., 59.

4. Ibid., 60.

5. Ibid., 68.

6. Ibid., 69.

7. Ibid., 70.

8. Ibid., 76.

9. Ibid., 72.

Chapter 23: Prayer Preparation

1. R. B. Jones, *Rent Heavens* (London: Stanley Martin & Co., Ltd., 1930), 36.

Chapter 24: The Vision of Evan Roberts

1. Mrs. Jessie Penn-Lewis, *The Awakening in Wales* (London: Marshall Bralters, Keswick House, Paternoster Press, E.C., 1905), 58.

2. Jones, *Rent Heavens*, 43.

3. Ibid., 43–44.

4. Ibid., 45.

5. Eifion Evans, *Revival Comes to Wales*, 70.

6. Ibid., 73.

7. Ibid., 74.

Chapter 25: Songs of Revival in South Wales

1. D. M. Phillips, *Evan Roberts* (London: Marshall Brothers, Keswick House, Paternoster Row, 1923), 239–40.

2. Ibid., 227–28.

3. Evans, *Revival Comes to Wales*, 95.

4. Ibid., 102.

5. Ibid., 104.

6. Phillips, *Evan Roberts*, 299.

7. Ibid., 299–302.

8. Ibid., 303.

Chapter 26: The Spreading Flame

1. Evans, *Revival Comes to Wales*, 113.

2. Ibid., 114.

3. Ibid., 115–16.

4. Ibid., 141.

5. Ibid., 171–73.

6. Ibid., 180, 181, 182.

Chapter 28: Harvest in America

1. J. Edwin Orr, *The Flaming Tongue* (Chicago: Moody, 1973), 70.

2. Ibid., 74.

3. Ibid., 74.

4. Ibid., 73–75.

5. Ibid., 81.

6. Ibid., 81.

Chapter 29: Revival at Ramabai's Mukti

1. Padmini Sangupta, *Pandita Ramabai Saraswati—Her Life and Work* (London: Asia Publishing House, 1970), 286.

2. Dyer, *Pandita Ramabai*, 102–3.

3. Ibid., 109–10.

Chapter 30: Prayer Transforms Central and Northern India

1. Basil Miller, *Praying Hyde* (Grand Rapids, Mich.: Zondervan, 1943), 36.

2. Ibid., 48–49.

Chapter 31: A Year of Blessing for Southern India

1. Orr, *Evangelical Awakenings in India* (New Delhi: Masiki Sahitya Sanstha, 1970), 88.

2. Ibid., 88–89.

3. Ibid., 89.

4. Ibid., 89.

5. Ibid., 90–91.

6. Ibid., 90.

7. Ibid., 91.

8. Ibid., 92–94.

9. Ibid., 95–96.

10. Ibid., 96–97.

11. Ibid., 100.

12. Ibid., 106.

Chapter 32: Revival in Andhra State

1. J. Edwin Orr, *Evangelical Awakenings in India* (New Delhi: Masihi Sahitya Sanstha, 1970), 75–76.

2. Ibid., 76.

3. Ibid., 79.

4. Ibid., 80.

5. Ibid., 81.

6. Ibid., 82.

7. Ibid., 85.

Chapter 33: Mighty Waves of Revival in Northeast India

1. No author listed, *Calling to Remembrance* (Atlantic City, N.J.: The World-Wide Revival Prayer Movement, n.d.), 66.

2. Ibid., 81–82.

3. Ibid., 86.

4. Ibid., 90–91.

Chapter 34: Korean Presbyterian Pentecost

1. William Blair & Bruce Hunt, *The Korean Pentecost* (Edinburgh: The Banner of Truth Trust, 1977), 67.

2. Ibid., 73.

3. Ibid., 74.

Chapter 35: Goforth and the North China Revival

1. Goforth, *By My Spirit*, 19–20.

2. Ibid., 31.

3. Ibid., 34.

4. Ibid., 41–42.

5. Ibid., 41–45.

6. Ibid., 48–49.

Chapter 36: The Great Chinese Harvest

1. Goforth, *By My Spirit*, 86.

2. Ibid., 131.

3. Ibid., 138.

Chapter 37: Revival Fires in Africa

1. Norman Grubb, *Rees Howells Intercessor* (London: Lutterworth Press, 1952), 166.

2. Ibid., 173–74.

Chapter 38: The Shantung Revival

1. Marie Monsen, *The Awakening* (China Inland Mission/Overseas Missionary Fellowship, 1986), 83.

2. C. L. Culpepper, *The Shantung Revival* (Dallas: Crescendo Book Publications, 1971), 13.

3. Ibid.

4. Ibid., 27.

5. Ibid.

6. Ibid., 28.

7. Ibid., 41.

8. Ibid., 55.

9. Ibid., 57–58.

10. Ibid., 60.

11. Ibid., 63.

Chapter 39: The East Africa Revival

1. C. R. Thompson, *Revival in Africa* (Calcutta, India: Evangelical Literature Depot, n.d.), 4.

2. J. E. Church, *Quest for the Highest* (United Kingdom: The Paternoster Press, Ltd., n.d.), 68.

3. A. C. Stanley Smith, *Road to Revival* (London: Church Missionary Society, n.d.), 71.

4. Gerald E. Bates, *Twentieth Century African Renewal* (Monograph, 1988), 13.

5. Ibid., 2.

6. Ibid., 18.

Chapter 40: The Revival in the Hebrides

1. Andrew Woolsey, *Duncan Campbell* (London: Hodder and Stoughton and The Faith Mission, 1974), 115.

2. Ibid., 118.

3. Ibid., 119–20.

4. Ibid., 122–23.

5. Ibid., 133.

6. Woolsey, *Duncan Campbell*, 134.

7. Ibid., 139–40.

8. Ibid., 140–41.

9. Ibid., 134–35.

10. Duncan Campbell. "When God Stepped Down from Heaven" (audio cassette taped message).

11. Ibid., 172.

12. Ibid., 173.

13. Ibid.

14. Ibid., 191.

Chapter 41: Revival Fire on Campuses

1. J. Edwin Orr, *Campus Aflame* (Glendale, Calif.: G/L Regal Books, 1971), 19.

2. Ibid., 65–66.

3. Ibid., 108–9.

4. Ibid.

5. Ibid., 111.

6. Mary Dorsett, "Revival," *Wheaton Alumni Bulletin* (April–May 1989): 5.

7. Stephen F. Olford, "Breakthrough in Wheaton" (paper), 1.

Chapter 42: The Spirit Comes to Asbury

1. E. Stanley Jones, Chapel address at Asbury Theological Seminary, September 28, 1966.

2. Orr, *Campus Aflame*, 122.

3. Z. T. Johnson, "Asbury College Revival," *The Herald* (March 22, 1958).

4. Dr. Bob Schuler's Page, *The Methodist Challenge* (May 1950): 9.

5. J. C. McPheeters, "The Revival Again," *The Herald* (March 12, 1969).

Chapter 43: The 1970 Asbury Revival

1. Robert E. Coleman, *One Divine Moment* (Old Tappan, N.J.: Fleming H. Revell Company, 1970), 74–75.

2. Ibid., 76–80.

BIBLIOGRAPHY

For those readers interested in discovering more about revivals in history, the books listed in the notes are excellent resources. Here are additional books that may also be helpful.

Brown, Michael L. *The End of the American Gospel Enterprise.* Shippensburg, Pa.: Destiny Image Publishers, 1989.

Carson, John T. *God's River in Spate.* Belfast: Church House, Publications Board, Presbyterian Church in Ireland, 1958.

Coleman, Robert E. *Dry Bones Can Live Again.* Old Tappan, N.J.: Fleming H. Revell Company, 1969.

_____. *The Spark That Ignites.* Minneapolis: World Wide Publications, 1989.

Evans, Eifion. *The Welsh Revival of 1904.* Evangelical Press of Wales, 1969.

Kulp, George B. *The Calloused Knees.* Cincinnati: God's Revivalist Office, 1909.

Lloyd-Jones, D. Martyn. *Revival.* Westchester, Ill.: Crossway Books, 1987.

Mallalieu, Willard Francis. *The Why, When, and How of Revivals.* New York: Eaton and Mains, 1901.

Matthews, David. *I Saw the Welsh Revival.* Chicago: Moody Press, 1951.

Morgan, George E. *Mighty Days of Revival.* London: Morgan and Scott, 1922.

Nicholson, Martha Snell. *His Banner Over Me.* Westchester, Ill.: Christian Readers Club, Division of Good News Publishers, 1957.

Olford, Stephen F. *Heart Cry for Revival,* rev. ed. Memphis, Tenn.: Encounter Ministries Inc., 1987.

_____. *Lord, Open the Heavens!* Wheaton, Ill.: Harold Shaw Publishers, 1980. (Formerly published as *Heart Cry for Revival,* 1962, 1969.)

Orr, J. Edwin. *The Eager Feet.* Chicago: Moody Press, 1975.

_____. *Evangelical Awakenings in Eastern Asia.* Minneapolis: Bethany Fellowship, Inc., 1975.

Prime, Samuel. *The Power of Prayer.* Edinburgh: The Banner of Truth Trust, 1991 (first published 1859).

Ramabai, Pandita. *Pandita Ramabai.* Melbourne: George Robertson & Co. Proprietary Limited, 1903.

Ravenhill, Leonard. *Revival God's Way.* Minneapolis: Bethany House Publishers, 1983.

____. *Revival Praying.* Zachary, La.: Ravenhill Books, 1962.

Rice, John R. *We Can Have Revival Now!* Wheaton, Ill.: Sword of the Lord Publishers, 1990.

Shearer, John. *Old Time Revivals.* London: Pickering & Inglis. No date.

Simon, John S. *The Revival of Religion in England in the Eighteenth Century.* London: Robert Culley. No date.

Stevens, Abel. *The History of the Methodist Episcopal Church in the United States of America, Vol. I.* New York: Eaton & Mains; Cincinnati: Curts & Jennings. September 1864.

____. *The History of the Religious Movement of the Eighteenth Century Called Methodism, Vol. III.* New York: Eaton & Mains; Cincinnati: Jennings & Graham. No date.

Tarr, Charles R. *A New Wind Blowing.* Anderson, Ind.: The Warner Press, 1972.

Wallis, Arthur. *In the Day of Thy Power.* London: Christian Literature Crusade, 1956.

____. *Revival: The Rain from Heaven.* Old Tappan, N.J.: Fleming H. Revell Company, 1979.

Watson, Eva M. *Glimpses of the Life and Work of George Douglas Watson.* Cincinnati: God's Bible School and Revivalist, 1929.

Watt, Eva Stuart. *Floods on Dry Ground.* London: Marshall, Morgan & Scott, Ltd., 1939.

White, John. *When the Spirit Comes with Power.* Downers Grove, Ill.: InterVarsity Press, 1988.

Wood, Arthur Skevington. *And with Fire.* London: Pickering & Inglis Ltd., 1958.

Woods, Grace W. *The Half Can Never Be Told.* Atlantic City, N.J.: The World-Wide Revival Prayer Movement, 1927.

INDEX

OTHER BOOKS
BY DR. DUEWEL

Touch the World Through Prayer—A challenging, very readable manual on prayer that has been used by God to "revitalize" the prayer life of thousands. A Christian "bestseller."

Let God Guide You Daily—A manual on guidance to help you enter into the joy of God's guidance as the daily experience of your life. (Available from author.)

Ablaze for God—A book to challenge all Christians, especially Christian workers and lay leaders, to a life and service Spirit-filled, Spirit-empowered, and mightily used by God.

Mighty Prevailing Prayer—Let the Spirit use this powerful volume to make your intercession mighty before God. A guide to intensified intercession and prayer warfare.

Measure Your Life—Seventeen ways God may measure you when He decides your heavenly reward. A challenge to invest your life totally for God.

Some 676,000 of Dr. Duewel's books are already in circulation. Available from Christian bookstores.

If God has made this book a blessing to you and you wish to share a testimony, or if you wish the author to remember you in a moment of prayer, feel free to write:

Dr. Wesley L. Duewel
P.O. Box A
Greenwood, IN 46142–6599

CPSIA information can be obtained
at www.ICGtesting.com
Printed in the USA
LVHW040225240520
656357LV00006B/37